D0915561

Dorothy L. Sayers

Solving the Mystery of Wickedness

Berg Women's Series

Gertrude Bell	SUSAN GOODMAN
Mme de Staël	RENEE WINEGARTEN
Emily Dickinson	DONNA DICKENSON
Elizabeth Gaskell	TESSA BRODETSKY
Mme de Châtelet	ESTHER EHRMANN
Emily Carr	RUTH GOWERS
George Sand	DONNA DICKENSON
Simone de Beauvoir	RENEE WINEGARTEN
Elizabeth I	SUSAN BASSNETT
Sigrid Undset	MITZI BRUNSDALE
Simone Weil	J. P. LITTLE
Margaret Fuller	DAVID WATSON
Willa Cather	JAMIE AMBROSE
Rosa Luxemburg	RICHARD ABRAHAM
Sarah Bernhardt	ELAINE ASTON
Mme de Sévigné	JEANNE A. and WILLIAM T. OJALA

In preparation

Mary Wollstonecraft	JENNIFER LORCH
Else Lasker-Schüler	RUTH SCHWERTFEGER
Natalia Ginzburg	ALAN BULLOCK
Mary Anderson	GRENDA HORNE HURT
Olive Schreiner	RUTH GOWERS
Harriet Beecher Stowe	LISA WATT MACFARLANE
Harriet Martineau	SUSAN HOECKER-DRYSDALE
Louise Labé	DAVID CAMERON
Erika Mann	SHELLEY FRISCH

Dorothy L. Sayers

Solving the Mystery of Wickedness

Mitzi Brunsdale

BERG *New York / Oxford / Munich*

Distributed exclusively in the U.S. and Canada by
St. Martin's Press, New York

Published in 1990 by
Berg Publishers, Inc.
Editorial offices:
165 Taber Avenue, Providence, RI 02906, U.S.A.
150 Cowley Road, Oxford OX4 1JJ, UK
Westermühlstraße 26, 8000 München 5, FRG

© Mitzi Brunsdale

Library of Congress Cataloging-in-Publication Data

Brunsdale, Mitzi.
 Dorothy L. Sayers : solving the mystery of wickedness / Mitzi
Brunsdale
  p. cm. — (Berg women's series)
 Includes bibliographical references.
 ISBN 0–85496–249–2
 1. Sayers, Dorothy L. (Dorothy Leigh), 1893–1957. 2. Women and
literature—Great Britain—History—20th century. 3. Detective and mystery
stories. English—History and criticism. 4. Authors, English—20th
century—Biography. 5. Good and evil in literature.
 I. Title. II. Series.
 PR6037.A95Z625   1990
 823′.912—dc20   89–18454

British Library Cataloguing in Publication Data

Brunsdale, Mitzi
 Dorothy L. Sayers: solving the mystery of wickedness
 – (Berg women's series).
 1. Fiction in English. Sayers, Dorothy L. Biographies
 I. Title
 823′.912

 ISBN 0–85496–249–2

Printed in Great Britain by
Billing & Sons Ltd, Worcester

Contents

Preface

Anyone who approaches the life and works of Dorothy L. Sayers had best be aware that she had no mercy on superficial or slipshod scholarship. She did not want her biography written until she had been dead for fifty years, and in her introduction to *Unpopular Opinions*, essays written when she was at the peak of her creative powers, she observed, "how easy it is for an unscrupulous pseudo-scholar to extract fantastic and misleading conclusions from a literary text by a series of omissions, emendations and distortions of context." She chose to shield herself formidably: her literary agency still maintains a policy on the use of both her published and unpublished works that effectively restricts quotation of them even in scholarly discussion. The only accounts of her self and her work Dorothy L. Sayers would have tolerated would have to be truthful, warts and all, and producing one at this time poses a considerable challenge. The prohibitive cost of extensive direct quotation from her works necessitates citation through more accessible sources, especially the Brabazon and Hone biographies, and neither the voluminous Sayers correspondence, opened in early 1989 to research, nor her important unpublished works of fiction and nonfiction are as yet available in scholarly editions. Nevertheless, the moral message of her literary legacy is the strongest possible justification for an introduction to her powerful writings, each arising from a life uncompromisingly lived out in the conviction of the sanctity of work.

What Dorothy L. Sayers had to say about the thorny moral problems of her day – the question of whether women are indeed human, the dilemma of a democratic system eye-to-eye with totalitarian expansion, the exhausting struggle of good to survive in the face of evil – was never less than the truth as she saw it through her Christian faith, and she always voiced or wrote that truth with keen intelligence and pungent wit. Today both scholarly and popular interest in her works are steadily growing, an indication, perhaps, that our world needs reminding that constants like faith and truth exist. This book was written in the hope of awakening new readers not just to her enormously good murder mysteries, but to the remarkable breadth of Dorothy L. Sayers's work as a whole – fiction and criticism, religious drama, aesthetic theory, and the magnificent Dante translation that climaxed her achievements – all carried out despite anguishing personal difficulties. To treat her work and her times with the accuracy they deserve, I owe profound thanks to the following individuals and groups who have most generously provided support, assistance, and permission to cite their works at such length as will, I hope, demonstrate conclusions consistent with Dorothy L. Sayers's uncompromising devotion to the truth:

Most of all, to the Dorothy L. Sayers Historical and Literary Society, Malthouse Lane, Hurstpierpoint, West Sussex, England BN6 9JY, for the wealth of information and photographs so efficiently and cordially provided, and in particular to the Society's Chairman, Dr. Barbara Reynolds, for permission to quote from *The Passionate Intellect*, and for her suggestions and corrections, as well as for her vital help in determining an appropriate means of referring to Miss Sayers: "Dorothy L. Sayers" in regard to her professional life, "Dorothy" in discussing her youth, and otherwise "Dorothy Sayers"; to Ralph Clarke, President of the Society, who contributed important chronological material and checked my work for accuracy; and to Philip Scowcroft, the Society's Research Officer, whose meticulous attention to detail has greatly enriched this study;

to the Very Reverend John Simpson, Dean of Canterbury Cathedral, for permission to quote from his moving Sermon of Thanksgiving for Dorothy L. Sayers's life and work;

to Alzina Stone Dale, for her unstinting permission to use material from her books and for scholarly commiseration when it was most needed;

to James Brabazon, for his gracious permission to cite passages from his authorized Sayers biography;

to J. T. Hubbell and Kent State University Press and to Ralph E. Hone and Margaret Hannay, for their generous permission to quote from their authoritative Sayers studies, and to Kent State University Press for permission to quote from Barbara Reynolds's *The Passionate Intellect*;

to Humphrey Carpenter, Jessica Mann, and Jan Morris, for their

delightfully unselfish cooperation, the mark of genuine seekers
after truth;

to Betty Karaim, Director; Margit Eastman; and the Mayville
State University Library staff, who again have exhaustively demonstrated the unflagging service research cannot do without;

to John, Margaret, Jean and Maureen, for their heroic endurance
of yet another writing project;

and to Luci and Joey, who deserve an "Aunt Sayers."

Any errors are of course my responsibility, and mine alone.

Mitzi Brunsdale
1989

Acknowledgments

Permission to quote from the following works of Dorothy L. Sayers has been given by David Higham Ltd. for the Estate of Dorothy L. Sayers:

"Are Women Human?" in *Unpopular Opinions* (London: Gollancz, 1946; New York: Harcourt, Brace, 1947)

Begin Here (London: Gollancz, 1940; New York: Harcourt, Brace, 1941)

"City of Dis, The," in *Introductory Papers on Dante* (London: Methuen, 1954; New York: Harper, 1954)

Clouds of Witness (London: T. Fisher Unwin, 1926; New York: Dial Press, 1927)

"Comedy of the Comedy, The," in *Introductory Papers on Dante* (London: Methuen, 1954; New York: Harper, 1954)

"Cornice of Sloth, The," in *Further Papers on Dante* (London: Methuen, 1957; New York: Harper, 1957)

"Creed or Chaos?" in *Creed or Chaos?* (London: Methuen, 1947; New York: Harcourt, Brace, 1949)

"Dante's Imagery: I. Symbolic," in *Introductory Papers on Dante* (London: Methuen, 1954; New York: Harper, 1954)

"Dante's Imagery: II. Pictorial," in *Introductory Papers on Dante* (London: Methuen, 1954; New York: Harper, 1954)

Devil to Pay, The (Canterbury: H. J. Goulden, Ltd., 1939; London: Gollancz, 1939; New York: Harcourt, Brace, 1939)

"Divine Comedy," in *Unpopular Opinions* (London: Gollancz, 1946; New York: Harcourt, Brace, 1947)

Documents in the Case, The (London: E. Benn, 1930; New York: Brewer and Warren, 1930)

"Faust Legend and the Idea of the Devil, The," in the English Goethe Society, *Papers Read Before the Society*, 1923+; *The Poetry of Search and the Poetry of Statement* (London: Gollancz, 1963)

Gaudy Night (London: Gollancz, 1935; New York: Harcourt, Brace, 1936)

"Gaudy Night" (essay), in Howard Haycroft, (ed.), *The Art of the*

Mystery Story (New York: Simon and Schuster, 1946)

Introduction to *Great Short Stories of Detection, Mystery and Horror* (U.S.: *The Omnibus of Crime*) (London: Gollancz, 1928; New York: Payson & Clarke, 1929; Harcourt, Brace, 1929)

Introduction to *Great Short Stories of Detection, Mystery and Horror, Second Series* (U.S.: *The Second Omnibus of Crime*) (London: Gollancz, 1931; New York: Coward-McCann, 1932)

Introduction to *Great Short Stories of Detection, Mystery and Horror, Third Series* (U.S.: *The Third Omnibus of Crime*) (London: Gollancz, 1934; New York: Coward-McCann, 1935)

"Greatest Drama Ever Staged is the Official Creed of Christendom, The," in *Creed or Chaos?* (London: Methuen, 1947; New York: Harcourt, Brace, 1949)

Have His Carcase (London: Gollancz, 1932; New York: Brewer, Warren & Putnam, 1932)

Introduction to *Hell*, in *The Comedy of Dante Alighieri, the Florentine* Harmondsworth, Middlesex: Penguin Books, 1949–1963)

"Living to Work," in *Unpopular Opinions* (London: Gollancz, 1946; New York: Harcourt, Brace, 1947)

Love All, in *Love All* and *Busman's Honeymoon* (Kent, Ohio: Kent State University Press, combined ed. 1984; *Love All* copyright 1984 by Anthony Fleming)

Man Born to Be King, The (London: Gollancz, 1943; New York: Harper, 1943)

"Meaning of Hell and Heaven, The," in *Introductory Papers on Dante* (London: Methuen, 1954; New York: Harper, 1954)

Mind of the Maker, The (London: Methuen, 1941; New York: Harcourt, Brace, 1941)

Murder Must Advertise (London: Gollancz, 1933; New York: Harcourt, Brace, 1933)

"Mysterious English, The," in *Unpopular Opinions* (London: Gollancz, 1946; New York: Harcourt, Brace, 1947)

Nine Tailors, The (London: Gollancz, 1934; New York: Harcourt, Brace, 1934)

Strong Poison (London: Gollancz, 1930; New York: Brewer & Warren, 1930; New York: Harcourt, Brace, 1936)

Tristan in Brittany (London: E. Benn, 1929; New York: Payson & Clarke, 1929)

Unnatural Death (in U.S. *The Dawson Pedigree*) (London: E. Benn,

1927; New York: Dial Press, 1928)

Unpleasantness at the Bellona Club, The (London: E. Benn, 1928; New York: Payson & Clarke, 1928; New York: Harper, 1928)

Introduction to *Unpopular Opinions* (London: Gollancz, 1946; New York: Harcourt, Brace, 1947)

To the memory of my mother, who raised me to believe it, and to my daughters Margaret, Jean, and Maureen, for whom I hope I have done the same:

> . . . a woman is just as much an ordinary human being as a man, with the same individual preferences, and with just as much right to the tastes and preferences of an individual.
> Dorothy L. Sayers, "Are Women Human?"

1 The Many Worlds of Her Christian Universe

Thirty years after Dorothy L. Sayers's death in 1957 and a half century after she wrote her mysteries, these twelve novels stand as classics of a popular and profitable genre for which British women writers have shown particular genius, entertainingly combining comedy of manners with psychological insight and ingenious forms of murder. Worldwide, women write about one-third of all mystery novels published today,[1] and why respectable matrons have proved so good at plotting and executing heinous crimes, at least on paper, has given many critics (and possibly many husbands) considerable food for thought.[2] Significant clues to this productive absorption with the grisly may lie in the personal and literary development of Dorothy L. Sayers, one of the most important writers responsible for raising quality detective fiction to the respected position it holds today. Dorothy L. Sayers was unquestionably the right person for the job when she helped bring the murder mystery to its Golden Age between the two World Wars, but how she arrived there and where she went afterwards are far less familiar today than her novels are, even though all of the other worlds she shaped for herself bear her own vivid stamp. Born in Oxford, England, on 13 June 1893, she was intellectually precocious, intrigued by language and its possibilities; a brilliant student, receiving in 1920 one of the first degrees granted to women at Oxford; a mother and wife battling prejudice and entrenched social attitudes under trying circumstances; a religious dramatist and lay theologian; a masterful translator and re-creator of the medieval world; and perhaps not least important to revealing her character, soft-touch "Aunt Sayers" to most of the animals, hers and everyone else's, near her home at Witham.[3]

The theory of literature that Dorothy L. Sayers evolved and lived out was remarkably thorough and consistent, considering the various forms of uproar in which she had to work. Nearly everything she wrote centered upon the conflict of Good and Evil, seen from the standpoint of the traditional Christian belief which

1

she uncompromisingly professed and practiced. Evil as the twentieth century came to know it was daily growing more evident in the world about her; during her lifetime, Britain's involvement in conflict after conflict, from the Boer War to the Cold War, turned the Empire into a Commonwealth, drained British resources, and irretrievably lowered British prestige. In her personal life too she faced serious difficulties: a tall, somewhat plain, shatteringly bright girl, who entered school considerably later than her classmates and who, furthermore, detested athletics, was fated to suffer agonies at boarding school; a middle-class woman of few financial resources, badly disappointed in love, who became pregnant in the 1920s and had to keep her out-of-wedlock child a painful secret; a wife whose husband's equilibrium had been shattered in the Great War not only had to support him but had to bear his growing animosity toward the necessity of her doing so. Faced with such calamities great and small, most human beings would ask Job's everlasting "why?" Only a few could roll up their sleeves and make the best of the situation as effectively as Dorothy Sayers did, and she did it by linking religious faith to her creative impulse in her concept of the sacramental nature of work. The combination led her throughout her life to undertake successively more challenging artistic attempts at solving the "question of questions" in human existence, which she called the "mystery of wickedness."[4]

A sublimely appropriate – and generally devilishly pungent – choice of words was always one of Dorothy L. Sayers's artistic trademarks. The causes and reasons of evil, especially the kind that afflicts the innocent, continually baffle men and women, often forcing them to attribute their sufferings to some mystery of existence – the world, or the flesh, or the Devil. In the religious sense, however, a mystery demonstrates a truth comprehensible only through divine revelation, while in literary history the term applies specifically to a medieval drama based on a scriptural event. Interestingly, through a linguistic corruption, the archaic meanings of "mystery" include "a guild," a "trade," or an "occupation." The derivation of "evil" originally conveyed the sense of overreaching, demonstrating the awe-filled consequences of Original Sin, a knowing choice to pluck the forbidden fruit of knowledge and thereby earn expulsion from Paradise. "Wickedness," however, implies a deliberate human choice of wrongdoing that may have something ingenious or playfully malicious about it, unquestionably sinful, but nonetheless juicily attractive to what Mark Twain liked to call "the damned human race." By describing the central issue of human life as the mystery of wickedness and making it the core of her artistic and moral message, Dorothy Sayers implied the great paradox of the Fortunate Fall, a truth that can only be grasped through divine revelation: that mankind, in a kind of spiritual as well as physical predilection marked by varying degrees of proficiency, has sinned and keeps on sinning, and indeed enjoys looking forward to more sinning, so that Christ could come bringing eternal redemption. What was more, she felt it the obligation of the Christian artist, whose gifts should enable him to recognize truth more clearly than could his fellows, to tell them so, and she did it in no uncertain terms.

When she was turning from her highly successful murder mysteries to religious writings, Dorothy L. Sayers described human artistic creativity as a reflection of Divine Creativity. She felt that genuine art must arise from human integrity, that gift which allows the intellect to recognize truth and to proclaim and defend it, and she believed that theme to have been present from the very beginning in her own literary efforts,[5] even before she began pitting a contemporary detective knight-errant against ogres of lust, avarice, and pride, prototypic confrontations of Good against Evil.

Dorothy Sayers once said that everyone was "either 'gothic' or 'classical' by instinct."[6] Christian theology of the Middle Ages was firmly rooted in the doctrine of St. Paul that while Christ perfectly redeemed mankind, man's tendency toward sin remains, and so man must share in Christ's suffering before joining with Him in the Resurrection.[7] Dorothy Sayers knew her own inclination lay toward soaring medieval spires, "prayers in stone" that lift men's eyes and souls to God, and while, like any human being, she might have sinned, she seems never to have abandoned that essentially medieval Pauline position on sin and redemption. Whatever suffering human imperfection might have caused her, she seemed to try to face it and work it through by solving the mystery of wickedness on the intellectual level in her various writings.

3

Dorothy Sayers also had one of those minds that rejoices in grasping the overall significance of a piece of gothic art by integrating the meanings of its thousands of decorations. She delighted in jigsaws and crosswords, the more fiendishly complicated the better, evidence of a painstaking talent for synthesis that made her excel in the use of involved poetic forms, in learning and translating languages, in creating flamboyant murder cases and their solutions, and in grasping the immensely complex allegory of Dante's *Divine Comedy*, the culmination of her creative life. She thus framed her series of solutions to the mystery of wickedness as demonstrations of religious truth as she saw it. Even if she decked out some of them, like the Wimsey novels, in modern dress, all of them are riotously alive with the panache and pageantry, the heroics, the humor, the robust faith, and most of all, the clear knowledge of Right and Wrong, Good and Evil, which attracted Dorothy Sayers to the Middle Ages.

As both a famous author and as a private person, Dorothy Sayers would likely have agreed with Dr. Arbuthnot that the thought of biography lent a new horror to the prospect of dying. She was profoundly convinced that work was central to the artist's being, and so she would have preferred to have had superficial commentators who ignored her work in favor of gossipy surmise about her personal life "fried in boiling oil." She specifically insisted that she wanted no biography written about her until fifty years after her death, when all those who could be affected would be beyond caring,[8] but she did leave two incomplete and as yet unpublished autobiographical statements, "My Edwardian Childhood" and "Cat o'Mary," dating from the early 1930s, which provide much of what is known about her childhood and early youth.[9]

Heredity and environment inevitably affected the first literary world Dorothy shaped for herself. Her father, Henry Sayers, was an Anglican clergyman who loved to teach music and the classics, and her mother's uncle, Percival Leigh, had been an early contributor to *Punch*, Britain's celebrated humor magazine. Dorothy was an only child, and her parents educated her much the same as were boys of that time; about the age of five she began to study Latin with her father, and by seven she had begun to write her own poetry, producing a considerable body of juvenilia – poems, plays, drawings, and stories – before she was fifteen.[10] Dorothy's friendship with her cousin Ivy Shrimpton began in 1906, when Ivy was eighteen and Dorothy thirteen, the latter already comfortable enough with French to have read Dumas's *The Three Musketeers* in the original language. Dorothy saw herself as the gallant Athos, and over the next several years she exchanged poems and letters with Ivy in that persona, never as long as she lived quite abandoning her rapture at Athos's sweeping gestures and his poignant, doomed devotion.

As a youngster Dorothy loved to read about romantic adventures and such glorious defeats as Thermopylae and Roncevaux, but when she entered the Godolphin School at Salisbury in 1909, she discovered new outlets for her talents with words. She overcame her social difficulties enough to become involved with the school's debating society, and she also edited the *Godolphin School Magazine* for two terms, attended performances of Molière's plays, and even played Shylock in a student production of *The Merchant of Venice*. Illness forced her to leave Godolphin in December of 1911, but her encounters there with drama and satire seem to have made such lasting impressions on Dorothy that as an adult she used these forms to express some of her own most profound convictions.

As holder of the distinguished Gilchrist Scholarship in Modern Languages, Dorothy Sayers came to Somerville College in the fall of 1912 and for three years honed her fine mind under the guidance of Mildred Pope, a medievalist and one of the leading women scholars of the early twentieth century. Settling into medieval French as though she had been born speaking it, Dorothy took First Class Honours and the Degree Course Certificate that in 1915 represented women's highest achievement at Oxford. She also had had time for plenty of fun, and for her fun meant putting her wicked penchant for parody to use; no one was safe from it. In 1913 she participated in a takeoff of *Hamlet*, and just before leaving Oxford with the equivalent of her degree, she wrote and acted in a spoof of Dr. Hugh Allen, the choral director who was the object of her schoolgirl crush.

No matter how golden one's college days have been, at graduation they have to give place to harsher realities, and even the most devoted mutual admiration societies are split apart when college

5

friends have to face up to earning a living. Dorothy was fortunate in being able to enjoy the companionship of several of her old Oxford friends throughout much of her life, but the world into which they had been born was starting to come to pieces in August 1914. The following spring Somerville College was turned into a military hospital, and its students were sent to a men's college, Oriel, causing considerable consternation, even in a national emergency. Some of Dorothy's friends left to become army nurses, facing new battlefield horrors the world could hardly comprehend, and Oxford's male student complement dropped between 1914 and 1915 from 3,000 to 1,000.[11] Oxford men who went to war suffered as much as any other segment of their generation; only a painfully small number returned, and most of those who did were damaged for life. Nearly an entire generation was lost, and by 1922 the British government was paying more than 900,000 war pensions.[12]

Dorothy had been happy at Oxford, perhaps happier than she had ever been before or would ever be again, and after leaving, she began to write poems again. Some she circulated among her friends from Oxford who would understand best:

> Therefore, God love thee, thou enchanted town,
> God love thee, leave me, clutch me not so fast;
> . . . .
> Sweet friends, go hence and seek your own renown,
> Now that we have gone down – have all gone down.[13]

She was also experimenting with technical poetic effects, using various arrangements of lines and rhymes probably taken from medieval French and notoriously difficult to employ in English verse. On 8 October 1915 she wrote to her friend Dorothy Rowe that she was tiring of the intense contemporary scene, wartime "things that meant a powerful lot." She said she needed to escape by writing in the medieval mode, to "revel a bit in the dear old obvious glories of scarlet cloaks & dragons & Otherworld Journeys, & in the clank and gurgle of alliteration, & the gorgeousness of proper names" [sic].[14] Her urge to escape wartime misery probably also helped lead her to read detective stories, and soon she learned to combine these two kinds of literature in order to support herself.

In the meanwhile, she had taken a job teaching modern languages at Hull High School, but she found teaching unsatisfying. Much more gratifying, she had also began to publish some of her poetry in the *Oxford Magazine*. In March 1916, during the Battle of Verdun, one of the longest and bloodiest engagements of the war, Blackwell's accepted *Op. I*, a selection of her poems, for *Adventurers All*, a series of books written by "Young Poets Unknown to Fame." Probably one of the best presents she had ever had was seeing her work in print by Christmas of that year. By the end of the following January, Dorothy accepted a position in publishing at Blackwell's offices in Oxford, far more to her liking than teaching had been.

When Dorothy was a girl, Tennyson's Victorian standards still received at least outward approbation in England:

> Man for the field, woman for the hearth,
> Man for the sword and for the needle she;
> Man with the head and woman with the heart,
> Man to command and woman to obey.[15]

During final examinations throughout Dorothy Sayers's years at Oxford, university officials asked Somerville's principal "to keep the young ladies from exposing their ankles because it distracted the men."[16] In 1915, Margaret Sanger was jailed for *Family Limitation*, the first book advocating birth control. As a mature woman, Dorothy Sayers commented that she had hardly ever seen or spoken to any men her own age until she was around twenty-five.[17] By today's relaxed standards, such straitlaced segregation of the sexes might seem conducive to spontaneous combustion, and in fact Dorothy was engulfed after she had been out of school for about a year.

At that time, she was doing entry-level publishing tasks like reading manuscripts, proofreading, and copyediting for Blackwell's in Oxford. She was also working on her translation of Thomas of Britain's medieval French epic of illicit passion, *Tristan*, and writing poetry, much of it religious in nature. It was

7

then that she met Eric Whelpton, who had returned from military service to Oxford in the spring of 1918, just when Dorothy's poem on Christ, "Rex Doloris" ("King of Sorrow"), was published in G. K. Chesterton's *New Witness*. Being a person whose passions were never lukewarm, Dorothy fell – and fell very hard. Her feelings for Whelpton showed her another side to the problem of suffering, for one of Dorothy Sayers's problems with men was that she not only had a fervent heart, she had a head and a very good one at that, and she was never a "woman to obey."

Whelpton always did what he could to foster the notion that he was Dorothy's model for Lord Peter Wimsey, the aristocratic hero of her detective novels, but most Sayers scholars believe that whatever qualities Whelpton shared with Lord Peter were coincidental or superficial. Whelpton was debilitated from illness, and Dorothy enthusiastically pitched in to take care of him. Her *Catholic Tales and Christian Songs*, a collection of devotional poems which included "Rex Doloris," appeared in September 1918, followed by other verse and the essay "Eros in Academe," but her biographer Ralph Hone concludes that between 1918 and 1919, when she was twenty-six, Dorothy was caught between the religious sensibilities her upbringing and nature enjoined upon her and the demands of her senses.[18] Hormones won a round; in the spring of 1919, her job with Blackwell's ended, and when Whelpton took a position with L'Ecole des Roches, a classy boys' boarding school in Normandy, Dorothy followed not long afterward as his secretary.

The magnetism Dorothy felt seems hardly to have been mutual. Whelpton seems never to have reciprocated or even appreciated her devotion, and his infatuation for a stunning divorcée he had met in London precipitated his return to England in early 1920. Dorothy came home herself that fall at the start of the Roaring Twenties, unhappy, "a virgin and unmarried,"[19] and badly in need of a job.

Dorothy was then forced to build another, and as it proved, a most pragmatically successful literary world for herself. Poetry writing, teaching, publishing, and Whelpton had all disappointed her, and even though she did receive her Bachelor of Arts and Master of Arts from Oxford in October 1920, one of the first women to do so, the honor did not pay her bills. In that year sales of detective stories of all stripes were on the upswing, from Agatha Christie's first published novel, *The Mysterious Affair at Styles*, to shrieking "penny dreadfuls," and Dorothy had astutely told Whelpton that that was where the money lay. She had been devouring mysteries for some time, and while she was recuperating from a bad bout with mumps in France, she and her friend Muriel Jaeger had concocted by mail an elaborate mock-scholarly historical analysis of Sexton Blake, then a popular series detective figure. Once back in London, Dorothy settled down in Bloomsbury, a district full of rampant creative personalities, and took what odd jobs she could get. She even endured another brief teaching stint, this time at London's Clapham High School. During a boring summer vacation at Bluntisham, she launched her first Wimsey novel, *Whose Body?*, and completed it by October, but her life became complicated by another passion, this time for the exotic Russian-born, Jewish-American writer John Cournos, who, as Dorothy later put it, spelled his "Art with a capital 'A'."[20] Her London life-style – playing jazz on the saxophone, buying a motorcycle, and worshipping Cournos – may have influenced the Reverend Sayers to change his will, leaving everything to his "dear wife";[21] but during the Christmas holiday of 1921, her parents staked Dorothy to six months' support to get her novel sold on condition that if nothing came of her writing by the next summer, she would settle down to teaching. That spring she found her first agent and took her first significant job, a position with S. H. Benson's, then one of England's most prominent advertising firms. In July an American publisher made an offer for *Whose Body?*, and Dorothy L. Sayers's career was under way.

Just when Dorothy's professional future was becoming more hopeful, her affair with Cournos soured. He left England and Dorothy without a word in October 1922; testifying to her pain are eleven embittered, as yet unpublished letters she later wrote him. James Brabazon discusses these letters in his authorized Sayers biography. On the angry rebound, Dorothy quickly took up with another man, but in early 1924 she emerged from that relationship not quite alone again; the man was gone, but she now had John Anthony, the child whose existence was unsuspected by her public and even her friends until the 1970s and

9

whom she inconspicuously placed with Ivy Shrimpton near Oxford. Through it all, she managed to finish her second book, *Clouds of Witness*, published in February 1926, and on 13 April, having under the circumstances quite astonishingly asked John Cournos to find her a "companionable man,"[22] Dorothy married Oswald Atherton ("Mac") Fleming, a retired army officer who wrote articles on auto racing. The ceremony took place in the registrar's office on Clerkenwell Road, Holborn, in London.

Dorothy Sayers seems never to have done anything halfway. For the next ten years, as Mac's health deteriorated, she turned out novel after novel for an audience that apparently could never get enough of Lord Peter Wimsey. After *Unnatural Death* (1927) and *The Unpleasantness at the Bellona Club* (1928), she acquired a new agent, David Higham, whose firm still controls access to her work, and began her association with Victor Gollancz, an aggressive young publisher, who issued many of her subsequent works. In 1928, Gollancz published *Lord Peter Views the Body*, a highly successful collection of short stories; and her translation of the medieval Anglo-Norman poem *Tristan*, the only work of hers that Eric Whelpton ever said he liked or, indeed, had read, appeared elsewhere as well. Soon she was able to leave Benson's and devote herself completely to her writing.

The British Broadcasting Company had begun programming in 1922, and Dorothy Sayers plunged into her long-standing association with them in 1930. For a woman frequently accused of being difficult to work with, she had remarkable success with projects requiring a high degree of cooperation. Besides various radio appearances, both on her own and with other members of the Detection Club she had helped to found, she collaborated with Robert Eustace on *The Documents in the Case*, her only full-length, non-Wimsey mystery novel. The following year saw *The Floating Admiral*, the first of the collectively authored novels Dorothy Sayers initiated to meet the Detection Club's expenses.

By this time, Dorothy L. Sayers had also made herself an authority on the history and theory of detective fiction, producing superb critical articles that set the standards of the genre for years to come. The 1930s were ripe for mystery stories; after the worldwide economic disaster of 1929, readers needed to escape to a realm where problems, unlike those that were harassing them every day, did have attainable solutions. After her initial successes, Dorothy Sayers began to experiment with various approaches to the detective novel. *The Five Red Herrings* (1931) is an elaborate puzzle built scientifically on railway timetables; its Scottish setting excluded several members of the Wimsey entourage, and some of Sayers's readers found the book insupportably dry without them. She wrote *Murder Must Advertise* (1933), based on her years at Benson's, to support her household and her son during trying economic times; the pound had just been devalued for the first time, and 2.5 million Britons were unemployed. *The Nine Tailors*, one of Sayers's most powerful mysteries and one that cost her years of research into change ringing, appeared in 1934 and in Britain alone sold 100,000 copies in seven weeks.

The other detective novels Dorothy L. Sayers wrote between 1930 and 1935 arose from literary experimentation much closer to her personal life. In *Strong Poison* (1930) she introduced a romantic interest, Harriet Vane, to Lord Peter Wimsey and immediately polarized her audience. Some adored Harriet, who shared many of Dorothy's own talents, attitudes, and characteristics, while others found they could not abide sharing Lord Peter with her. The strong urge toward autobiographical expression that impelled Dorothy Sayers to create Harriet for Lord Peter also seems to have resulted in her two attempts in the early 1930s at putting her own life onto the printed page. "My Edwardian Childhood" deals directly with her earliest recollections up to about the age of four. On the other hand, "Cat o'Mary" is a fragmentary novel she subtitled "The Biography of a Prig," and according to Brabazon, it treats matters about her youth that she never otherwise revealed.[23] Dorothy Sayers abandoned both projects, but in 1934, after attending the Annual Somerville Gaudy to give the University Toast, she settled down to the novel that many feel represents her best as a mystery author and incorporates the greatest degree of self-analysis that she could muster. *Gaudy Night's* first edition of 17,000 sold out upon publication, and by April 1936, it was in its sixth printing; it remains one of Dorothy L. Sayers's best-loved novels.

The heavy burdens Dorothy Sayers was carrying in the early 1930s took their toll. After finishing *The Nine Tailors* in November

11

1933, she came to a crossroads in her life. She debated leaving Mac, whose emotional state was becoming precarious, but she decided against it. She also chose to pretend to "adopt" young Anthony, since it had become apparent that otherwise she could never officially take him into her home. At the same time, because Dorothy had become tired of his old self, her popular hero Lord Peter Wimsey was also undergoing crucial changes throughout the novels in which Harriet appears. Unable to kill him off in the face of his besotted admirers, she determined to execute the next most effective means of eradicating an attractive bachelor's personality – marriage. In *Busman's Honeymoon*, which began as a play written in collaboration with her good friend Muriel St. Clare Byrne and published in novel form in June 1937, Dorothy did just that. She tossed off a few more small morsels of Wimsey in short stories – an unfinished and unpublished novel called "Thrones, Dominations," and the "Wimsey Papers," written to beef up British backbones in the winter of 1939–40 – but by Christmas of 1936, Dorothy L. Sayers was scouting out a new mansion for herself in the literary "realms of gold." For fifteen years to keep body and soul together, she had been absorbed in creating modern-day confrontations of good and evil through Lord Peter Wimsey, her knight in a shiny black Daimler.[24] Now she would tackle wickedness head on through the older vehicle of the medieval mystery play.

One of the jokes Dorothy Sayers often delightedly told on herself came from a schoolboy who had written, "And then there was Miss Dorothy Sayers who turned from a life of crime to join the Church of England."[25] The anecdote implicitly voices the contradiction sometimes postulated between her life and her work: how a woman who had reveled in a shock-the-bourgeois Bohemian existence could later produce intensely traditional and conservative Anglican religious drama and essays. Dorothy Sayers not only could laugh at the way the irreverent babe presented the truth about her position, she relished telling people about it, something one hardly does when one is ashamed of the difference between what one says and what one does. To her, there probably never seemed any contradiction at all; since all human beings, even such notable saints as Paul and Augustine, were sinners, she would never have claimed to be anything else. She may have kept certain personal matters private, but she made no bones about her religious preferences and even her own short-comings. So far as is known, all her life she adhered to the Anglican faith in which her father had baptized her at Christ Church Cathedral. Her childhood was steeped in the magnificent imagery and rhythms of the King James Bible and the Book of Common Prayer, two of the most powerful influences upon her style. Her twenty-four poems in the 1918 collection *Catholic Tales and Christian Songs* reveal a spiritual innocence and intimacy with Christ that her reviewer in the *Times Literary Supplement* found "characteristic of the Middle Ages."[26] They also foreshadow Sayers's treatment of Christ-as-Man in her radio dramas. Her coworkers at Blackwell's had noticed that she was "religious" because she kept a crucifix on her desk and habitually made the sign of the cross before meals,[27] and for most of her life she went alone to early Communion services at St. Thomas's Church in Regent Street, London, and at All Souls' Church at Witham.[28] Whatever choices she made – and lived with and suffered for – in her personal life, she remained a deeply devout woman of an Anglo-Catholic persuasion.

In 1936, as Dorothy Sayers was completing the stage version of *Busman's Honeymoon*, friends began to urge her to write a play for the Canterbury Festival, like T. S. Eliot's *Murder in the Cathedral*, presented at Canterbury the preceding year. The chance to combine her first literary love, poetry, with the medieval story of William of Sens, the French architect chosen to restore the Canterbury Cathedral Choir after the fire in 1174, proved irresistible, and she completed *The Zeal of Thy House*, her first religious drama, for performance in June 1937. Her old delight in theatrics, dormant while she was writing her detective stories, had revived when she and Muriel St. Clare Byrne had been working on *Busman's Honeymoon*, and it took solid hold of her. Dorothy Sayers not only helped supervise the staging of *The Zeal of Thy House* at Canterbury, but she later took it to London and on a tour of the provinces. She financed the project by Lord Peter Wimsey's endorsement of Horlick's Malted Milk, much to the consternation of Wimsey's admirers.[29]

Dorothy Sayers's enthusiasm for religious drama blazed throughout the tense prewar years and the finest British hours that followed. She wrote a nativity play, *He That Should Come*, for a BBC broadcast on Christmas, 1938, beginning her long association with producer Val Gielgud. For the 1939 Canterbury Festival she reworked the medieval Faust legend into *The Devil To Pay*, updating the old story by redefining the sin to which Faust falls, while insisting that he chose to be punished for it to save his integrity.

When Prime Minister Neville Chamberlain's policy of appeasement failed and Hitler's Blitzkrieg fell upon Poland on 1 September 1939, bringing Britain into another world war, Dorothy Sayers rose nobly to her country's spiritual defense. After a brief stint with the Ministry of Information, which both parties found unsatisfactory, she set about letting her nation know what it needed to do to save the best in Western civilization from an enemy that had chosen to sin against the Holy Ghost – to believe that Evil was Good. She indefatigably produced more plays, speeches, poems, book reviews, essays, and entire books, some of her finest, all intended to support British morale and define her nation's Christian purpose. Possibly as early as 1939, she started on another stage comedy, *Love All*, important to her personal development; but even earlier that year she had begun thinking about a cycle of plays based on the life of Christ for the BBC Children's Hour. During some of the blackest days in England's history, she toiled away at this massive project, developing a colloquial approach based solidly on conservative church dogma. Finally, after a clash of wills with the BBC and pitched battles with evangelistic religious groups – she beat them all hands down – Val Gielgud's production of the twelve episodes of *The Man Born to Be King* aired from December 1941 to October 1942. Its immense popular success has been repeated as recently as 1975.[30]

Just as she had done in "The Wimsey Papers," eleven sketches in letter form published in *The Spectator* during the winter of 1939–40, Dorothy Sayers attempted to bolster home front morale in speeches and poems calling on the traditional English virtues of fortitude, determination, and Christian values. Her long essay *Begin Here*, published in January 1940, accepted the worldwide crisis of war as an opportunity to rebuild Western culture, whose failings she did not hesitate to point out in such

14

polemics as "Creed or Chaos?" "Christian Morality," "The Church's Responsibility," "The Religion behind the Nation," and "Forgiveness and the Enemy." Dorothy Sayers typically preached and practiced with equal zeal, and her hectic wartime schedule included touring factories, knitting for the war effort, adopting the African porcupines at the London Zoo, accepting refugee children into her home, and raising pigs in her Witham backyard – the females were all called Fatima, and the males Sir Francis Bacon.

The most important of Dorothy L. Sayers's wartime literary achievements was *The Mind of the Maker* (1941), in which she set forth her doctrine of human work in general and art in particular as a reflection of a connection to Godhead Itself in the Holy Trinity. This preoccupation led her to her last enormous undertaking; after the Allies had turned the tide of war in 1942–43 at Midway, El Alamein, and Stalingrad, she became increasingly absorbed with the problem of artistic creativity in the context of religious belief. In August 1944, inspired by *The Figure of Beatrice*, her friend Charles Williams's book on Dante, Dorothy Sayers began to read the *Divine Comedy*. She instantly recognized the work of a master she could at last obey, and she rapturously embraced it; Dorothy Sayers was in love again.

All of Dorothy L. Sayers's professional interests coincided in her absorption with Dante.[31] While V–1 rockets bombarded London during August 1944, she swallowed the *Divine Comedy* whole, reading at first from a bilingual edition, but because she knew Latin well and could follow Dante's pristine Italian without much difficulty, a few weeks later she was reading the original text fluently. Many qualities of Dante's work moved her deeply: his immense erudition and a soaring poetry that a mind like hers found irresistible; a Christian context that fit her own religious sense like a finely crafted Florentine glove; the hypnotic power of a master storyteller and a sublime sense of history; and perhaps most surprising of all, a cosmic sense of humor that she felt chalky scholarly renditions had purged from the *Divine Comedy*. Being Dorothy L. Sayers and totally smitten, what else could she do but set about translating him – and in his own demanding form, *terza rima*?

By that Christmas, Dorothy Sayers's version of the *Inferno* was

15

under way, and the next April E. V. Rieu of Penguin Books offered her a contract for the entire *Divine Comedy*, calling for the *Inferno* translation to be ready on 1 January 1946, with *Purgatory* and *Paradise* in 1947 and 1948, respectively. This schedule proved too ambitious even for Dorothy Sayers, and in fact her translation of the *Inferno* did not appear until November 1949. *Purgatory* was published in May 1955, and she worked on *Paradise* until she died in 1957, leaving it to be completed by her good friend Barbara Reynolds and published in 1962. Though greeted with some hesitation by the community of Dante scholars because she was not one of them, Dorothy L. Sayers's translation of the *Divine Comedy* remains very much everyman's Dante, with introductions and notes that have never been surpassed for their brilliance, forthright good sense, and thorough scholarship.

Her work on Dante might have gone more quickly if Dorothy Sayers had not been heavily involved with a multitude of other activities. At the time she began the *Inferno*, Mac's blood pressure and sciatica were giving serious problems, and he had to be hospitalized several times before his death in 1950. In 1945, she undertook yet another festival play, *The Just Vengeance*, for the Cathedral at Lichfield, written under the idiosyncratic influence of Charles Williams, who had guided her to Dante. At Barbara Reynolds's invitation, she spoke at the Summer School of the reopened Society of Italian Studies, and she maintained annual appearances there for the rest of her life. At the end of that year, she also spearheaded the resurrection of her beloved Detection Club. In 1949, while she was at work on *Purgatory*, she was deep in a revival of *The Zeal of Thy House* when the Bishop of Colchester asked her to write the 1951 Festival Play for his Cathedral.

Mac's death in 1950 left Dorothy a few years of productive widowhood, and she made the most of them. Besides Dante, she was still devoting a good deal of time to church-related activities. For the subject of her Colchester play, she chose the pivotal fourth-century Council of Nicea, which established the official creed of Christianity; her result was *The Emperor Constantine*, a monumental drama which took four hours of performance time and a cast of ninety-six. She also was a church warden of her London parish and played an energetic role in its affairs.

Just after World War II, Britain's postwar climate was chilly

16

in several respects. Fuel shortages beset the nation after the nationalization of the coal industry in 1947, and food rationing went on until 1954. A considerable shift was also occurring in religious attitudes; the 1954 Derby Study showed that 30 percent of the British population was going to the cinema in a given week, while only 12 percent attended church services in the same period. The general decrease in participation in organized religion accompanied a dramatic rise in consumerism; and the 1948 British Citizenship Act, which granted British passports to all Commonwealth citizens, encouraged successive waves of non-white immigration to Britain. Self-consciousness among the younger generations ran amok, with Beatles and Angry Young Men becoming the lions of popular British culture and with the era of the civilized literary murder rapidly giving way to the brutal incoherence of Mike Hammer's paperback mayhem. Dorothy L. Sayers and her traditional English values had abruptly become passé.

In 1954, the religious position which had earned Dorothy Sayers nationwide acclaim and even an offer nine years earlier of an honorary doctorate in divinity from the Archbishop of Canterbury, which she had declined, made her the target of savage attacks from two quarters. Kathleen Nott vented considerable agnostic spleen in *The Emperor's Clothes*, an assault on conservative Anglican writers, accusing T. S. Eliot, T. E. Hulme, C. S. Lewis, and several others – Dorothy L. Sayers prominently among them – of gullibility in defending Christian faith rather than rational scientific humanism. If any writer's intellectual equipment precluded gullibility, Dorothy Sayers's did, and the book must have galled her deeply. Even closer to her religious home, one of her fellow parishioners at St. Anne's denounced her for allegedly caring more about religious dogma than about the Church's social responsibilities. Dorothy refuted both of these assaults with her usual thoroughness, but doing so probably cost her considerable effort and soul-searching, a kind of professional and spiritual purgation.

Her work with Dante must have helped her put such problems into perspective. While working on her translations and notes for *Purgatory*, she published her *Introductory Papers on Dante* in 1954 and *Further Papers on Dante* in 1957. She had also returned to her

17

old fascination with medieval French, and her distinguished translation of *The Song of Roland* appeared in the fall of 1957. Not for the first time in her career, she was also doing some writing for children: Advent and Easter calendars telling the stories of Christ's coming, His Passion and Resurrection, and the tale of Noah's Ark, when the Almighty punished the wicked so forcefully.

In early December 1957 Dorothy Sayers was asked to be one of Barbara Reynolds's witnesses (Dorothy observed that the Book of Common Prayer called them "Godparents")[32] when her friend joined the Anglican Church, a gesture that must have brought Dorothy a sense of family absent during her adult life. She spent a little time with Dr. Reynolds's family at Cambridge and then shopped for Christmas gifts in London. Just after she returned to Witham on December 16, without even having time to change her clothes or feed her cats, she succumbed to a massive heart attack at her home.

Dorothy Sayers was cremated and her ashes placed under the floor of the tower of St. Anne's in Soho, where a plaque was at last dedicated to her memory in June 1978. Six bishops of the Church of England attended her memorial service on 15 January 1958 at St. Margaret's Church, next door to Westminster Abbey, and at the close of the service, all who attended received a white leather-bound copy of her essay "The Greatest Drama Ever Staged."[33]

She had made her will in 1939, leaving everything – about £35,000 – to her son Anthony under the executorship of Muriel St. Clare Byrne. Anthony had discovered that Dorothy Sayers was his mother when he had applied for a passport just after the war,[34] and shortly after her death he revealed the truth about his parentage to Muriel. While some of Dorothy Sayers's friends in England came to share this knowledge, it did not reach the general public until Janet Hitchman unearthed it and published it in her unauthorized 1975 biography, *Such a Strange Lady*, a phrase Hitchman claimed she had heard used repeatedly among Dorothy Sayers's English acquaintances.[35]

Genius in any field of human endeavor runs the risk of being thought strange; those who don't possess it are generally unfamiliar with and hence usually unsympathetic to its gifts and its demands. If the determination required to succeed in a man's world – adopting a barely feminized business suit with porkpie hat and eschewing handbags for much more practical pockets – marked Dorothy Sayers as strange, so be it, as she probably would have said. To support her husband and her son and to accomplish everything she had, Dorothy Sayers had to sacrifice the customary pastimes of women of her time and class, like babies, benevolent societies, and bridge. Anyhow, in the famous comparison from *Gaudy Night*, she likely would have been as suitably employed at them as a Derby winner hauling a coal cart.

What her temperament, her talent, and her training did suit her for was confronting the eternal force of evil in its stylish new manifestations. The twentieth century no longer afforded direct opportunities for knight-errantly quests or heroic rearguard last stands, but Dorothy Sayers undertook to give battle with the armor of laser-bright logic, piercing common sense, and her lifelong shield of committed Christianity. In her struggle, she shaped successive literary worlds: detective stories where good triumphs not only inevitably but with musketeerish panache; morality plays that pose eternal truths about mankind's foolish willingness to sin; translations that bring the average reader close to great achievements of the Age of Faith, when the results of man's choices between Good and Evil were far more easily discernible than in our muddled modern times. The time that has passed since her death is beginning to allow sufficient perspective to view Dorothy L. Sayers's various works as integral literary worlds of one mighty universe, centered on that exasperating and crucial puzzle: the everlasting mystery of wickedness.

Notes

1. Nevertheless, in 1987 the *New York Times Book Review* reviewed ninety-seven mysteries by men and seven by women – 7 percent, a proportion that seems to hold true throughout the United States. An organization called the Sisters in Crime, founded in 1987, has

launched a Book Review Project to scrutinize several major U.S. review pages for their coverage of mystery novels written by women. Sisters in Crime publishes a newsletter obtainable from Kate's Mystery Books, 2211 Massachusetts Avenue, Cambridge, Mass. 02140 USA. Lenore Fischer, "Talk of the Trade," *Publishers Weekly* (28 October 1988), p. 57.

2. On the other hand, United Kingdom novelist Reginald Hill opened the Fourth International Congress of Crime Writers in New York on 9 May 1988 by quoting one of his neighbors who pitied Hill's wife for being "married to a man who can think like *that*." Walter Wager, "500 Cunning Authors Assemble for Tough Talk and Sociability," *Publishers Weekly* (3 June 1988), p. 27.

3. Alzina Stone Dale, *Maker and Craftsman: The Story of Dorothy L. Sayers* (Grand Rapids, Mich.: William B. Eerdmans Publishing Co., 1978), p. 125.

4. Dorothy L. Sayers, *The Devil to Pay*, in *Four Sacred Plays* (London: Victor Gollancz, 1959), p. 111.

5. Dorothy L. Sayers, *The Mind of the Maker* (London: Methuen, 1941), p. 207.

6. Dale, p. 3.

7. See Barbara Reynolds, *The Passionate Intellect: Dorothy L. Sayers' Encounter with Dante* (Kent, Ohio: Kent State University Press, 1989), p. 87.

8. Ralph E. Hone, *Dorothy L. Sayers: A Literary Biography* (Kent, Ohio: Kent State University Press, 1979), p. x. This and subsequent citations are used by permission of the Kent State University Press.

9. James Brabazon, *Dorothy L. Sayers: A Biography* (New York: Charles Scribners' Sons, 1981), p. 301.

10. Anthony Fleming, Preface to Brabazon, p. xi.

11. Dale, p. 47.

12. Asa Briggs, *A Social History of England* (New York: Viking, 1983), p. 258.

13. Dale, p. 49.

14. Hone, p. 22.

15. Alfred, Lord Tennyson, "The Princess," quoted in Briggs, p. 243.

16. Dale, p. 40.

17. Dorothy L. Sayers, *Are Women Human?* (Grand Rapids, Mich.: William B. Eerdmans Publishing Co., 1971), p. 35.

18. Brabazon, p. 82.

19. Brabazon, p. 6.

20. Dorothy L. Sayers, quoted in Brabazon, p. 90.

21. Hone, p. 38.

22. Brabazon, p. 113.

23. Ibid., pp. 301, 15.

24. Lord Peter Wimsey seems to have changed cars each year and thus had a succession of Daimlers, each of which he called "Mrs.

Merdle." The first of these, a specially built Daimler Twin-Six, with racing body, useful gadgets, and "no row" (presumably meaning a gorgeously purring engine), appeared in *Unnatural Death* (1927), p. 61.

25. Dale, p. xiv.
26. Hone, p. 30.
27. Brabazon, p. 67.
28. Dale, p. 103.
29. Ibid., p. 154.
30. Robert B. Harmon and Margaret A. Burger, *An Annotated Guide to the Works of Dorothy L. Sayers* (New York: Garland, 1977), pp. 133, 135.
31. The vital area of Dorothy L. Sayers's life and work involved with her encounter with Dante is discussed in rich detail by Barbara Reynolds in *The Passionate Intellect*. Dr. Reynold's analysis is indispensable to understanding Dorothy Sayers's achievement in her work with Dante, and it deserves meticulous attention.
32. Reynolds, p. 149.
33. Dale, p. 107.
34. Brabazon, p. 174.
35. According to Dr. Reynolds, none of Dorothy Sayers's acquaintances would have used the phrase because of its lower-class connotations; "lady" instead of "woman" indicates in Dr. Reynolds' opinion that the speakers might have been charwomen or shopkeepers (letter from Barbara Reynolds to the author, 29 February 1989).

2 Her Edwardian Childhood 1893–1915

> One day I will show them.
> Dorothy L. Sayers, "Cat o'Mary"

When she was around thirty-nine, Dorothy L. Sayers began her only directly autobiographical statement, "My Edwardian Childhood." She left it unfinished and unpublished, and only those portions and comments which appear in James Brabazon's authorized biography are currently available in print. Its title is a puzzle in itself; Sayers's thirty-three-page fragment covers her first four years, from her birth on 13 June 1893 to 1897, the year Queen Victoria celebrated her Diamond Jubilee. Victoria died on 22 January 1901 when Dorothy was seven, and Victoria's son Edward VII, who liked to claim he succeeded the "Eternal Mother," took the throne at fifty-nine and ruled until 1910, two years before Dorothy began her studies at Oxford. Why then did Dorothy Sayers describe her early childhood as Edwardian rather than Victorian? Just possibly this fragment is merely an introductory section of a much longer intended autobiography, but as scrupulously as she always chose her words, it seems more likely that she might have wanted to stress differences between herself as a child and the majority of other English girls of her position and time.

Both of Dorothy's parents were members of that stable middle class which had formed the backbone of English society for generations. Like his father before him, Henry Sayers was a clergyman of the Church of England, but he had also served as headmaster at two schools for boys before taking the same position at the University Cathedral Choir School of Christ Church College, Oxford. He was a classics scholar and a capable musician who scored hymns for his church;[1] the portraits of tall, gentle, rather unworldly clergymen brimming with the milk of human kindness appearing in several of his daughter's novels testify to her fondness for him. Dorothy's mother, whose maiden name was Helen Mary Leigh, came from a Hampshire family which claimed to trace its pedigree to the reign of Henry III in the thirteenth century.[2] Several commentators feel that Dorothy's famous insistence upon the "L." which stood for "Leigh" in her professional name stemmed from her pride in her mother's side of the family. She was particularly fond also of her Aunt Mabel Leigh, who, until she died at eighty-five, lived with Dorothy and her husband at Witham. Dorothy was born when her father was nearly forty and Mrs. Sayers over thirty years of age, and she was their only child.

Families like Dorothy's were representative of the remarkable stability of the British national character in the first half of the twentieth century. According to Edward Schils, an American sociologist, British culture contained a "centre" that remained intact until 1945 and consisted partly in its authority structure and partly in "the order of symbols, of values and beliefs, which govern the society."[3] English historian Michael Bentley has also observed that even though British social values prior to 1950 were sustained more heavily by secular than by spiritual roots, those values remained strikingly cohesive, and that while bitter class divisions spawned serious strikes in 1911 and 1920, very little communist or fascist reaction took hold in the nation at those times.[4]

Dorothy Sayers inherited many of the symbols, values, and beliefs of the late Victorian period whose child she was. As the daughter of a clergyman, she grew up in a high-minded atmosphere, with education unquestioningly accepted as a function of religion. The habit of preaching also permeated every sphere of Victorian activity, not only from the pulpit but in various secular manifestations, like the philanthropic phraseology which allowed colonial adventurers to sound amazingly like missionaries while pursuing rewards quite different from the Kingdom of Heaven.

Victoria's long reign from 1837 to 1901 also saw an immense upsurge in most forms of human knowledge. The British Empire's scientists and engineers received their training at the Scottish universities, because philosophy and religion prevailed at Oxford and Cambridge, where the Anglican clergy dominated education until the university reforms of the 1850s and restricted the creation of research facilities in science and technology. Until about the 1880s, a passionate amateurism also prevailed among educated Britons. They fervently believed that the sheer love of knowledge equipped any amateur to operate on an equal footing in a given field with the person who made his living at it, and so when Dorothy Sayers was a girl, there were still only faint rumblings of the degree of specialization which today makes communication on technical subjects among scholars of different areas difficult at best and often embarrassingly impossible between professionals and lay people. For the most part, Victorian thinkers had to set their theories before the general public in blessedly plain language, and the popularization of even the most abstruse areas of the liberal arts, like theology and philosophy, lent confidence to the Victorian belief in the power of logical argument to improve their society.[5]

Large families – Queen Victoria herself had nine children – were the approved norm in the nineteenth century, and militant domesticity ruled prosperous Victorian middle-class life, at least on the surface. When released from their upstairs nurseries or from Nanny's custody, children were rigorously restricted to being seen and not heard. Like Jane Austen's heroines, girls almost always received their education at home, learning a little French or German, drawing and music, before setting about their real work of finding suitable husbands. Boys went off to boarding school around eight years of age, entering Oxford or Cambridge at nineteen. When they did spend time with their parents in the evenings, Victorian offspring helped make their own entertainment by playing musical instruments or parlor games like Charades, or most often reading aloud, a pastime which demanded that novelists produce material fit for tender ears; Anthony Trollope commented that his profession "seem[ed] to me to be as serious as the parson's own."[6] In this edifying atmosphere, aired – or even hinted – moral transgressions sealed the fate of any public figure unwise enough to commit them.

Much Victorian reading material also promoted the chivalric ideal that the Victorians had resuscitated from the Middle Ages and modified to suit their views on propriety. According to Mark Girouard, the chivalrous gentleman of the nineteenth century was "brave, straightforward and honourable, loyal to his monarch, country and friends, unfailingly true to his word . . . a natural leader . . . fearless in war [and] gentle to the weak; above all . . . tender, respectful and courteous to women . . . an honourable opponent and a good loser . . . an ardent and faithful lover, but hated loose talk, especially about women."[7] As an ideal deliberately created by such proponents of Galahad-clean living as Lord Baden-Powell, founder of the Boy Scouts, the prototypic Victorian gentleman deserved to rule because he had the moral fiber and sense of responsibility necessary to do so. Gentlemanliness derived from both birth and public school education; Sir Arthur Conan Doyle, for example, preferred to think of himself not as a great-grandson of a Dublin silk merchant but as a descendant of Norman Doyles who came to Ireland in the twelfth century.[8] Extracurricular reading buttressed the pedagogic efforts of Eton and Harrow, and well-to-do Victorian boys swallowed the principles of chivalric behavior in delectable coatings of fiction: Malory's original or (more likely) modernized *Morte d'Arthur*; Sir Walter Scott's medieval novels, like *Ivanhoe* and *The Talisman*; contemporary tales celebrating British pluck, like W. H. Fitchett's *Deeds That Won the Empire*; and even the new thrillers and romances, vividly written, moving faster than a speeding bullet, and impossible to put down, like the adventure tales Conan Doyle preferred to be known for rather than his Sherlock Holmes stories; and the exploits of Baroness Orczy's dashing *Scarlet Pimpernel*.[9] All of these were available to Dorothy Sayers when she was growing up, and she loved them. The chivalric impulse sometimes led Victorian gentlemen to band together as "fellowship knights," like the Arthurian Knights of the Round Table, or to act as individual knights-errant who might pursue quixotic quests to the point of eccentricity.[10] Whether practiced in genteel moderation or carried to extremes, though, the Victorian chivalric ideal perished in the murderous leveling of the Great War and dwindled off into escape literature – the romances, the fantasies, and the detective stories of the twentieth century, among which Sayers's Lord Peter Wimsey novels were to take such a prominent place.

For her first four and a half years, Dorothy Sayers lived amid Oxford's medieval architecture, and her father taught her to love it as much as he himself did. She was born at #1 Brewer Street, St. Aldate, just across from the gates of Christ Church College, and soon thereafter her family moved into the new Choir House, a little further down the same street. Christ Church possesses several architectural distinctions: it contains Oxford's largest, single, eighteenth-century edifice; it displays the university's largest Gothic Revival range; and it enjoys the largest Oxford quadrangle, an area of immaculately manicured lawn surrounded by the college's buildings, containing Sir Christopher Wren's Tom Tower. At 9:05 every night Dorothy spent in Oxford, she would have heard its bell strike one hundred and one times – once for each original member of the college – to send all undergraduates within doors. By a singular historical circumstance, Christ Church's chapel also serves as Oxford's cathedral; founded in 1524 by Cardinal Wolsey on the revenue he had confiscated from twenty-one monastic houses he closed, the college received a new lease on life after Wolsey's downfall, when his one-time master Henry VIII reestablished it as the Cathedral Church of Christ. The church dates from about 1200, but its most prominent feature, the elaborate vault of the narrow choir where Dorothy's father spent a good deal of his time, dates from the 1500s and is adorned with multiple tiers of Gothic arches and windows. Henry Sayers baptized Dorothy there, and she must have visited the church often.

Oxford's ancient buildings, closed away from the gaze of the uninitiated into secret gardens of knowledge and self-discipline, exude their own special atmosphere of excellence; John Ruskin, elected first Slade Professor of Fine Art at Christ Church in 1869, maintained, "All our colleges – though some of them are simply designed – are yet *richly* built [Ruskin's italics], never pinchingly. . . . [And] a wealthy and worthy completion of all appointed features . . . [gives younger scholars] respect for the branches of learning which these buildings are intended to honour, and increasing, in a certain degree, that sense of the value of delicacy and accuracy which is the first condition of advance in those branches of learning themselves."[11] Although she would not have made full use of such perceptions until after she had returned to Oxford as a scholar, Dorothy's first experiences of the old heart of Oxford, with its cramped, twisted streets, its "dreaming spires," and its great carillons, remained as the "real Oxford" in her memory long after William Morris started the Cowley factory of the British Motor Company in 1922,

26

swelling the town's population and altering a good deal of its character.

When she was four and a half, Dorothy's father accepted the position of parish priest at Bluntisham-cum-Earith, which carried a good salary of more than £1500 per year, compensation in part for moving out of lovely Oxford to the swampy, often flooding Fen Country of Cambridgeshire, and into a country rectory that had only oil lamps, primitive plumbing, and fireplaces for sporadic heating.[12] The remains of a Roman camp lay not far from Bluntisham, and her biographers note that Dorothy's father told her the romantic legend that the yellow flowers – monksbane – brightening the rectory lawns that January could grow only where the ground had been wet with Roman soldiers' blood.

Dorothy's father undertook her first lessons in Latin when she was five. Even though Dorothy later suspected he had not been wholeheartedly dedicated to teaching "small demons with angel-voices" at the Christ Church Choir School,[13] Mr. Sayers's experience and her natural aptitude for languages produced impressive results. Dorothy was thrilled with the sense of power the understanding of another language gave her, and soon French and German lessons augmented the Latin. She seems to have read almost anything she could lay her hands upon, and the Sayers household was well stocked with reading material, from biblical history to the novels of Dickens and Scott, romantic adventures like *The Scarlet Pimpernel*, and detective stories about Sherlock Holmes and a popular investigator of the time, Sexton Blake[14] – in short, all the things an inquisitive boy her age might have been expected to read.

"A Vote of Thanks to Cyrus," an essay Dorothy Sayers wrote as a mature woman, reveals a sophisticated insight she had as a youngster, linking the world of the classics, which she read about in a children's magazine called *Tales from Herodotus*, with the stories of the Old Testament she was no doubt encouraged by her parents to read; all at once she realized that Cyrus of Persia had played a role in the story of Daniel, and the King Ahasuerus who allowed his Jewish wife Queen Esther to save her people was one and the same with the Persian emperor Xerxes, against whom the Spartans had made their courageous stand at Thermopylae. Far earlier than most children and entirely on her own, Dorothy was already assembling the jigsaw pieces of history.

Since she was the child of a devoted clergyman, Dorothy's imagination was constantly stimulated by the powerful language and embellishments of Anglican worship. In the formal services to which she would have been taken and the regular prayers the family held at eight-fifteen each morning with their servants,[15] she would have heard repeated some of the stateliest religious cadences in the English language. The Church of England, the famous middle road between Roman Catholicism and Protestantism, came into being when Henry VIII broke with Rome and in the 1534 Act of Supremacy declared himself the "only supreme head on earth" of the English Church – a matter of regal policy, not religious doctrine. Thomas Cranmer, Archbishop of Canterbury, produced the Anglican Book of Common Prayer under Henry's short-lived son Edward VI in the mid-sixteenth century, and its 1662 version was used by the Church until 1965. During the first half of the nineteenth century, the Oxford Movement had reaffirmed the Catholic and apostolic character of the Anglican High Church tradition (Anglo-Catholicism), with an emphasis on ritual and belief in the doctrines of the Real Presence and apostolic succession, as opposed to the Low, or Evangelical, Church faction, which stressed the Bible and preaching and was the prevalent body of the Church throughout the nineteenth century. Dorothy Sayers's family was orthodox and conservative, taking a moderate stance between High Church and Low; but according to Alzina Stone Dale, some of the Reverend Mr. Sayers's parishes were "probably more Protestant than he would have liked,"[16] indicating that his preferences possibly helped to shape his daughter's Anglo-Catholicism. While the Church of England is "established," meaning that its bishops are appointed by the Crown, its parishes and clergy receive their support from their parishioners, not from the state. Until the mid-1850s, only members of the Church of England could attend a university, hold office, or even vote, and when Dorothy was growing up, English law required everyone in the country to be a member of a specified parish.

In the years when a child is most susceptible to language, especially a girl with a good ear for music and words, Dorothy was inundated by the powerful diction and rhythms of the King James Bible and the Book of Common Prayer. Much later she remarked that while a writer is struggling to set down his own ideas, he either consciously or unconsciously draws on "sources of power" from what he has read and stored in his memory,[17] and much of her writing, especially her religious dramas and even her detective novels, resounds with echoes of those majestic religious works. Dorothy's upbringing also included fine classical music, and both her training and her preferences considerably exceeded the tinkling "accomplishment" of the average young Victorian lady. Her father had bells installed in the tower of his parish church, and Ralph Hone has demonstrated that the quintessentially English art of change ringing, which played an important role in the setting and plot of *The Nine Tailors,* was familiar in Bluntisham while Dorothy was growing up there.[18] She inherited her father's musical ability; she studied both the piano and the violin, and she also enjoyed singing, especially anthems of the Church Militant, with strong thumping rhythms and glorious images: sapphire thrones and angel armies appealed far more to her than being reminded that little children are weak, or being indoctrinated with the concept of a meek, gentle Saviour.[19]

Still more unusual for a youngster, even one who grew up in a rectory, was Dorothy's preoccupation before the age of thirteen with the Athanasian Creed. Today, this creed is by far less well known among Christians than the simpler Apostles' Creed or the Nicene Creed. An English translation of the Athanasian Creed, called the *Quicunque Vult* (whoever wishes [to be saved]), appears in the Book of Common Prayer; it was formulated by an unknown Western author of the sixth century in response to lingering Arian heresies which claimed the Son was not of the same substance as the Father. The Athanasian Creed precisely and elaborately defines the teaching of the Church upon the Mysteries of the Incarnation and the Trinity: "The Son is of the Father alone, neither made nor created, but begotten"; and Father, Son, and Holy Ghost "are not three eternals, but one eternal . . . and the whole three Persons are co-eternal together and co-equal."[20] Most Christians, whatever their ages, accept their creeds as formal professions of matters they take on faith, letting the theologians worry about trying to explain such mysteries logically, but at this very young age Dorothy had an "over-mastering fascination" with the Athanasian Creed which she kept to herself, afraid that the adults around her would scoff at her claim to understand it. Her reticence seems to indicate the depth of her feeling. Brabazon indicates that as a child she also took intellectual issue with one of its verses, which warned that "there is one Father, not three Fathers," because her common sense told her that a nine-in-one deity would be an absurdity.[21] Since a creed is the believer's formal profession of faith and his guide to what his faith believes is right and wrong, Dorothy's interest would seem to reveal a concern with exactitude of language and a religious sensibility few twelve-year-olds seem to possess; she wanted to be very sure, even then, that she knew precisely what she was promising to God, and that it satisfied her intellect.

Many of the mature interests which Dorothy Sayers later drew upon for her creative work appeared in her early childhood – her passion for the Middle Ages and her love for its architecture, especially for the old town of Oxford; her fascination with languages, beginning with her father's Latin lessons and a little later her studies of French and German with her governesses; her ability to link disparate pieces of knowledge into an intelligible whole, together with a romantic absorption with the great lost causes of history; her delight in music and the glorious style of her Bible and the Book of Common Prayer; and her stubborn determination to grasp her faith, not through her emotions or by someone else's authority but through the logical working of her own mind.

Up to a point, Dorothy's early life was much like that of any other girl of her time and station; she lived comfortably, received a conventional Anglican religious training, learned her lessons from her father and her governesses, showed her achievements off to her admiring relatives – her parents, Aunt Leigh, Grandmother Sayers, and frequent visitors – and the captive audience of the six Sayers servants, and enjoyed the status her father's position gave her. But in some respects she must have been a lonely child, since there was no one her own age in the rectory to play with; and associating closely with the village children, let alone going to their school, would have been out of the question. Her intellectual precocity, as often happens, probably tended to make the adults who surrounded her treat her as if she were a little grown-up, one that was definitely both seen and heard. Dorothy's relative isolation from youngsters of her own age may also have contributed to the intensity which she brought to her friendship with her cousin Ivy Shrimpton, five years older, who came to visit when Dorothy was thirteen.

James Brabazon provides a detailed account of their relationship at that time, drawn from letters Dorothy wrote to Ivy and from "Cat o'Mary," Dorothy's fictionalized and unpublished fragmentary novel about her childhood and adolescence.[22] Ivy and Dorothy exchanged poems and short stories as well as letters in which Dorothy attempted to "improve" her friend's religious attitudes, her French, and even her spelling; Ivy must have had considerable patience along with "rough and ready" wisdom about ordinary life which Dorothy, just entering puberty, might have needed badly. Brabazon notes one especially intriguing passage in a letter Dorothy wrote to Ivy early in 1908, in which she took her friend a little to task for Ivy's supposed tendency toward intolerance of moral lapses; if Ivy had indeed possessed such intolerance, she would hardly have been alone in Victorian society. In her letter Dorothy expressed the hope that if someday she "sinned a great sin," she would not have to be afraid to come to Ivy for help.[23] The comment is certainly uncanny in the light of subsequent events, but it also shows that Dorothy at fifteen frankly acknowledged her own capacity for wrongdoing, something an indulged only child might not have been expected to do.

When Ivy was staying with Dorothy's family in the summer of 1907, Dorothy hit upon the notion of staging Dumas's *Three Musketeers*, her most recent literary infatuation, and she dragooned her family and the staff into the production. Ivy played the Duchesse Marie de Chevreuse, Dorothy's father took the part of the King of France, and her mother became the scheming villain, Cardinal Richelieu. Dorothy not only took the role of Athos, the disguised nobleman, but became Athos, assuming his swagger, his air of unhealed sorrows, and his unquenchable spirit; and for more than a year, she poured out passionate letters and poems in that role, some of them in French, to Ivy. Brabazon attributes Dorothy's lifelong preference for the hero's role rather than the heroine's to her essentially analytical mind – generally,

31

he claims, a male characteristic – but like all of her most reliable commentators, he insists that no evidence whatsoever indicates that Dorothy's sexual preferences were not entirely female.[24]

In Dumas's novel the dashing Athos was only melancholy when a little drunk; and when he was himself, he was "the most shrewd and impenetrable of men."[25] Dorothy in her early teens might have acted as though she were intoxicated by literary swashbuckling, but she had a tough core of native shrewdness and an ability to keep her real self to herself. In the 1930s, when she was experimenting with various kinds of autobiographical revelation, she created a striking miniature portrait of herself at fifteen as Hilary Thorpe in *The Nine Tailors*. As her father lay dying, young Hilary told him she knew exactly what she was going to do with her life; she would get a scholarship to Oxford and make her own living as an independent woman and a writer – not poetry, which didn't pay very well, but best-selling novels, the kind that "everybody goes potty over."[26]

Dorothy's first step toward authorship required that she attend boarding school, where she could prepare for the rigorous entrance examinations for Oxford. Virtually no coeducational schools existed at that time in England, and Godolphin School at Salisbury had about two hundred female students, half of them residential. It enjoyed a reputation for training the career women of the day, though not many of its students could take advantage of the opportunity. They were, of course, ferociously segregated from young men, and Godolphin's redoubtable headmistress, Miss Mary Alice Douglas, believed firmly in regimentation and hard work. Godolphin was Victorian with a vengeance, and Dorothy observed later – an understatement – that she had not been happy there.[27]

Dorothy's parents could not have failed to recognize her brilliance, and they probably felt they were preparing her for Oxford as best they could by sending her to Godolphin, but she faced some almost insurmountable problems in adjusting to life there. On the physical level, her virtual isolation at Bluntisham had shielded her from the usual childhood diseases, which are generally harder on adolescents than on youngsters. Chicken pox kept her from entering Godolphin in the fall of 1908, and she did not arrive there until January – fifteen years old, tall, a little ungainly, with new glasses and possibly a chip on the shoulder. Most Godolphin girls entered much earlier, at eight or ten, and they already had their social groups staked out. Dorothy had spent those years as the center of attention in the Bluntisham household, doing mostly as she pleased and being applauded, even when she shocked her audience, something she increasingly liked to do. Dormitory living must have been as difficult for her as were the prescribed rigid march formations and the subdued Godolphin uniform, a blue pinafore over a blouse and blue skirt, dull attire for a girl who had just been decking herself out in the plumes and satins and laces of a seventeenth-century French musketeer. Under Miss Douglas's formidable administration, Godolphin operated on Spartan principles; students were limited to a pound per week for spending money, the buildings had no central heating, and, even more difficult for Dorothy, Godolphin followed the hallowed tradition of the British boys' public schools and set about molding their students' characters through outdoor team sports like field hockey. Dorothy detested such things, and it showed.

Academically, she excelled in some areas, like languages, but had to be placed behind her age group in others, like mathematics. Even worse for her acclimatization, her intellectual prowess set her apart from her fellow students, and she did not mind letting them know it, a combination rarely conducive to social acceptance. Much later Dorothy described her adolescent self as egotistical, absorbed with herself, and passively disobedient.[28] Circumstances at Godolphin even tempted her to take active measures against those who failed to appreciate her ability. In one notable example recorded in "Cat o'Mary," her French class was grappling ineffectually with background on Molière; Dorothy bided her time and then let fly a volley of dates, works, and highlights of his career – all in perfect French. She recalled with relish that her teacher "reeled slightly from the shock" of hearing the subjunctive placed properly for the first time in her life from the lower fifth form.[29] What the other girls thought was doubtlessly uncharitable.

Dorothy Sayers's biographers agree that for the most part she remained an outsider during her three years at Godolphin. Brabazon notes that she resorted to "slyness, defiance, and buffoonery" to survive, and he even feels that she did her best to try to forget the place.[30] Besides her problems with her peers and teachers, Dorothy felt uncomfortable with Godolphin's Low Church approach to religion, a puritanical pietism which crept furtively around "Gawd" and seemed to drain all the vigorous glory that she loved out of Christianity. Her parents sent instructions that she was to be confirmed at services in Salisbury Cathedral, and what elsewhere might been a joyous spiritual occasion equipping a young adult to take arms against evil as a new soldier of God turned into one of Dorothy's unhappiest moments. In a 1930 letter to Ivy, Dorothy observed that having been confirmed "against her will" had made her resentful about religion for a long time.[31] Quite possibly it was the emotionalism and lack of intellectual rigor connected with Salisbury's religious practices that bothered her most – to the dangerous degree, she later wrote, of nearly driving her away from Christianity completely.[32]

Despite all of her unhappiness at Godolphin, however, Dorothy probably took away more lasting benefits than would have been easy for her to admit. Miss Douglas inculcated hefty doses of the Protestant work ethic into her students, exhorting them to rejoice in work done well for its own sake. Accustomed to unanimous approval at Bluntisham, where she could study what she liked at her own pace, Dorothy once had to be summoned by Miss Douglas for an "improving" talk on character reformation, in the course of which the headmistress suggested that Dorothy learn to accept criticism and to cease making excuses for herself.[33]

One of the music mistresses at Godolphin, Fräulein Fehmer, made a much more positive impression on Dorothy. Fräulein Fehmer taught a Teutonic insistence on pianistic accuracy fully in line with Miss Douglas's precepts, but the musician's ravishing interpretations of Chopin's Nocturnes remained vivid all the rest of Dorothy's life. Fräulein Fehmer went back to Germany before World War I and, according to Ralph Hone, later became a Nazi;[34] but Dorothy never forgot her and, in 1944, wrote a poem about what her old teacher must be feeling as the Allied bombs pounded Germany. After locating her address, Dorothy sent food and clothing packages to Fräulein Fehmer until she died at the end of 1948. Loyalty was always one of Dorothy's – like Athos's – noblest qualities.

As well as showing up both her good and not-so-good traits, Godolphin also opened up areas where Dorothy could and did excel. Dorothy won distinctions for the yearly Oxford and Cambridge Joint Board Higher Certificate Examinations in 1909 and 1910, and in language examinations in the fall of 1911, she beat out all other candidates in England who had studied both French and German.[35] Since Dorothy preferred not to explore athletic fields any more than she had to, she pursued her dramatic and literary interests – acting in student productions, reviewing professional performances of Molière for the *Godolphin School Magazine*, which she eventually edited for two terms, and participating in the school debating society. While she probably enjoyed these activities, there would have been dark times at Godolphin when the conflicts between Dorothy's personality and those around her stung her into adolescent alienation. Almost worse, she knew what a gift she had for words and how little it was appreciated. The pain of not having her talents understood or appreciated, and her angry reaction to these misperceptions, lasted a long time. Writing around 1934, Dorothy put words that might have flashed frequently through her own mind on the lips of Katherine Lammas, the autobiographical heroine of "Cat o'Mary": "One day I will show them. . . . I will build, build, build. . . . It is in me. It is not in them and I know it."[36]

The stress Dorothy suffered at Godolphin took its toll. In February of 1911, measles struck the school, and according to Brabazon, Miss Douglas returned from a trip to countermand the quarantine that a subordinate had placed on the girls who were ill and to impose a regimen of winter air, exercise and "positive thinking."[37] It nearly killed Dorothy, whose acute measles were followed by pneumonia. She was sick for two months; her mother came to nurse her, and then she was moved to a convalescent home. All her hair fell out from the high fever, and coming back to take her exams that spring nearly bald must have been a brutal strain for an eighteen-year-old girl well aware she was already something of a misfit.

Dorothy spent the summer at home and returned to Godolphin that fall to prepare for her scholarship exams for Oxford, and as a senior she was named a house-prefect. This added to her troubles, as she proved better at telling others what to do than at

35

doing it herself, and teenaged girls are scorpion-quick to rebel against hypocritical authority. Before the term was over on 20 December, Dorothy fell ill again – Brabazon conjectures a nervous breakdown[38] – and she left Godolphin for good. She studied at home, and the following spring she won the Gilchrist Scholarship in Modern Languages, one of the highest scholarships in England, to Somerville College, then considered the most academically rigorous of the women's colleges at Oxford.

From "Cat o'Mary," which Dorothy broke off at February –March 1911, the time when she was down with pneumonia, Brabazon concludes that the inner turmoil Dorothy experienced during her years at Godolphin resulted not just from ordinary adolescent angst, but more from an essential lack of contact with reality, in the sense that her experience of life had to be filtered through her literary intellect. Brabazon claims that throughout her life "she felt no direct assurance even of the reality of her own personality,"[39] but this observation does not seem to agree with the self-portraits she created in her fiction.

Until "Cat o'Mary" and Dorothy Sayers's entire correspondence are available for examination and discussion, it is impossible to debate Brabazon's opinion, but a number of other considerations about her childhood and adolescence need to be taken into account. First, at least some of her difficulties were not of her own making. As the headstrong only child of older parents, growing up without contemporaries in a household with servants and an attentive aunt and grandmother, Dorothy was indulgently allowed occasionally to be as raucous as Aunt Leigh's parrot and encouraged to practice a kind of infant tyranny by granting or withholding demonstrations of affection.[40] She was galloping toward trouble, and the adults who should have stopped her were smoothing her way.

In addition, Dorothy's problems in adjusting to life at Godolphin were probably also exacerbated by her innate difference from her fellows; a brilliant mind usually causes tension between the student who possesses it and less talented schoolmates who realize they do not. Paint a monkey green, said Freud, and the others will tear it to pieces; in a closed environment, whether the painted monkey chooses to hide or fight, he inevitably suffers punishment at his fellows' teeth and claws because of a condition he cannot change.

Nevertheless, a radical shift in England's cultural patterns was beginning when Dorothy was at Godolphin. Ironically, her keen mind was isolated from the intellectual ferment gathering force in the first years of the new century. Bluntisham, for all its crowded library shelves, and Godolphin, under Miss Douglas's firm management, were hardly affected by the seminal works that were rocking intellectual circles in Britain, in America, and on the Continent. Freud's *Studies on Hysteria* (1895) and his *Interpretation of Dreams* (1905) were bitterly opposed by conservative thinkers; they would have been unthinkable additions to the Reverend Mr. Sayers's collection. No indication exists that Dorothy Sayers had any youthful exposure to the plays of Ibsen, then breaking the windows of stuffy Victorian sensibilities with a hammering Norse confirmation of the individual's responsibility to himself – and herself – instead of to society. The English translation of Marx's *Das Kapital* began appearing in 1907, as did the French philosopher Henri Bergson's *L'Évolution Créatrice*, which provided a foundation for modern stream-of-consciousness fiction; but in the same year England's traditional cultural values were reaffirmed by the selection of Rudyard Kipling for the Nobel Prize in Literature.

Young Dorothy Sayers had a boy's analytical mind, and the kind of reading she liked best had given her a boy's love of great chivalrous deeds, a boy's stubborn determination, a boy's ambition – and at the same time she faced all the limitations late Victorian custom placed upon a well-bred girl. She would have been raised to feel that the study of the Bible was the central preoccupation of educated persons, and Miss Douglas's insistence on the joy of work would have strengthened the conviction common in the Victorian middle class that service to one's fellow man was a standard of public activity. Dorothy's "improving" letters to Ivy manifested the rampant Victorian belief in the efficacy of preaching, something Dorothy never quite lost. Her insistence on being able to understand anything she read – later as a critic she had no patience with foggy writing or thinking – was also an outgrowth of the era's respect for the learned amateur. Dorothy would have been expected to take an accepted place in her society as a bright and devout young teacher or wife, dedicated to improving her environment and its inhabitants

37

through womanly demonstrations of her faith – praying with the servants before meals, perhaps, or running jumble sales to raise funds to convert the heathen. In the eyes of most of her parents' contemporaries, it would have been reprehensible that where mealy-mouthed piety and Victorian standards of deportment were concerned, Dorothy might well have sided with the heathen. In the years just prior to World War I's obliteration of the self-satisfaction of England's educated classes, a young woman of Dorothy's position who wanted any other kind of life would have been considered unnatural. The symptoms of defiance which she had begun to practice – and enjoy – in response to her misery at Godolphin, like her excuse making and showing off her French, probably would have been considered downright wicked by most of the older generation.

There was one area of Dorothy's life during her adolescence, however, where she knew she could excel. In the writing that already was becoming an outlet for her energy and talent, Dorothy was by now beginning to develop her sense of humor and a gift for satire. She could unerringly spot incongruities, strip them of Victorian camouflage and lay them out wittily, and, what is more, she could do it in her writing, a challenge even for experienced authors, as many fizzled attempts at literary humor can testify. Although she claimed she wanted it all destroyed, her son Anthony preserved a large body of her early work – poems, short stories, little plays – and when these are made generally available, they will likely reveal that much of the grown-up Dorothy Sayers was already descernible in her youthful writing. "The Gargoyle," a poem probably written in her mid-teens, hints at Dorothy's mature wit; it also demonstrates her satisfaction with things that however much rejected for their surface appearance, could still rejoice in being themselves. The gargoyle, an ugly beast sculpted to serve as a rainspout on medieval buildings, plays "cheerfully on rainy days," Dorothy wrote, but preachers "are awful dampers when they're dry."[41] The poem shows Dorothy's willingness to shock, her defiance of entrenched custom, and her delight in poking fun at whatever she felt needed deflating. Putting such notions into literary form might have started as revenge against persons or institutions that had hurt her, but Dorothy's ability to do so also indicates that she badly needed a change from Godolphin's stuffy atmosphere, possibly accounting many years later for her forthright description of her childhood as Edwardian rather than Victorian.

Often, loosened societal customs follow years of straitlacings. After England's seventeenth-century experiment with the dour Puritan Commonwealth (around the time of the musketeers who had captured Dorothy Sayers's imagination), the "Merry Monarch" Charles II returned home to England from his exile in France, renowned for its reputation of sexual license, and an era of unbridled pursuit of pleasure ensued in England. The term "Victorian" has come to rival "puritanical" in denoting unhealthy repression, and the double standard reigned supreme in nineteenth-century England; until 1882, women did not even possess rights to property gained either before or after marriage. The prevailing Victorian attitude toward sex was that sexual appetites and intellectual qualities were incompatible,[42] but by the end of the century, opposition to such notions had begun to swell. The celebrated trial of Oscar Wilde in 1895 had dealt a two-sided blow to conventionality, smiting both marital fidelity and sexual norms, and by the time of Victoria's death in 1901, sexuality had become a matter of social consciousness and was even being discussed in print. The personal preferences of England's new king also strongly buttressed this revolution. As Prince of Wales, Edward VII had been goodnaturedly philandering for years, and the British public had as goodnaturedly tolerated it. Now that he was king, a whole new life-style among the upper classes suddenly was not only acceptable, it was chic.

Edward VII, known publicly as "The Peacemaker" and to his friends as "Tum-Tum,"[43] came at the age of fifty-eight to the throne of an Empire that had enjoyed astonishing economic success for the past thirty years, a "super-wealth" that continued to burgeon. More was being spent on sport, mostly hunting and racing, than on the entire Royal Navy.[44] As British agriculture was in a depressed condition, the fortunes of the old wealthy – the landed aristocracy – dwindled, and the nouveaux riches poured into the creamiest top level of society, where money had become the measure of most things. The new king was lowering social barriers to a level that made the Old Guard shudder, and the awesomely expensive country house afforded the British leisure class an entirely different kind of "Saturday-to-Monday" than wealthy Victorians had enjoyed. (The term "weekend" was considered vulgar, since it implied the necessity of working for a living.) In the 1800s, a stay in the country had meant wholesome fresh air, shooting, and the hostess's greatest convenience, a stable guest list at her mercy for the duration because of the restrictions of horse and buggy travel. The advent of the automobile allowed guests to come and go at their pleasure, adding a new dimension to the possibilities of country-house flirtation.

Although Dorothy Sayers belonged to a far more conservative and far less well-to-do segment of her society than the smart Edwardian set, she was as a young person nonetheless allowed, at least at home, to shock the bourgeois, and she could not have helped but hear about and even be affected by the change in upper-class standards; the goings-on of the rich and Royals have always enjoyed an avid audience. One of the best of the salacious tales that went the rounds about Edwardian houseparties was about Lord Charles Beresford, who while reconnoitering a darkened bedroom presumably containing his current flame, vaulted onto the bed with a hearty "cock-a-doodle-doo" – and found himself between the Bishop of Chester and the Bishop's wife.[45] Her departed Majesty Queen Victoria most certainly would not have been amused, but the young Dorothy Sayers who entered Oxford in the fall of 1912, eager to learn to be herself and full of a wicked sense of humor, might well have been.

Notes

1. James Brabazon, *Dorothy L. Sayers: A Biography* (New York: Charles Scribners' Sons, 1981), p. 4.
2. Ibid., p. 5.
3. Michael Bentley, "Social Change: Appearance and Reality," in *The Cambridge Historical Encyclopedia of Great Britain and Ireland* (Cambridge: Cambridge University Press, 1985), p. 331.
4. Ibid., p. 330.
5. W. E. S. Thomas, "Culture: Revolution, Romanticism, and Victor-

ianism," in *The Cambridge Historical Encyclopedia of Great Britain and Ireland* (Cambridge: Cambridge University Press, 1985), pp. 285–86.

6. Ibid., p. 285.
7. Mark Girouard, *The Return to Camelot: Chivalry and the English Gentleman* (New Haven: Yale University Press, 1981), p. 260.
8. Ibid., p. 263.
9. Ibid., pp. 265–66.
10. Ibid., p. 271.
11. John Ruskin, quoted in *The Oxford Book of Oxford*, ed. Jan Morris, (Oxford: Oxford University Press, 1978), pp. 230–31. Morris does not supply the source of this Ruskin quotation.
12. Alzina Stone Dale, *Maker and Craftsman: The Story of Dorothy L. Sayers* (Grand Rapids, Mich.: William B. Eerdmans Publishing Co., 1978), p. 5.
13. Dorothy L. Sayers, quoted in Ralph E. Hone, *Dorothy L. Sayers: A Literary Biography* (Kent, Ohio: Kent State University Press, 1979), p. 1.
14. Dale, p. 18. None of Sayers's biographers identifies the author of the then-popular detective stories whose hero was "Sexton Blake." These stories probably had much the same kind of appeal as series thrillers or Westerns do today.
15. Brabazon, p. 11.
16. Dale, p. 17.
17. Dorothy L. Sayers, *The Mind of the Maker* (London: Methuen, 1941), p. 94.
18. Hone, p. 5.
19. Dorothy L. Sayers, *Begin Here*, quoted in Hone, p. 5.
20. The Athanasian Creed, as quoted in Hone, p. 186.
21. Letter of Dorothy L. Sayers to Dr. James Welch 7 December 1940, BBC Achives, quoted in Hone, pp. 5–6.
22. Brabazon, pp. 22–30.
23. Letter of Dorothy L. Sayers to Ivy Shrimpton 23 February 1908, quoted in Brabazon, p. 29.
24. Brabazon, p. 26.
25. Alexander Dumas, *The Three Musketeers* (New York: Grosset and Dunlap, n.d.; rpt. 1922), p. 275.
26. Dorothy L. Sayers, *The Nine Tailors* (New York: Harcourt Brace and World, 1934; rpt. 1962), p. 59. Alzina Stone Dale has also noted this point; see *Maker and Craftsman*, p. 27.
27. Hone, p. 8.
28. Brabazon, p. 26.
29. Dorothy L. Sayers, "Cat o'Mary," quoted in Brabazon, p. 32.
30. Brabazon, p. 33.
31. Letter of Dorothy L. Sayers to Ivy Shrimpton 15 April 1930, quoted in Brabazon, p. 33.
32. Brabazon, p. 35.
33. Brabazon, p. 34.

41

34. Hone, p. 8.
35. Ibid., p. 10.
36. Dorothy L. Sayers, "Cat o'Mary," quoted in Brabazon, p. 34.
37. Brabazon, p. 38.
38. Ibid., p. 40.
39. Ibid., p. 37. For Brabazon's discussion of "Cat o'Mary," see Chapters 1–4 of *Dorothy L. Sayers: A Biography*.
40. Ibid., p. 16.
41. Dorothy L. Sayers, "The Gargoyle," quoted in Brabazon, p. 20.
42. Asa Briggs, *A Social History of England* (New York: Viking Press, 1983), pp. 242–43.
43. Clive Aslet, *The Last Country Houses* (New Haven: Yale University Press, 1982), pp. 16, 70.
44. Ibid., pp. 185–88.
45. Anita Leslie, *Edwardians in Love*, quoted in Aslet, p. 72.

3 Oxford
1912–1915

> There's something about this place ... that
> alters all one's values.
> Dorothy L. Sayers, *Gaudy Night*

When Dorothy L. Sayers wrote her "Oxford novel," *Gaudy Night*,
she chose John Donne's phrase "gardens that are walled in" to
describe the university she loved. She had found that not all walls
are made of stone. To the uninitiated, especially Americans
accustomed to equating a university's achievements with its
research endowments or the record of its football team, Oxford
might seem unprepossessing; narrow, congested streets, ancient,
grey buildings streaked in black, a few glimpses of lawn beyond
medieval gates, and nondescript middle-aged men on bicycles or
afoot – but among them some of the world's most renowned
scholars. C. S. Lewis, Dorothy Sayers's contemporary, remarked
that immaculately dressed students fresh from British public
schools "think we have come to clean the windows when they see
us."[1] Such protective coloration can make keys to Oxford's
gardens difficult to acquire or even perceive. Although Dorothy
Sayers had all the intellectual equipment to succeed there, the
institution she entered in the fall of 1912 was a world that did not
share its secret beauties easily. The majority of its inhabitants
came from Britain's upper middle class and aristocracy, then starting
to feel the first tremors in their grip on Britain's social structure.

Two years before World War I erupted, England's economic
boom of the early 1900s was beginning to falter. The Liberals had
come to power in 1906 and had implemented costly social legislation. The Royal Navy had also launched a massive new program
of dreadnought building, and to pay for it all, Lloyd George, then
Chancellor of the Exchequer, introduced the "People's Budget,"
smiting the pocketbooks of the landed aristocracy with hefty new
taxes.[2] Bitter opposition from the House of Lords caused Lord
Asquith, the prime minister, to threaten to create enough new
Liberal peers to pass any legislation he wanted. The Lords

43

capitulated and were defanged, losing nearly all their veto powers and swallowing tax measures that put many of the landed aristocracy out of their estates. Nonetheless, between 1911 and 1913 one percent of the population of Great Britain owned 65.5 percent of the nation's personal capital, and many of that ruling elite called Oxford their spiritual home.

They were a breed apart. One of their hallmarks was the "Oxford voice," capable of enraging those who were not able to acquire it. D. H. Lawrence, a product of Nottingham's teacher-training institute, savagely observed,

> When you hear it languishing
> and hooing, cooing, sidling through the front teeth,
> . . . .
> and oh, so seductively superior, so seductively
> self-effacingly
> deprecatingly
> superior
> . . . .
> you don't even laugh any more, you can't.[3]

The "in crowd" of Edwardian Oxford also had their own idiom, well-nigh incomprehensible to outsiders. Jan Morris has culled this specimen from the diary of a Worcester College freshman, Willie Elmhirst, 1911: "After Toggers brekker went to divvers leccer, then to eat at the Ugger" (After he had breakfast with the Torpids racing crew, Willie went to a divinity lecture and had lunch at the Oxford Union).[4]

Dorothy Sayers had had the Oxford voice from the start, and she had no trouble picking up the dialect – she later used it to good effect for local color in *Gaudy Night* – but she was a woman, and her sex was as yet not widely tolerated at Oxford, whose all-male beginnings were lost, some said, in the mists of early English history, founded perhaps by King Alfred in the ninth century or even by the legendary Trojan refugee Brutus. By the end of the twelfth century, Oxford was well established as a haven for clerical scholars, who studied for seven years in the seven liberal arts leading to the Master of Arts degree.[5] Merton, the first of the Oxford colleges, was founded in 1264; its superior, called the Warden, had to be "a man of circumspection in spiritual and temporal affairs," and its scholars, chaste and of good conduct and dressed "as nearly alike as possible," were to "live meekly in fellowship."[6] For over six hundred years, Oxford remained what Harold Macmillan in 1975 wistfully recalled as "an entirely masculine, almost monastic society."[7] A woman occasionally might intrude but only as a necessary evil, like a servant or (later) a wife; or as a temptress such as Max Beerbohm of Merton described in his uproarious novel *Zuleika Dobson* (1911), in which the entire male student body of Oxford plunged like lemmings into the Isis bellowing, "Zuleika!"

The woman-free life of Oxford's male scholars received its first major jolt in 1875 when women over eighteen years of age were admitted to examinations. "The other place," as Oxonians refer to Cambridge, already had established two colleges for women by 1879, when Oxford's Lady Margaret Hall, attached firmly to the Church of England, and Somerville Hall, just as rigorously nondenominational, were founded. Somerville became a college in 1881, priding itself on stringent scholarly standards and the success of its graduates both in and beyond academia; these have included, besides Dorothy Sayers, the novelist Iris Murdoch; the social reformers Margaret Fry and Barbara Ward; and Prime Minister Margaret Thatcher. *Somerville College 1879–1921*, by Catherine Hope Mansfield and Muriel St. Clare Byrne – the latter was Dorothy Sayers's close, lifelong friend – provides a charming contemporary view of Somerville's early history and customs.[8]

In 1886, Oxford first officially admitted women to "responsions" or "Smalls," entrance examinations in Latin and Greek taken during the first year of study, and in 1888 to "Greats," the Honour School of *Literae Humaniores*, Oxford's most famous School, or major subject area. The Oxford Home-Students Society had also been established in 1879, and two more women's colleges arose, St. Hugh's in 1886 and St. Hilda's in 1893. The women's colleges admitted only students reading for honors; Somerville went a step further and required almost all of its students to qualify for the Bachelor of Arts.[9] All Oxford qualifying examinations for the Bachelor of Arts degree were opened to women in 1894, a major step toward awarding them Oxford

45

degrees, although that Rubicon was not crossed until 1920, two years after British women – over thirty – had received the vote. Somerville far outstripped its sister institutions by having about three hundred students, Dorothy Sayers among them, qualify for the Bachelor of Arts degree that memorable year.

The college had taken its name from Mary Somerville, an eighteenth-century scientist who, in deference to male sensibilities, had had to learn her Euclid and algebra from behind a curtain.[10] From the outset, the college deliberately had fostered "a progressive conception of woman . . . clothed discreetly in the hereditary feminine garb of modest manners and watchful tact," powerful feminine weapons that present-day liberated advocates of women's rights might do well to get out of mothballs. Somerville's first principal, Miss Madeleine Shaw Lefevre, unleashed the college's tactics to heroic effect on Christ Church's eminent Victorian art critic John Ruskin, who might have been considered an impressive challenge since he was the son of a domineering mother and party to a four-year unconsummated marriage. Ruskin at first found the notion of a women's college "repugnant," but after tea at Somerville, he gallantly presented the college with some of his own books and paintings and the sapphires and rubies which were later set into a pendant worn by Somerville's principals.[11] Miss Shaw Lefevre's successors evidently enlarged upon her successful maneuvers, because when Dorothy Sayers arrived at Somerville twenty years later, the college had just experienced a welcome rise in its financial support and was completing a sizable building program. Nevertheless, Dorothy found out that admitting women and accepting them were still two quite different matters at Oxford.

C. S. Lewis described the "real Oxford" of his day and Dorothy's as "a close [sic] corporation of jolly, untidy, lazy, good-for-nothing, humorous old men, who have been electing their own successors ever since the world began and who intend to go on with it."[12] For years the real Oxford imposed horrendous social conditions upon women that today would seem comic if one overlooked the deadly double standard behind their enforcement. At first women students could not be seen walking to dinner parties on Oxford streets, and so Somerville kept a bath chair for such use; and not until 1893 could women attend lectures without chaperones beside them, knitting industriously on white cotton garments.[13] The situation had improved by 1906, when bicycles were recommended equipment for "undergraduettes," but even after British nurses had endured harrowing overseas conditions in the Great War, the 1924 Oxford *Intercollegiate Rules for Women* still insisted that women undergraduates could enter men's rooms only with permission and when accompanied by approved chaperones; permission also had to be obtained for evening invitations and mixed parties at any time, and women had to report to the proper authorities upon their return. Mixed café parties were allowed only between two and half past five in the afternoon and had to include at least two women.[14]

During the Roaring Twenties, Oxford's Vice-Chancellor ("Vigger-Chogger") Dr. Lewis Farnell, Rector of Exeter, waged a passionate rearguard action against encroachment by women on his sacred precincts. When he discovered that the lamentable "trench-habit" of "taking coffee or chocolate . . . about eleven in the morning" had come home with young officers from the Great War and had been "eagerly caught up by our lazy and self-indulgent boys and girls," Dr. Farnell sought to put the cafés out-of-bounds, just as the bars were, between ten in the morning and one in the afternoon. He soon received "an earnest and anxious petition" from all the lady Heads "begging us not to do anything so severe against their poor girls." Outflanked by the special difficulties of a bisexual university, Dr. Farnell had to retreat, but he claimed that he had "put it to the Proctors, in the wise words of Antony's Enobarbus, 'Under a compelling occasion, let women die'."[15]

To what Dr. Farnell called his "perpetual regret," he lost the entire battle, and women did not drop out of Oxford in the 1920s. A decade earlier, though, Dorothy Sayers and her fellow women students must have needed plenty of grit and backbone to survive. A healthy sense of humor, as several memoirs besides Dorothy's indicate, no doubt also helped.

Somerville is located on the Woodstock Road leading northwest out of the city, just south of the Radcliffe Infirmary and slightly north of the heart of Oxford, where almost all of its hallowed colleges and monuments lie. From the college's narrow Woodstock Road entrance, two small quadrangles precede a large open area of lawn and trees, and Maitland, one of two large buildings to the east completed by October 1913, linked the older parts of the college together. Maitland, where Dorothy Sayers lived, houses the College Hall, about seventy feet by thirty-five feet, where students, their tutors, and the administration take their meals. A heroic fund drive for its construction was started in March 1910, producing paneling for the Hall and a Jacobean oak chair for the principal, Miss Penrose, who herself donated the Hall's "beautiful lightoliers,"[16] but compared with the venerable men's institutions, the women's colleges had minimal endowments. Whereas college "scouts" (servants) could fetch such amenities as plovers' eggs and champagne to peckish young gentlemen, Oxford women got by on cocoa and Kia-Ora, perching on convertible divans in tiny chilly bed-sitters rather than savoring claret and port on deep sofas beside coal fires.[17] Somerville's rooms did not even have hot water when Dorothy first was a student there.

Early twentieth-century university education for women, like any adolescence, had its blemishes. Christopher Hobhouse uncharitably observed that Oxford women of the time ignored both their appearances and their comfort, decking themselves in "hairy woolens and shapeless tweeds" and braiding their hair into "stringy buns."[18] The Viscountess Rhondda, a Somerville graduate who became one of Britain's first women magistrates, recalled she had disliked Somerville's "frousty" smell, its ugliness, its food, the dowdiness of both dons and girls, the isolation from men, and "the slightly deprecating and dowdy, and again very self-conscious, atmosphere of ladylike culture that hung about the dons at play."[19] Usually, however, the women of all five female Societies worked together harmoniously "whether in a common defence, or from a common policy," especially in matters involving university teaching.[20]

While Dorothy was at the university, women were not allowed to take degrees, but even a degree equivalent certificate from Oxford could open up better economic opportunities for them than ordinary women could achieve almost any other way. The forty to forty-five women a year who entered Somerville before 1920 could look forward to the possibility of careers in the law, like Lady Rhondda, or jobs in Civil Service, mainly administrative and social work, which were starting to become available to them. Most Somerville students still prepared to teach, a few moving into university positions, and their Oxford credentials allowed many of them a small degree of luxury which otherwise a teaching career could never provide.[21] Dorothy Sayers's fine mind seemed to destine her for teaching, but she also had a flair for combining scholarship with creative activity, something she called a "congenital disease" that lasted her entire life. In her scholarship examinations, taken at Oxford in the spring of 1912, she not only translated a sonnet, but made her translation an entirely new piece of art in strict Petrarchan form.[22]

Dorothy had to tackle the Latin and Greek responsions before she could indulge her love of modern languages. Her coach for her first two terms at Oxford was one Herbert May, for whom she seems to have had respect and affection, even though he did perpetually fortify himself with snuff.[23] During her second term she also passed the dreaded "Divvers," a difficult examination in Divinity, which many students barely scraped through. Dorothy then had the good fortune to be assigned Mildred Katherine Pope, about twenty years her senior, as her tutor in medieval French. Miss Pope herself had a brilliant academic career; when on 7 October 1920 the women's degree statute came into force allowing women to be admitted to all Oxford degrees except Theology, to wear academic dress, and to serve the university under the same conditions as did men, Miss Pope became the first woman don to be appointed as a university lecturer, and she was also named a deputy professor during the absence of a male Professor Studer that Michaelmas (autumn) term.[24] In 1934 Mildred Pope was awarded the chair of Romance Philology (modern languages) at Manchester University, a notable achievement for any scholar, since British universities generally have only one professor for each subject, and an honor virtually unheard of for a woman at that time. According to Alzina Stone Dale, Miss Pope's portrait in Somerville's dining hall shows "a plain, humorous face with intent, bespectacled eyes under tightly combed hair and rather dowdy clothes." Unlike her famous pupil, Miss Pope was devoted to field hockey,[25] one of the few sports available to Somerville students. The other was punting, which offered hours of "exquisite pleasure" on the river,[26] the

49

backdrop for an unforgettable love scene between Sayers's Lord Peter Wimsey and his Harriet in *Gaudy Night*.

Mildred Pope was lecturing on "epic and romance" during the 1913–14 university year,[27] and while Dorothy was studying at Oxford, she attended lectures and followed Miss Pope's reading lists in medieval French, producing weekly essays – the accepted mode of Oxford teaching – which Miss Pope would thoroughly critique a few days later for style and structure as well as content. This scrupulous one-on-one attention not only fostered Dorothy's habit of literary excellence, it established a warm bond between Dorothy and Miss Pope, to whom Dorothy dedicated her translation of Thomas's *Tristan* begun at Oxford and published in 1929. When Dorothy Sayers returned to Oxford as a well-known author in 1934 to give the University Toast at Somerville's Gaudy (reunion) Dinner, she paid Mildred Pope one of the finest tributes a pupil could offer her teacher: "She has always seemed to typify some of the noblest things for which the University stands. The integrity of judgement that gain cannot corrupt, the humility in the face of the facts that self-esteem cannot blind; the generosity of a great mind that is eager to give praise to others; the singleness of purpose that pursues knowledge as some pursue glory."[28] Working with Mildred Pope at Oxford had at last given Dorothy the chance to stretch her mind by dealing professionally with the Middle Ages she loved, and that circumstance alone must have helped make her years at Oxford some of the happiest in her life. More than twenty-five years after she left Oxford, Dorothy Sayers described all she had learned there as some basic Old French grammar and "a respect for intellectual integrity"[29] – the latter being nothing less than the theme of one of her most popular and most self-revealing novels, *Gaudy Night*. James Brabazon feels that she also received the traditional legacy of a liberal education at Oxford, the ability to discipline her mind so that she could effectively cope with the problems the world presented her.[30]

Socially, too, Dorothy could at last be herself at Oxford. Somerville had no discernible single type of student, although the Viscountess Rhondda had found two sorts to dislike, "the cocoa-cum-missionary-party-hymn-singing girls" with their "air of forced brightness and virtue," and "those who reacted from this into smoking cigarettes and feeling wicked," with their "self-conscious would-be naughtiness."[31] At college Dorothy did drink cocoa and liked to belt out the more militant hymns, but she also smoked and cultivated an appearance of disreputability. Edwardian and early Georgian daywear for the lady of fashion involved long gored and fitted skirts equipped with bustles and dust-ruffles and topped by lace-and-linen Gibson girl blouses with leg o'mutton sleeves. These ensembles required hours of tedious and frustrating combat with fourteen-pound irons that had to be heated up on stoves and rushed precariously to the ironing table, "a heart-breaking, back-breaking business";[32] no wonder "hairy woolens" and shapeless jerseys appealed to women students making do without ladies' maids and battling fearsome "essays" customarily put off until the last moment.

Dorothy loved clothes, and her taste, previously smothered under the blue Godolphin pinafore, ran rather wilder than the prevailing Oxford norm. With her blue eyes and dark hair – still not completely grown back from her illness – she preferred forceful colors, bold shapes, dangling earrings, and sleeves that daringly revealed her arms – at a time when the sight of a shapely ankle was widely believed to send young men into dangerous spasms of sexual excitation. She was thin and stood five feet seven inches, tall for a girl at that time, and to compensate for the difficulties with her hair, she had to resort to wigs. Perhaps as overcompensation for her difficulties at Godolphin, she refused to hide her problem, and instead flaunted her solutions to it, adding immense hairbows and other effects which fellow students who knew nothing about Dorothy's pneumonia found bizarre; her contemporary Vera Brittain described them as "extravagant indoor head-gear which varied from shrill colours by day to gold or silver by night."[33] Dorothy appeared one morning for breakfast in Hall with a wide red hair ribbon and earrings that swept her shoulders – each a tiny gilt cage holding a red and green parrot. The appalled principal could not violate her own policy of noninterference with her students' personal lives, but she did ask another third-year student to try to persuade Dorothy to remove the earrings.[34] It seems unlikely that Dorothy would have done so.

Dorothy's flamboyant dress now was probably less a symptom

of rebellion than a means of self-expression, like her musketeer costumes, since she delightedly found herself among talented women friends at Oxford. Her Oxford friend Dorothy Rowe recalled that when they went to Oxford for their scholarship tests, Dorothy Sayers began to quote in French from Rostand's *Cyrano de Bergerac*, the tale of the musketeer with the gigantic nose who made his life into one grand gesture. By finishing the quotation, Dorothy Rowe started off a solid friendship.[35] At Godolphin the talents Dorothy had not been able to resist flaunting had closed her off from her schoolmates, but at Oxford she met kindred spirits. In the fall of 1912, Dorothy Rowe and Charis Barnett founded an exclusive literary group, one of those ephemeral organizations that pop into the life of a college and as suddenly disappear, having lent their times unique flavors and leavening. Dorothy Sayers provided its name, the "Mutual Admiration Society," on the grounds that if its handful of members did not call it that, the rest of Somerville's one hundred students certainly would.[36] M.A.S. members went on to important careers, and all of them published books in later life. Besides Dorothy Rowe, Muriel St. Clare Byrne, who entered Oxford in 1914, and Muriel Jaeger, nicknamed "Jim," became Dorothy Sayers's close friends. The M.A.S. admitted only those girls its members liked, Charis Barnett said,[37] but Dorothy was genuinely popular. Vera Brittain, who also started in 1914, recalled that Dorothy was "exhuberant" and kind to "freshers," continually bustling around the top floor of Maitland getting ready for tea parties.[38]

During her first year at Somerville, Dorothy also took part in the amateur theatricals accepted as being in Somerville's blood.[39] One of her first dramatic efforts was a satiric skit for entering students in February 1913 called *Hamlet, the Pragger-Dagger*, apparently a smash since it had to be repeated in front of the entire college. (The Prince of Wales – the "Pragger-Wagger," later the Duke of Windsor – was then also in attendance at Oxford.)[40] That December Dorothy acted the role of John Gaunt in the Henley-Stevenson play *Admiral Guinea*, which Dorothy Rowe stage-managed.

In 1915, Dorothy Sayers reached the pinnacle of her college dramatic career with the "going-down" (graduation) play, "Somerville's clever comment on herself,"[41] always an antidote for the "Schools" examinations third-year students had just survived. Dorothy had sung contralto with Oxford University's illustrious Bach Choir throughout her college years, and she had developed a well-publicized flaming crush on its director, Dr. Hugh Percy Allen, who was later knighted. Dr. Allen's peculiar mannerisms and unbridled opinions allowed rich opportunities for parody, and Dorothy made the most of them. "Pied Pipings or The Innocents Abroad," which Dorothy directed while playing "Dr. H. P. Rallentando" herself, was set to Gilbert and Sullivan tunes. She kept her portrait in makeup for that role on the wall of her study at Witham until she died.[42]

Just then Oxford could have used some levity, because the assassination of Archduke Ferdinand at Sarajevo on 28 June 1914 had ignited a war like nothing the world had ever seen. England's Victorian ideals of chivalry had helped promote the idea that nothing could be nobler than dying in a just cause for one's country, and a fight with Kaiser Wilhelm's Germany had been brewing for a long time. Mark Girouard has observed that Britain's imperialism and faith in its manifest destiny, its sense of the "White Man's Burden," its public school tradition, and even the Boy Scout organization and adventure stories boys (and some girls, like Dorothy Sayers) read had engendered "giant forces of loyalty to king and country . . . ready to be triggered off, submerging all doubts in the process."[43] "People could approach the war in a black-and-white, yes-or-no spirit because they lacked the faintest prevision of what it was going to be like."[44] Rudyard Kipling was more realistic. His "Recessional," composed for Queen Victoria's Diamond Jubilee in 1897, noted the Victorian tendency to be "drunk with sight of power":

> For frantic boast and foolish word,
> Thy mercy on Thy people, Lord![45]

Aside from the Crimean War, Britain had not fought a major enemy since Napoleon. The American Civil War had shown that in modern warfare a massed infantry assault on a fortified position was doomed, but that horrifying lesson had yet to be grasped in the trenches of France and Flanders. From August 1914 to January 1916, 2,467,000 British men volunteered[46] – and more continued to do so, even after it had become apparent that the life expectancy of an English subaltern at the front was measured in weeks.

Between 1914 and 1915, Oxford's male population dropped from 3,000 to 1,000,[47] and over 2,700 of Oxford's men were killed in World War I.[48] Of the eight scholars and exhibitioners who came up to Balliol with Harold Macmillan in 1912, only two were alive at the end of the war. Oxford rapidly became a city of ghosts, not only of the dead but even more shattering, the shell-shocked living.[49]

A 1917 survey of all 700 members of the Somerville Student Association indicated that the half who replied were engaged in three types of wartime work: "active service" requiring new training, "war work" for which university education had provided preparation, and work not connected with the war effort, which was thought sometimes to be the most difficult of all.[50] Most of the Somerville women were doing various kinds of war work, and about a hundred in various capacities served in hospitals, like Charis Barnett, who lost both her brother and her fiancé in the war and left Somerville to become a nurse with the Quakers in France. Muriel St. Clare Byrne felt that Somerville's best contribution to war efficiency was administrative work carried out in social welfare areas and government positions, including the War Office and the Ministry of Munitions, which gave women a strong foothold when the British Civil Service was opened to them in August 1921.[51]

Dorothy Sayers had a close brush with the war at its very beginning. Ignoring the ominous news from Europe in the summer of 1914, she and two friends set out for Tours, an important center of medieval Christian learning in the lovely Loire Valley of central France, planning to stay all of August and the first two weeks in September. After the outbreak of hostilities on 4 August, they found France mobilizing and transportation around Tours limited to military traffic. A letter to her parents on 11 August shows that Dorothy maintained her detachment under the trying circumstances, noting that the French seemed calmer than the English did about the situation.[52] Brabazon believes she must have had some difficulty getting back to England around the middle of August, but her French could pass for a native's, and once home she must have had some exciting stories to tell.[53]

Dorothy considered active war work but decided against it, so she remained in Oxford. Just after the 1915 spring term, Somerville's students were moved to the Rhodes Block and the St. Mary Quadrangle of Oriel, a college by then half empty of its men, so that Somerville could be used as a military hospital. It was close enough to the Radcliffe Infirmary for surgical patients to be carried directly into operating rooms there, and many Oxford men entered Somerville as casualties.[54] This exceptional arrangement placed a heavy public relations responsibility on Somerville's women, who were now in closer proximity to Oxford men than they ever had been before. Apprehension about unspecified disasters abounded in the male community. Some industrious Oxford men did try to tunnel into the women's lodgings one night,[55] but the enterprise collapsed. Overall, Oxford women conducted themselves with unimpeachable decorum, enduring the inconvenience of basement bathrooms and the sadly limited number of gas rings for tea parties, and created a generally favorable impression.[56] One of the greatest professional benefits to them, of course, was living in the heart of Oxford, and for born scholars like Dorothy Sayers, working in the "arms of Duke Humphrey" – the oldest part of the Bodleian Library – would have been a special joy.

Many years later in her "Oxford novel" *Gaudy Night*, Dorothy's famous detective Lord Peter Wimsey voiced her mature opinion of her alma mater: "There's something about this place . . . that alters all one's values."[57] At eighteen, Dorothy had left Godolphin sick and exhausted, unable to fit in with her classmates and most of her teachers; she emerged from Somerville four years later as a healthy young woman with many of her grown-up values already well established. Oxford made a remarkable difference in Dorothy's life, one that affected nearly every kind of work she later did and almost every relationship that she had.

The Mutual Admiration Society proved that Somerville offered Dorothy Sayers the best kind of companionship she could have had at that important stage in her life, young women secure enough with their own intellectual talents not to feel threatened by hers. It furnished her an outlet for the writing she did on her own, like a fictional conversation of the Three Wise Men that

Charis Barnett felt foreshadowed *The Man Born to Be King*.[58] Moreover, meeting weekly with this audience of her peers – unlike Bluntisham, with its undemanding familial appreciation, and Godolphin, in some respects just the opposite – gave Dorothy the chance to hear their criticism of her work, vital to the development of any creative person; no one can produce significant art in a vacuum.

Dorothy's Gilchrist Scholarship paid for her school fees, but she likely did not have much money to spend for fun. Harriet Vane, the autobiographical figure Dorothy created to marry and thus exterminate Lord Peter Wimsey, had five pounds or so (around twenty-five dollars) each six-week Oxford term for recreation, and Dorothy's friend Charis Barnett had as little as two.[59] Even though prices in the early 1900s seem ridiculously low by today's standards, Dorothy and her friends had to make much of their own amusement from scratch – hence the amateur dramatics and the tea parties in their own accommodations or the Junior Common Room, sometimes inviting their favorite dons, generally unmarried women like Miss Pope who wholeheartedly gave their lives to their profession. Oxford also has many lovely areas accessible by boat or bicycle for picnics, like the Botanic Garden, conservatories and walled rose gardens, perfect for spending a romantic afternoon. Oxford boat races were great free spectacles, and university festivals often provided splendid music gratis, like the May Day performance of the Magdalen College choir Dorothy mentioned in *Gaudy Night*.

Outside of her writing and the M.A.S., music probably gave Dorothy more pleasure – and some well-exhibited pangs – than any other extracurricular activity she pursued at Oxford. Dr. Allen had peculiarities – he was widely known for discarding items of clothing in the course of practice sessions, a "strip tease act" which, Dorothy observed, left almost nothing but his trousers to come off – but under his idiosyncratic direction the Bach Choir undertook not only medieval hymns and Baroque cantatas but highly demanding works, like the Verdi *Requiem* and Bach's *B-minor Mass*, the pièce de résistance of one week-long festival that left Dorothy swooning, "simply mad,"[60] under the combined influence of the music and Dr. Allen.

Brabazon suggests that Dorothy's infatuation with Dr. Allen, which lasted most of the time she was at Oxford, culminated in invitations to his choir loft toward the end of her last year. She let him know she was not afraid of him, and whatever happened in the choir loft – her letters to her parents are not specific, Brabazon says – she did not intend to be the latest addition to Dr. Allen's "little tame cats."[61] Her crush, widely known in Oxford, may have been another devil-may-care musketeerish pose, like her dashing wigs and the offending parrot earrings. Rather than making herself sick, she had found fun in shocking the world around her, and her dramatic activities afforded the perfect vehicle. The parody of Dr. Allen that she staged at the end of her college years marked an important step in her relations with men (admittedly limited under Oxford conditions) because it showed that she had learned to view herself objectively and laugh at herself, one of the notably difficult lessons of growing up.

The focus of Dorothy's concerns was shifting outward from adolescent self-absorption while she was at Oxford. Besides her generally pleasant attitude toward underclassmen, she joined a group of "Somerville charitables" who volunteered to sing at the Radcliffe Infirmary, where the patients' choices of lugubrious hymns convinced her that "all simple minds love gloom."[62] When Oxford was filling with Belgian refugees in the fall of 1914, she also undertook to help some of them find places to live, an exercise in social work considerably beyond the call of her duties just then.[63] Dorothy seems to have been developing an often-overlooked streak of genuine charity, the kind that never seeks or wants any kind of publicity.

Oxford also affected her religious views. She came out of Godolphin so angry at its Low Church practice, its emotionalism and its furtive references to "Gawd" that she might have abandoned Christianity wholesale, as do many young people. Fortunately for her faith, Oxford at this time was in the grip of a modish Anglo-Catholicism, and Dorothy began to read the religious works of G. K. Chesterton, a conservative and prolific Anglican writer who would convert to Roman Catholicism in 1922. She already knew his widely read "Father Brown" detective series, which had begun in 1911, and while she was a student at Somerville, she also heard Chesterton lecture and reveled in his logical and forceful defense of orthodoxy against heresy, which he found in such popular authors as Kipling, George Bernard Shaw and H. G. Wells. Dorothy found Chesterton irresistible, a "Christian liberator" who blasted the Church with fresh air and made Christianity seem the most exciting adventure possible.[64] She always loved to debate and would often stay up well past midnight arguing over the eternal problems of youth – sex, politics, art, and especially religion. Brabazon suggests that the religious position she took at this time strangely combined freethinking and orthodox Christian belief as Chesterton was revealing it to her, a vivid and even humorous spiritual adventure perfectly suited to her intellect and temperament.[65] Chesterton's religious conservatism, which included a sense of sin and its wages so powerful as often to be called reactionary, seems not to have bothered her at all.

The most practical contribution Oxford made to Dorothy's development, however, might seem the most fundamental: she learned how to work. Besides all the fun, she studied several hours a day or night, and she was producing solid results. By the end of the Michaelmas (autumn) Term, 1913, Mildred Pope observed that Dorothy genuinely liked thoroughness and tackled the more technical philological aspects of her subject with as much enthusiasm as she addressed the literary ones.[66] Dorothy finished in Trinity (spring) Term, 1915, after a brilliant perform-ance on her final honors examinations (Schools), which covered everything she had studied for the past three years and culmi-nated in an oral examination determining whether one received First or Second Honors. Dorothy made only one small slip by sacrificing meaning for metrical effect in one word of a translation of a poem, sailing nobly with an impressive First through an examination process that justifiably terrorized many students.

If as John Donne had put it, Oxford was a garden walled off from the rest of the world, Dorothy had had to struggle to enter it, overcoming some serious emotional and social problems along the way. Once inside, however, she found herself enthralled by Oxford's dedication to excellence, its respect for intellectual integrity, and the humility it engendered in fine minds – all of the qualities she admired in Mildred Pope. Oxford was the one place on earth Dorothy Sayers was happiest, because it reinvigorated her Anglican faith that had been seriously shaken at Godolphin, and it taught her that hard work at her writing could make people both laugh and think, a job she now knew she could do well enough to earn her share of the joy of creation. When she had to leave, she wrote as though she felt cast out of Eden:

> . . . the thing that I remember most of all
> is the white hemlock by the garden wall.
>
> June 23, 1915[67]

Notes

1. W. H. Lewis, *The Letters of C. S. Lewis*, quoted in Jan Morris, *The Oxford Book of Oxford* (Oxford: Oxford University Press, 1978), p. 339.
2. Peter Clarke, "Government and Politics in England: Realignment and Readjustment," in *The Cambridge Historical Encyclopedia of Great Britain and Ireland*, ed. Christopher Haigh (Cambridge: Cambridge University Press, 1985), p. 294. Seven new taxes were imposed on the wealthy.
3. D. H. Lawrence, "The Oxford Voice," in *Pansies* (1929); *The Complete Poems of D. H. Lawrence*, ed. Vivian deSola Pinto and Warren Roberts (New York: Viking, 1971), pp. 433–34.
4. Willie Elmhirst, *A Freshman's Diary*, quoted in Morris, p. 329.
5. Morris, p. 6.
6. Oxford's original Statutes, quoted and translated from the Latin by Morris, p. 21.
7. Harold Macmillan, in *The Times*, quoted in Morris, p. 361.
8. Muriel St. Clare Byrne and Catherine Hope Mansfield, *Somerville College, 1879–1921* (Oxford: Oxford University Press, 1927).
9. Ibid., p. 65.
10. Ibid., p. 34. Dorothy Sayers made the patroness of fictional Shrewsbury College in *Gaudy Night* the ominous holy-terror daughter of Bess of Hardwick. As described in Chapter 3, Mary, Countess of Shrewsbury, had an outstanding talent for invective and "every alarming quality which a learned woman is popularly credited with developing." A portrait of the redoubtable sixteenth-century Countess hanging in St. John's College, Cambridge, was Sayers's inspiration. (See the Sayers Society Tour of Cambridge, p. 1.)

11. Ibid., pp. 15, 12–13.
12. Lewis, quoted as above in Morris, pp. 338–39.
13. Byrne and Mansfield, pp. 74, 76.
14. Oxford's *Intercollegiate Rules for Women*, 1924, quoted in Morris, p. 358.
15. Lewis R. Farnell, *An Oxonian Looks Back*, quoted in Morris, p. 359.
16. Byrne and Mansfield, pp. 32–33.
17. Christopher Hobhouse, *Oxford*, quoted in Morris, p. 360.
18. Ibid.
19. Viscountess Rhondda, *This Was My World*, quoted in Morris, p. 360.
20. Byrne and Mansfield, p. 62.
21. Ibid., p. 85.
22. Alzina Stone Dale, *Maker and Craftsman: The Story of Dorothy L. Sayers* (Grand Rapids, Mich.: William B. Eerdmans Publishing Co., 1978), p. 30.
23. Ralph E. Hone, *Dorothy L. Sayers: A Literary Biography* (Kent, Ohio: Kent State University Press, 1979), p. 13.
24. Byrne and Mansfield, pp. 66–68.
25. Dale, pp. 44–45.
26. Byrne and Mansfield, p. 82.
27. Ibid., p. 87.
28. Dale, p. 45.
29. James Brabazon, *Dorothy L. Sayers: A Biography* (New York: Charles Scribners' Sons, 1981), p. 47.
30. Ibid., p. 48.
31. Lady Rhondda, quoted in Morris, p. 360.
32. Clive Aslet, *The Last Country Houses* (New Haven, Conn.: Yale University Press, 1982), p. 106.
33. Vera Brittain, *The Women at Oxford: A Fragment of History*, quoted in Hone, p. 17.
34. Dale, p. 35. See also Hone, p. 18.
35. Brabazon, p. 42.
36. Hone, p. 17.
37. Brabazon, p. 44.
38. Hone, p. 17.
39. Byrne and Mansfield, pp. 80–81.
40. Hone, p. 18.
41. Byrne and Mansfield, p. 81.
42. Dale, p. 40.
43. Mark Girouard, *The Return to Camelot* (New Haven, Conn.: Yale University Press, 1981), p. 281.
44. Ibid., p. 282.
45. Rudyard Kipling, "Recessional," in *British Literature*, ed. Hazelton Spencer et al., II (Lexington, Mass.: D. C. Heath and Co., 1974), p. 978.
46. Girouard, p. 283.
47. Dale, p. 47.

48. Morris, p. 335.
49. Macmillan, quoted in Morris, p. 336.
50. Byrne and Mansfield, pp. 46–47.
51. Ibid., pp. 53–55.
52. Brabazon, p. 52.
53. Ibid.
54. Byrne and Mansfield, p. 44.
55. Dale, p. 47.
56. Byrne and Mansfield, pp. 42–43.
57. Dorothy L. Sayers, *Gaudy Night* (1936; rpt. New York: Avon Books, 1968), p. 382.
58. Hone, p. 17.
59. Dale, p. 40.
60. Brabazon, p. 50.
61. Ibid., p. 52.
62. Letter of Dorothy L. Sayers to Dr. James Welch, quoted in Hone, p. 19.
63. Brabazon, p. 52.
64. Dale, pp. 37–38.
65. Brabazon, p. 39.
66. Ibid., p. 54.
67. Dorothy L. Sayers, "Last Morning in Oxford," quoted in Dale, p. 49.

4 Eros In and Out of Academe 1915–1922

> ... men and women both have got
> Too great an itch for novelty ...
> And change their mind too easily,
> And change desire, and change their will
> Clean against reason and their skill.
> Dorothy L. Sayers, *Tristan in Brittany*

No matter how much she had loved being there, Oxford let Dorothy Sayers and women students of her time down in one vital respect: the standards of conduct drawn up by the male authorities of the university and accepted by its women's colleges (whether they liked them or not) considered men and women two mutually exclusive species. On one end of the 1915 British social scale, flirtations – and more – might be taking place in the darkened boudoirs of Edwardian country houses, and on the other, women might be offering time-honored solaces to soldiers, but the university intended to ignore them; such things had always happened and given human nature, always would, and for centuries Oxford's enclosed gardens had usually managed to shelter their male scholars from biological disruptions – except, of course, those of their own choosing. Significant changes in the position of women were beginning to emerge in Britain and America when Dorothy Sayers was an Oxford undergraduate, however, and no amount of ivory-tower disparagement was going to make them go away.

Europe's old feudal, aristocratic system had regarded women as men's inferiors both physically and intellectually. Secular law backed by the moral authority of the Church prevented women from possessing property, engaging in business, and making decisions regarding their children's futures or even their own, a situation which prevailed in much of Europe until well into the twentieth century. Regardless of the French Revolutionary demand for equality of the sexes, soon forgotten once the Empire was reestablished, the legal system based on the Code Napoleon

62

prevented French women from voting until 1944, and until twenty years after that, French wives could neither possess a checking account nor legally consult their physicians about contraception.[1] In Britain and the United States, though, the growth of industry-based democracy, inspired by eighteenth-century humanism and the Industrial Revolution, lent momentum to the notion of feminism, the movement toward the social, political, and educational equality of women with men.

The first great feminist document came from Britain, Mary Wollstonecraft's *Vindication of the Rights of Women* (1792). In America, Abigail Adams and Mercy Otis Warren had unsuccessfully pressed George Washington and Thomas Jefferson to include the concept of women's emancipation in the Constitution of the United States, and in 1848, Elizabeth Cady Stanton led a women's convention at Seneca Falls, New York. They declared women's independence, calling for full legal equality, full educational and economic opportunity with equal compensation, the right to collect wages, and the right to vote, issues which remained in doubt for many years.

In Britain, the Earl of Carlyle presented a resolution favoring female suffrage to the House of Lords in 1851, and pioneering efforts toward higher education for women began around 1867, the year of the Reform Bill, which enfranchised male urban workers, enacted the secret ballot, and opened the door to a national educational system. Feminism suffered two major setbacks in 1870, however, with defeats of a bill for women's suffrage in the House of Commons and of a similar bill before the United States Congress, which had just given the right to vote to black men but not to the white women who had worked for their emancipation.

While some advocates of women's rights, like the founders and early students of Somerville College, deliberately employed a nonthreatening approach, a militant British suffragette organization, the Women's Social and Political Union, rose up in 1903, led by Emmeline Pankhurst and her daughters. Until 1914, the suffragettes radically kept their cause in the public eye, heckling public speakers, holding street meetings, getting themselves jailed for inciting riots, and carrying out hunger strikes that forced prison authorities to conduct gruesome tube feedings

63

which were aired prominently in the British press.

Beyond the issues of women's economic and political rights lurked a touchier area, sexuality and birth control. In 1877, Annie Besant was tried as a criminal in America for selling *The Fruits of Philosophy*, a pamphlet outlining contraceptive methods. Aletta Jacobs opened the first birth control clinic in Amsterdam in 1878, but the first U.S. clinic did not appear until 1916, headed by Margaret Sanger, who was promptly given a thirty-day jail sentence. The British Empire's first contraception clinic, in London, was not established until 1921 and then only through the efforts of the distinguished eugenicist Marie Stopes, who also promoted similar installations elsewhere. During and after World War I, information about increasingly reliable means of birth control freed women for the first time from the threat of unwanted pregnancies, dramatically changing sexual attitudes.

Even after thousands of Britons had "seen Paree," though, Oxford's establishment firmly intended to keep those it could down on the traditionally double-standard farm – and in many respects Oxford set and upheld the standards of the class which still ruled Britain. In a stinging essay she wrote in 1919, "Eros in Academe,"[2] Dorothy Sayers observed that Oxford deliberately fostered an unnatural atmosphere in which going to tea with a young man was "a thrilling dissipation," and inviting him back another time in the same term "too desperately exciting for all concerned."[3]

This artificial situation was not merely exciting, it was dangerous for all concerned. Until 1914, Oxford's authorities, wrapped in a golden scholarly haze, attempted to defuse the male sex drive by sublimating it into brotherly devotion or chilling it on the playing fields or rowing teams. Among male undergraduates real or feigned homosexuality had become stylish; the strictly segregated academic women in their utilitarian hairdos and serviceable woolens were decidedly not. While a man was free to experiment within the bounds of Oxonian discretion, a woman had little or no opportunity to discover that a man was anything but an alien being, or as Dorothy put it, a "cataclysm of nature,"[4] and thus the object of intense speculation. Theoretical discussions of "social wisdom," the euphemism for sexuality current in Dorothy's day, must have raged over the Somerville teapots and cocoa cups and probably everywhere else Oxford women gathered, but while the eternally knitting chaperones might have disappeared, the spirit that had installed them lingered wherever male and female students mixed and tended to dampen practical investigation.

The women of Dorothy's social class and time at Oxford had virtually nowhere to turn for advice about sex, one of the most bedeviling problems of the human race. Besides being away from home, they were at the age when daughters traditionally dismiss motherly opinions as hopelessly antediluvian. Many of the young women had been away at girls' boarding schools since the age of eight or ten, and in any case, most mothers and daughters had been conditioned to upholding the Victorian status quo. Dorothy might have had a slight advantage in experience since she had not gone to Godolphin until she was fifteen, but she had spent those years in the rarefied atmosphere of a country rectory, where Aunt Leigh's parrot, admittedly formidable, had probably supplied the coarsest language she had ever heard while growing up. Neither Somerville or any other women's college could offer its students much helpful counsel, because usually their tutors and administrators were women with backgrounds much like their students' own; the majority of the dons had sacrificed marriage and family responsibilities for demanding careers, and possibly they knew less about practical relations between men and women than did their students. Dorothy, like her contemporaries, would hardly have gone to her mentors with any kind of "social" problem; while she could have counted on their sympathy and kindness, she would have been aware that they would have had no idea of what to do or say, because such things were simply not supposed to happen to "nice girls." Typically, British Georgian society expected a well-brought up young man to gain experience where it pleased him, choose a virgin bride, and advise her at a tender moment that "nice girls don't wriggle."

Dorothy Sayers detested hypocrisy with her whole being. She knew that then, as now, "social difficulties" did happen to nice girls, and claiming otherwise, she insisted in "Eros in Academe," was "monstrous" and "a cowardly lie."[5] Furthermore, Somerville had made her a trained medievalist, and she realized that the Middle Ages, for all its celebrated insistence on religious faith, exhibited a forthright, even earthy, attitude toward sex that was more honest and hence more appealing to her than the mincing circumlutions of her own time. After three years at Somerville, Dorothy Sayers could meet and beat men on their own intellectual ground, but she had very little first-hand experience of what to do with them in any other respect, no resources for sound advice, and a raging curiosity about the whole matter. The combination proved inflammatory.

After Dorothy Sayers left Oxford in June of 1915, she spent a dull summer and fall at her parents' home in Bluntisham, enlivened only a little by a few visiting members of the M.A.S., a short shopping spree in London, then threatened by Zeppelin attacks, and a return visit to Somerville to help Vera Farnall with the library. It was hard for Dorothy to leave the people and the places that had made her happy, and she set her feelings down in poems which she circulated among her friends, a college habit that she kept throughout her life. Even though her First made her seem an ideal candidate for an eventual university position, Dorothy, like young Hilary Thorpe, her autobiographical character in *The Nine Tailors*, had already determined to become a writer, and with plenty of time on her hands at Bluntisham she started to try out some possibilities. Many of the poems she wrote then dealt with the past and all exhibit Dorothy's mastery of technique, though Brabazon finds them marked by Victorian sentimentality.[6] She was also continuing a college project which Miss Pope had declared promising,[7] translating the extant fragments from the medieval French romance of the fatal passion of Tristan and Iseut written by the Anglo-Norman monk Thomas of Britain.

At its best, writing is a chancy way to make a living, something that Dorothy at twenty-two needed to begin considering. Her friends were taking jobs; Dorothy Rowe was teaching English at Bournemouth High School, and Charis Barnett was going into nursing. For Dorothy, merely remaining at home in Bluntisham, doing her writing, reading Sherlock Holmes and scandalizing the countryside by smoking cigarettes in public now seemed out of the question. The war had reached into the Fen Country, and when two of Dorothy's male relatives, an uncle and a cousin, arrived to visit, they were still shaky from nervous breakdowns.

Dorothy's mother had also fallen ill with severe nervous attacks that prevented her at times from moving or speaking.[8] Dorothy was looking around for something constructive to do, and that December she heard of an opening for a teacher of modern languages at Hull High School in northeast England; she made up her mind quickly and took up her duties there in the fall term of 1916.

Dorothy lasted at Hull until April 1917. As first teaching jobs went at that time, it was not overly strenuous; she lived in a quiet, residential neighborhood at No. 86 Westbourne Avenue, so that she did not have full-time school duties, like supervising a dormitory, and Hull itself, founded late in the thirteenth century by Edward I, had many medieval architectural attractions, like Holy Trinity Church and the old mansion of the wool merchant De La Pole family.[9] It also offered Dorothy surprisingly nice shops and an acceptable café, and she found pleasant company among her fellow teachers, if not the sparkling comradeship of the M.A.S. As one of England's chief ports and a major outlet for goods manufactured in Yorkshire and Lincolnshire, Hull also had its share of attention from the enemy in 1916 and 1917, and Dorothy had to live through some real Zeppelin bombing raids. She put on a brave face in her letters home, but her hair started to fall out again, and she acquired a first-hand knowledge of fear – "brutal, bestial and utterly degrading."[10]

Teaching itself proved disagreeable, too. Comments Dorothy Sayers later made about education show that in her classroom at Hull High School, she had found herself almost on another planet. Her students might have been willing enough, and Alzina Stone Dale indicates that several recalled Dorothy as attractive and likable, helping them put on plays in French and organizing a school choir,[11] but she had to deal with adolescent girls of far less academic preparation, ability, and interest than she probably expected. That in itself would be disheartening enough, but to try one's best, as it would seem Dorothy did, and fail because of the students' ineptitude or apathy, and on top of that fall victim to the jealousy that all too often consumes colleagues and superiors of a brilliant, energetic, and worst of all, new young woman would be a bitter disappointment indeed. In a *Times* review of 1934, written when she was taking a long, hard look over her life, Dorothy Sayers commented:

> For some reason, nearly all school murder stories are good ones
> – probably because it is so easy to believe that murder could
> be committed in such a place. I do not mean this statement to
> be funny or sarcastic: nobody who has not taught in a school
> can possibly realise the state of nervous tension and mutual
> irritation that can glow up among the members of the staff at
> the end of a trying term, or the utter spiritual misery that a bad
> head can inflict upon his or her subordinates.[12]

Dorothy's writing would scarcely have paid her bills, but in
March 1916 she must have been thrilled to learn that the young
Oxford publisher Basil Blackwell had agreed to publish her first
collection of fifteen poems; she had written some while at Oxford
and the rest after finishing her work there, and a few had already
appeared in Oxford literary magazines. Dorothy's *Op. I* came out
in December 1916 in Blackwell's *Adventurers All*, a "Series of
Young Poets Unknown to Fame." Commentators seem to agree
that her style was fluent, but that the poems "are not always
understandable" because of references to the esoteric world of
medieval French literature, and are mostly "thin in thematic
strength."[13] Despite the critics, a young person as yet "unknown
to fame" but who had already determined to achieve it with her
pen would have been enormously encouraged by having her book
accepted. Possibly at Dorothy's urging, her father visited Blackwell at the end of 1916, and Dorothy joined the firm the next
April in a kind of apprenticeship her father had financed.[14]

In the course of her job with Blackwell's, Dorothy learned a
great deal about the practicalities of the publishing business –
reading manuscripts, proofreading, and copyediting – which
later stood her in good stead, though the major work she did for
the firm, editing the 1917, 1918, and 1919 volumes of *Oxford Poetry*
and contributing her own work to each, would likely have been
more to her taste. She was keeping up her own writing, too,
translating *Tristan*, contributing a short story, "Who Calls the
Tune?" to Muriel St. Clare Byrne's *Little Blue Moon*, a short-lived
periodical that aired the productions of the M.A.S. in 1917, and
preparing a second collection of her own poetry, this time religious in nature, for publication. Dorothy had had the satisfac-

tion of having her poem "Rex Doloris" printed in G. K. Chesterton's *New Witness*, and she hoped Chesterton, whom she admired greatly, would take the entire group, twenty-five devotional poems she titled *Catholic Tales and Christian Songs*. Chesterton could not accept the book, so she fell back on Blackwell's, who published it in 1918.

Catholic Tales and Christian Songs offers a vital clue to Dorothy Sayers's religious thinking, both then and later. "Catholic" refers to the traditional theology and dogma that High Church Anglicanism shares with the Church of Rome. Exemplifying the theory that the shoemaker's children often lack shoes, Dorothy had received surprisingly little training in formal Church dogma as a child; her autobiographical "Cat o' Mary" describes the heroine's mother as reluctant to bother her daughter with doctrinal matters and the girl's father as avoiding religious instruction entirely, except for requiring her attendance at weekly services.[15] By fifteen, Dorothy on her own seems to have worked out a theory of morality much like the "hate the sin but love the sinner" position common to Anglicanism and Roman Catholicism; taking the case of Ivy's cousin Freda, then thinking of converting to Roman Catholicism, as her springboard, Dorothy admonished Ivy against dismissing people simply because they had done something wrong – a kind of pharisaism that, Dorothy told Ivy, the Lord was always "down on." This was the very letter in which Dorothy had eerily foreshadowed a critical time in her own life when she would have to go to Ivy for help after sinning "a great sin."[16]

Disappointed and bitter toward the pietistic Christianity of Salisbury and then enthralled by Chesterton's vigorous religious outlook, Dorothy seems to have been working toward her own mode of belief at Oxford, and her poems which later appeared in *Catholic Tales and Christian Songs* show a variety of views on Christ and the religion He founded that is so far-reaching, Alzina Stone Dale claims, as to have shocked ordinary Christians like her father's parishioners.[17] Far from tiptoeing around "Gawd" as Evangelicals did, Dorothy used some unsettling innovations. She used modern speech patterns, for one thing, in her satirical verse drama "The Mocking of Christ" at a time when thee's, thou's and the obsolete English verb forms ending in "st" were de rigueur for devotional verse. In "Christus Dionysus" (Dionysus being the pagan Greek god of ecstasy and resurrection), she went so far as to postulate Jesus as the Lord of Laughter.

The brilliant variety of *Catholic Tales*, James Brabazon suggests, cannot be dismissed as insincerity, because in "Cat o' Mary" he finds evidence that Dorothy Sayers deliberately eliminated untrustworthy emotionalism from her work, relying instead on the belief she had received through intellectual conviction.[18] Upon publication of *Catholic Tales*, Louis Untermeyer praised Dorothy's portrayal of a "warm and altogether human godhead,"[19] and a reviewer for the *Times Literary Supplement* pointed out a "childlike spirit and familiar intimacy with Christ characteristic of the Middle Ages,"[20] qualities Dorothy would use again in her religious drama. Despite her innovations, Ralph Hone also indicates how very different Dorothy's poems were from other works of the time, like T. S. Eliot's world-weary "Love Song of J. Alfred Prufrock," which also appeared in 1917, and from the boisterous sexuality of James Joyce's *Ulysses*, which the United States Post Office seized and burned upon its arrival in 1918.

When she was his employee during 1917–18, Basil Blackwell recalls Dorothy making the sign of the cross before meals; this seems an outward symptom of her inward acceptance of traditional dogma. After the publication of *Catholic Tales and Christian Songs* in 1918, Dorothy and Muriel Jaeger entered into an elaborate hoax involving the placement of reviews and correspondence in religious journals to increase its sales by stirring up some theological controversy.[21] Sales did not skyrocket, but in the process Dorothy at twenty-six seems to have learned a great deal about theology. The spiritual upshot was that she declared unequivocally that Catholicism contained the "real truth" – or as much of it as man, being only a creature of God, could grasp. At this point whatever doubt or uneasiness Dorothy might have felt about her faith seems to have been resolved. Innate delicious wickedness might lead mankind, including herself, into sin; but God's forgiveness was there for the asking by the penitent once the truth about his or her actions was acknowledged. Here she stood, planted squarely on the firm ground of her intellectual conviction. Being Dorothy Sayers, she never could do anything less.

Her religious situation having been clarified in the midst of World War I, Dorothy could not have been in a more congenial atmosphere than Oxford, with its well-loved surroundings, her friends Muriel St. Clare Byrne and Muriel Jaeger still at Somerville, the Bach Choir, and work that allowed her to exercise her growing literary capabilities. According to Brabazon, Dorothy found it "positively sinful" to be having such a good time during a national tragedy, and he notes that when Somerville's principal met Dorothy in the street one day, Miss Penrose could not disguise her opinion that Dorothy ought to have been doing something "of national importance."[22]

There was more to the good time she was having in Oxford than a job she liked, her close friends, and even her writing. She had tried out a little flirtation on a handy curate in Hull, and during her first summer at Blackwell's, her *Op. I* aroused the sentiments of the vice-principal of St. Edmund Hall, a friend of Basil Blackwell's, to such a degree that after only a few encounters he proposed to her. Mr. Hodgson was apparently too smitten to realize that Dorothy had rejected him, and he went so far as to join the Bach Choir when he couldn't sing, an exercise in abject devotion Dorothy found revolting; what she really wanted, she wrote to her parents, was "somebody to fight with!"[23]

Someone more to Dorothy's taste was the Oxford surgeon Mr. Whitelaw, who removed her appendix that July. Once she was recovering, she enjoyed his banter, because both were sure neither was playing the game for keeps. Dorothy seems to have shared the "eat, drink, and be merry" mood across Britain in those dark days before the ambiguous dawn of the Armistice. After the bloody stalemate on the Western Front during the winter of 1917–18, a formidable German offensive pushed the British back forty miles the next March, and the unthinkable – a German victory – suddenly became a frightening possibility. Even the United States's reluctant entry into the war on 6 April 1917 did not help much at first. The British had no way of knowing that the enemy was as close to exhaustion as their own armies were: "The dismay that we experienced and the anxiety that racked us was far greater than at any time during the Second World War, even during the Battle of Britain when . . . we were virtually without allies."[24]

In the summer of 1918, the young officer invalided out of the war who later wrote those words became the first real love of Dorothy Sayers's life. Eric Whelpton, about Dorothy's age, was the son of a British clergyman who brought his family up in Boulogne, where Britons had formed a small colony, enjoying a lower cost of living and better educational opportunities for their children than they could have at home. Whelpton's 1974 memoir *The Making of a European* resounds not only with what D. H. Lawrence labeled the Oxford voice but also a self-congratulatory tone miles removed from Dorothy Sayers's forthright habit of the calling of a spade, however grimy, a spade.

As a child and youth, Whelpton had spent enough time abroad in places like Paris, Davos, and a Stuttgart suburb to have acquired a gloss of sophistication, and in the fall of 1912, he had come up to Hertford College at Oxford. Whelpton noted that about half the men there were Rhodes or open scholars, and he unblushingly observed that he learned enough Greek in six weeks to pass the Responsions.[25] He enjoyed the cosseted life of a male undergraduate at Oxford, with two scouts to light the sitting room fires for the nine men on his staircase, fetch their hot bath water from the basement, bring up wines from the buttery, and keep their rooms and their persons tidy. Whelpton's college bills for one Christmas term came to "only £43"[26] – a far cry from the two or three pounds a term Dorothy and her friends each could spend.

No indication exists that Whelpton met Dorothy Sayers while both were undergraduates between the fall of 1912 and the summer of 1914. Like many Britons, Whelpton had believed that the Royal Navy's dreadnoughts would deter German aggression, and the assassination of Archduke Ferdinand on 28 June caught him sitting for his examinations. Britain declared war on 4 August and by that evening had 80,000 men under arms, Whelpton among them with a commission as a second lieutenant in the Berkshire Territorials, a unit which followed the near-feudal organizational pattern common among British county units at that time. As an officer, Whelpton had a "family responsibility" for his men, who immediately were ordered to march across England "to weed out the weaklings."[27] Just after reaching Chelmsford, Whelpton himself was flattened by a vaccination for enteric fever that left him subject to inexplicable periods of unconsciousness, followed by a serious illness he attributed to polio. He was transferred to a home service battalion engaged in eastern coastal defense, mostly in Essex, where he commanded 900 soldiers unfit for active service and spent his days in the saddle checking seawall patrols.

Early in his memoir Whelpton describes himself as "a moral and physical coward,"[28] perhaps in reaction to having spent his war service in relative ease while the life expectancy of an English officer in France was about two weeks.[29] In any case, after eighteen months his health broke down completely, and in September 1916 he was invalided out with 85 percent disability, which the Army attributed to epilepsy. For the next year and a half, Whelpton lived in "great comfort" at Eastbourne, where his English-gentleman good looks, his physical difficulties (which did not prevent him from relieving the wartime stresses of local belles),[30] and an air that comes across in his memoir as self-consciously Byronic, all allowed him to enjoy what he calls his "susceptibility to women" to the fullest. "Often we lay in each others' arms in close embrace and this contact with the sun beating down upon us and the sheer warmth helped us to live for the moment."[31]

During his convalescence, living for the moment seems to be all that Whelpton wanted to do. He escaped several potential marital entanglements, and at last, thinking of training for the Foreign Office, he returned to Oxford in the spring of 1918. He found it almost unbearably changed. There were only four other male undergraduates at Hertford College; half of his friends at Oxford had been killed, and half of those that remained had serious injuries. The flu also struck Britain that June and again in October, causing a greater total of casualties than the war itself had done. That fall, Whelpton recalled, all four undergraduates at Exeter College, men who had survived the front, died of Spanish influenza.[32]

In his memoirs, Whelpton bestowed praise so faint as to be scarcely discernible on the "highly intelligent . . . remarkable women" he met then at Oxford. Whelpton was not sure "whether wartime conditions brought out [the] latent talent," of women like Vera Brittain, Doreen Wallace, Margaret Irwin, and Dorothy

Sayers, and he insisted "the academic girls did not rouse any passions," since he vastly preferred the male "companionship of early manhood."[33] Even allowing for the possible befuddlement of age – Whelpton was in his late seventies when he wrote his memoir – he seems not to have paid much attention to Dorothy's appearance, which he dismissed as "far from beautiful." He did observe her "exotic" beads and "pendulous necklaces," but he mistakenly recalled her blue eyes, one of her most striking features, as grey, and described her voice as "rather high pitched," when in fact she was a pronounced contralto. He called her manner towards him "protective and almost maternal" and ingenuously claimed he could not think why Dorothy and Doreen Wallace had befriended him.[34]

In fairness to Whelpton, he had had a good deal of experience in affairs of the glands and heart, and Dorothy had not – a textbook example of the Victorian double standard. Whelpton presented Dorothy with a challenge, just what she always found impossible to ignore or resist. He had left Oxford with his education incomplete, and she could introduce him to the poets she loved, like John Donne. Through his mother, Whelpton could claim descent from a titled family dating from the Holy Roman Empire;[35] and his Parisian upbringing, his military service, and even his "love 'em and leave 'em" performance with women were reminiscent of another wounded young romantic hero – Tristan, with whom she had figuratively been living for some time by translating his fatal love story. Dorothy fell hard.

She moved into a flat directly above Whelpton's at Bath Place that summer and allowed him to use her as a "pillow" – Dorothy's word for a woman on whose lap a young man could pour out his troubles with other girls,[36] hardly a compliment to someone who cared about him deeply herself, but a phenomenon that frequently plagues brainy women in their relationships with men. Whelpton found the Oxford winter too arduous, and that spring, having the type of degree granted under wartime conditions but little prospect of a job in England, he heard of a position as a part-time English master at L'Ecole des Roches in Normandy, an English-style boys' preparatory school with a prodigious reputation. It seemed the ideal solution to his problems.

In a letter to Ralph Hone dated 5 May 1975, Whelpton

claimed he did not know Dorothy Sayers was in love with him even when he engaged her as a bilingual secretary at Les Roches after her job at Blackwell's had evaporated.[37] (Having her working at mechanical tasks, Basil Blackwell said, was like hitching a racehorse to a cart.)[38] As for Dorothy, the troubles her unreciprocated infatuation with Whelpton caused her clearly show between the lines of the poems she was writing then, like the bitter grief in "For Phaon," thinly disguised as a monologue by Sappho: "Less than myself I give not, and am *I* a little thing?"[39] "Vials Full of Odours" also reveals that her longing for a physical relationship was affecting her deeply:

> . . . my love is in Normandy,
> And oh! the scent of the bean-flower
> Is like a burning fire in me.[40]

Perhaps the most significant testimony to the depth of Dorothy's feeling for Whelpton is that she did not flaunt this torch publicly, as she had her well-known interest in Dr. Allen, and her unrequited passion for Whelpton, buried out of the sight of most of the world, probably exacerbated the German measles that she caught around this time. She tried a religious retreat during January 1919, but spiritual solace did not suffice; and finally, Oxford itself failed to satisfy her any more. On 6 April 1919, she described everything around her to Muriel Jaeger as "quite horrid."[41] In this mood, she wrote the vehement essay "Eros in Academe," denouncing her upbringing and her college for leaving her "socially [that is, sexually] ignorant" in a world whose social norms were being turned upside down: women now were allowed to understand sex, but not to enjoy it.[42]

While Dorothy was miserable in Oxford, Whelpton, still susceptible, had been basking in the attention of two lovely sisters-in-law of the Protestant chaplain at Les Roches, and he narrowly escaped the machinations of Mme de Moleyns, widow of the school's founder, who fancied him as a son-in-law. Whelpton seems to have convinced the administration at Les Roches that he could pass on prospective employees, and he interviewed James Joyce for a position in the English Department but turned him down because of Joyce's shyness.[43] In order to secure Dorothy's services for the secretarial job, Whelpton had to present himself for inspection to her parents at the Christchurch rectory near Upwell which Dorothy's father had traded for Bluntisham. Whelpton took note of Mr. Sayers's comfortable income, allayed his paternal suspicions by declaring that his affections were otherwise engaged, and settled down to enjoy a five-course dinner and the spectacle of Dorothy in an evening gown which revealed her slim, bare, well-shaped arms. In his memoir, Whelpton also noted that the spacious rectory might have served as the locale of Dorothy's later novel *The Seven* [sic] *Tailors* (never having read the book, one of her best, he forgot that there were actually nine).[44]

Dorothy's situation at Les Roches would have satisfied the most stringent requirements of propriety. Whelpton lived about a mile away from the school, and Dorothy proved an efficient and dedicated secretary, running an exchange program for British and French students. She worked with Whelpton about six hours a day, and outside of their jobs, they seem to have discussed French literature and Whelpton's gastronomical as well as amatory adventures, one way a woman in Dorothy's position could pick up a little vicarious social knowledge. Whelpton found one of her tastes, at least, abhorrent, dismissing the detective novels which she was then voraciously reading as rubbish he would never touch – and he never did, although he insisted "some of his friends" recognized him as her aristocratic detective Lord Peter Wimsey.[45]

Dorothy weathered several crises in her year at Les Roches. A girl on the school office staff became pregnant by a soldier, and Dorothy, her Anglo-Catholic sensibilities afflicted, undertook to dissuade the unfortunate woman from abortion and with Whelpton's help settled her protégée in Paris that November. This emotion-laden situation marked a turning point; around this time Whelpton realized that Dorothy loved him. The attraction seems never to have become mutual, and on the evidence of her letters to her family, Brabazon suggests that Whelpton's concept of romance varied too greatly from Dorothy's for them to have made any kind of lasting match.[46] The question abruptly became academic during the 1920 Easter vacation when Whelpton accidentally sat next to a breathtakingly beautiful woman in a London theater, located her later through a newspaper advertisement, and proposed to her two days after it appeared – without so much as learning her last name.[47]

Whelpton had intended to remain at Les Roches, but his new amour, a divorcée suffering from an unidentified illness, required him to spend increasing amounts of time in England, scouting out more lucrative employment. Meanwhile, Dorothy fell victim to yet another childhood disease when mumps struck Les Roches. She had trouble with her hair again, and she had to spend a long time in bed recuperating. For amusement, she and Muriel Jaeger collaborated by mail on a mock-scholarly investigation into the life and achievements of Sexton Blake, the popular-fiction detective whose adventures most British youths, including Dorothy, had eagerly devoured while growing up. The fun allowed Dorothy to exercise her scholarly style, but more important to her future, it developed her fascination with the detective as a folk hero, the chevalier on the white horse who indefatigibly seeks out the truth, rescues maidens and punishes their evil tormentors.

Dorothy had already decided that detective fiction offered handsome moneymaking possibilities, but Whelpton spurned her generous offer to share them. After her hopes for Whelpton had been thoroughly dashed, London, the heart of British publishing, seemed the best place for Dorothy Sayers to put her literary aspirations into practice, and furthermore, it held out opportunities in areas where her abbreviated relationship with Whelpton had convinced her she needed experience. With some difficulty she got herself free of Les Roches, and by September she was back in England, a little older and quite a bit wiser, and still a spinster.

Life often provides compensations for disappointment, even though they often may be clouded by self-pity or depression. On 11 May 1919, the British Parliament had passed the Women's Statute, allowing women to receive university degrees and become full members of the university community, entitled to wear the gowns and special caps designed for their degrees. Oxford grants the Bachelor of Arts when students have completed their studies, and after a period of time and payment of the appropriate fees, they automatically receive the Master of Arts. Dorothy Sayers was eligible for both degrees, and on 14 October 1920 in Oxford's venerable Sheldonian Theatre, following the five principals of the women's colleges, Dorothy was among the first seven women to receive the bachelor's "rabbit-skins." A few moments later, to a cheering audience, she accepted the red-lined hood which marked her as an Oxford *domina*.[48]

After a few months had cooled the sting of Whelpton's rejection, Dorothy Sayers had to find a new way of supporting herself. Convention would have had her return to her parents' home or take another teaching position, but for a woman bent on becoming an author, rural Christchurch was out of the question, and a few months at Clapham High School in south metropolitan London in the winter of 1920 reinforced the opinion she had developed at Hull – that she would rather sweep streets than teach children.[49] She never actually resorted to manual labor, but her fortunes were at a very low ebb during her first months in London. She published two translated fragments of Thomas's *Tristan* with an introduction in *Modern Languages*, but all she could find was a series of odd jobs paying little or, at least in one case, nothing; she did a screenplay of Ibañez' popular novel *Blood and Sand* but never received anything for it at all.[50] She lived first in St. George's Square and then at 44 Mecklenburg Square in Bloomsbury, home to many artists and writers and a synonym in the bourgeois imagination for loose-living "Bohemia." For the first time in her life she had to do her own cooking, and she told her parents that food was her "most sinful extravagance,"[51] a claim about her life-style that did not seem to convince them. Mr. Sayers changed his will on 20 November 1920, leaving his entire estate to his wife Helen.[52]

Dorothy was disgusted with Whelpton, who also was taking what jobs he could get. He worked in Florence as a junior partner in a British real estate firm from September 1920 to January 1921, and he was teaching at an English boys' school in Hertfordshire[53] when the enigmatic Frances he idealized drifted in and out of his arms and died during Lent, 1922. Dorothy saw the affair as suicidal for Whelpton, describing it scornfully as "giving his heart to a dog to tear."[54] She apparently had given up on him, and by July 1921 she was almost ready to give up on herself. The plaintive letter with which James Brabazon chose to open his biography of Dorothy Sayers shows a twenty-eight-year-old woman close to the end of her rope: "I can't get the work I want, nor the money I want, nor consequently the clothes I

78

want, nor the holiday I want, nor the man I want!"[55] In the depths of that dreadful despondency, Dorothy went home to Christchurch for a vacation, and, egged on by her friend Muriel Jaeger, worked on a novel she had first thought of in January 1921 which she initially called "Lord Peter." By October, Dorothy had completed *Whose Body?*, the first of her enormously popular Lord Peter Wimsey detective series.[56]

Notes

1. Mavis Gallant, *Paris Notebooks: Essays and Reviews* (New York: Random House, 1988), p. 110.
2. Dorothy L. Sayers, "Eros in Academe," *Oxford Outlook* I (June 1919), quoted in Ralph E. Hone, *Dorothy L. Sayers, A Literary Biography* (Kent, Ohio: Kent State University Press, 1979), pp. 20–21, 30.
3. Ibid., quoted in Hone, pp. 20–21.
4. Ibid., quoted in Hone, p. 20.
5. Ibid.
6. James Brabazon, *Dorothy L. Sayers: A Biography* (New York: Charles Scribners' Sons, 1981), p. 58.
7. Alzina Stone Dale, *Maker and Craftsman: The Story of Dorothy L. Sayers* (Grand Rapids, Mich.: William B. Eerdmans Publishing Co., 1978), p. 51.
8. Brabazon, p. 58.
9. Philip L. Scowcroft observes that Dorothy Sayers's short story "Suspicion," from *In the Teeth of the Evidence*, "is set in Hull, and the topographical detail, remembered after twenty–odd years, is accurate." Letter to the author 6 February 1989. See also Dale, p. 51.
10. Dorothy L. Sayers, Letter to Muriel Jaeger 14 November 1916, quoted in Brabazon, p. 60.
11. Dale, p. 52.
12. Dorothy L. Sayers, Review in the *Sunday Times* 9 September 1934, p. 8; quoted in Hone, p. 24.
13. Robert B. Harmon and Margaret A. Burger, *An Annotated Guide to the Works of Dorothy L. Sayers* (New York: Garland Publishing, Inc., 1977), p. 149, and Hone, p. 26.
14. Brabazon, p. 61.
15. "Cat o'Mary," quoted in Brabazon, pp. 23–24.
16. Dorothy L. Sayers, Letter to Ivy Shrimpton, 23 February 1908, quoted in Brabazon, p. 29.

17. Dale, p. 58.
18. Brabazon, pp. 66–67.
19. Quoted in Harmon and Burger, p. 148.
20. *Times Literary Supplement*, 21 November 1918, pp. 570–71, quoted in Hone, p. 30.
21. Brabazon, p. 69.
22. Brabazon, p. 62.
23. Ibid., p. 63. Dorothy L. Sayers, Letter to parents 19 June 1917.
24. Eric Whelpton, *The Making of a European* (London: Johnson Publications Ltd., 1974), p. 118.
25. Ibid., pp. 99, 84.
26. Ibid., p. 95.
27. Ibid., p. 109.
28. Ibid., p. 28.
29. Dale, p. 55.
30. Whelpton, p. 115.
31. Ibid., p. 116.
32. Ibid., p. 122.
33. Ibid., pp. 123, 125.
34. Ibid., p. 126.
35. Dale, p. 57.
36. Brabazon, p. 71. Dorothy L. Sayers, Undated letter to parents.
37. Hone, p. 33.
38. Brabazon, p. 75.
39. Dorothy L. Sayers, "For Phaon," quoted in Hone, p. 27.
40. Dorothy L. Sayers, "Vials Full of Odours," quoted in Hone, p. 28.
41. Dorothy L. Sayers, letter to Muriel Jaeger 6 April 1919, quoted in Brabazon, p. 75.
42. Hone, p. 21.
43. Whelpton, p. 136.
44. Ibid., p. 138.
45. Ibid., p. 139.
46. Brabazon, p. 80.
47. Whelpton, p. 142.
48. Hone, p. 37.
49. Ibid., p. 24.
50. Brabazon, p. 84.
51. Dorothy L. Sayers, Letter to her parents 9 December 1920, quoted in Brabazon, p. 85.
52. Hone, p. 38.
53. Whelpton, p. 157.
54. Dorothy L. Sayers, Letter to her parents 1 July 1921, quoted in Brabazon, p. 86.
55. Dorothy L. Sayers, Letter to her parents 16 July 1921, quoted in Brabazon, p. 1.
56. Barbara Reynolds, *The Passionate Intellect* (Kent, Ohio: Kent State University Press, 1989), p. 236, note 1.

5 Sorrowful and Joyous Mysteries 1922–1929

> Never retreat. Never explain. Get it done and let them howl.
>
> Benjamin Jowett, Master of Balliol

While Dorothy Sayers was fighting her own battles for the work and the man she thought she wanted, World War I was taking a ghastly toll on her country and the world. At the Battle of Jutland, British dreadnoughts forced the German fleet back to their home ports for the rest of the war, but British land forces hemorrhaged for four years in the trenches of the Western Front. In the Atlantic, prowling U-boats caused shortages of food and raw materials that in 1917, prior to the adoption of the convoy system and the entry of the United States into the war that summer, almost brought Britain to surrender. After the collapse of Austria-Hungary and the severe deterioration of German morale, the war finally bled to a halt in November 1918, leaving a staggering 10 million dead and 20 million wounded. Britain lost 750,000, more than a tenth of those it had mobilized, and 2 million others were injured – blinded, gassed, shell-shocked.[1] The whole nation grieved – parents for children, wives for husbands, sweethearts for fiancés, women for the lovers they would never have. "Trench poetry" forever obliterated Britain's glorious chivalric view of war; Wilfred Owen, killed in France just before the Armistice, asked, "What passing-bells for those who die as cattle?"[2] prefiguring T. S. Eliot's 1922 vision of Europe as one vast wasteland.

Germany was not represented at the Paris Conference following the war. Britain's Lloyd George and President Woodrow Wilson of the United States argued for moderation of the French demands for revenge, but the resulting Treaty of Versailles, hastily drawn and heavily punitive, attempted to ensure that Germany would never again become a military power. The Allies limited the German army, confiscated German colonies and European territories, and enforced Allied occupation of the

Rhineland; the Versailles Treaty dangerously lulled Britain into a false sense of security and contributed to policies of appeasement that ensured another world conflagration.

Changes in the international climate at the end of the Great War, like the Soviet Revolution of 1917, led British politicians to begin talking about sweeping social changes, a trend reinforced by a dramatic wave of strikes at home. England was changing hands; over a million acres were sold, many by the aristocracy who could not afford land taxes and death duties. Lloyd George declared, "The nation is now in molten state. . . . We cannot return to the old ways, the old abuses, the old stupidities."[3]

Britain's suffragettes, who had dropped their campaign for women's rights to pitch with equal fervor into the war effort, could not have agreed more. Christabel Pankhurst called World War I "God's vengeance on the people who held women in subjection,"[4] and once the war with Germany had ceased, she and her fellow activists gathered forces to carry on the work they believed the Almighty had started. They still faced formidable obstacles: despite their contributions to the war effort, British women had little voice in politics at the opening of the twenties, when they constituted the same 21 percent of the labor force as they had ten years earlier.

While the war did help British women past thirty win the vote in 1918, the war had shattered "that sense of security which brooded over Victorian homes and made men buy estates and lay cellars against their old age and for the benefit of their sons."[5] The Housing Act of 1919 involved the state for the first time in providing new, subsidized home environments for women and children, influencing the future of British family life, which had been fractured by the war. With real and potential husbands and fathers gone, women were forced to seek employment outside the home to a greater degree than ever before. Victorian domestic discipline became another casualty of the twentieth century. The upper classes found that the "old race of servants who labored from six o'clock in the morning till eleven o'clock at night"[6] had almost become extinct; the social revolution demanded that ladies do much of their own housework and cooking themselves, creating a demand for labor saving machines and simplified clothing. One grande dame returning from a London ball and finding no servants available to undo her back-laced bodice was reduced to calling a hansom cab, handing the driver a pair of nail scissors, and asking him to cut the string.[7] Under such pressures, skirts were shortened dramatically and time-consuming crowning glories were bobbed and shingled. Women began to drink in pubs, religious restraints loosened, and one 1919 observer claimed in horror that every village chemist was selling contraceptives.[8] The twenties had begun to roar.

Nineteen twenty-one, the year of Dorothy Sayers's great depression, also saw the opening of "the golden age of detective fiction." Between the two world wars, an onslaught of the mystery novels Dorothy devoured and Eric Whelpton so deplored struck the public fancy head on, though fiction dealing with moral vicissitudes and fiendish psychological aberrations had been around for a long time. Even Lord Byron, whose own career was a delicious shocker, had professed himself horrified at Matthew Lewis's *The Monk* (1796), a crawly tale of gothic intrigue appearing long before Edgar Allan Poe gave the world its first genuine detective stories in the 1840s. Detective novels were beginning to appear in Great Britain by the 1860s, with popular mysteries involving the supernatural by the Irish writer Joseph Sheridan LeFanu and in Wilkie Collins's *The Moonstone* (1868), which became one of Dorothy Sayers's favorites. Women were prominent in this field from the start; an American woman, Seeley Regester (Mrs. Metta Victoria Fuller Victor), had beaten Collins to the draw with her detective novel *The Dead Letter* a year earlier. Anna Katherine Green, another American, is considered the ancestress of mystery fiction; her *Leavenworth Case* (1878), nine years before the first Sherlock Holmes story, was an immediate bestseller and remained in print a hundred years later.[9]

Mystery historian Jessica Mann records that detective fiction was denounced almost from the start as "bad reading." In 1801, Wordsworth claimed that cheap novels reduced the human mind to "savage torpor," and in 1874, the *Temple Bar* attributed the mental, physical, and moral deterioration of the human species to the quality and quantity of mystery stories. At the turn of the century, fiction comprised 65 to 90 percent of Britain's public library circulation, causing some guardians of public morals to call novel reading a greater curse than pubs. The *Evening Standard* thundered in 1891, "Many are the crimes brought about by the disordered imagination of a reader of sensational and often immoral rubbish, while many a home is neglected and uncared for owing to the all-absorbed, novel-reading wife."[10]

With her customary thoroughness, Dorothy Sayers read almost all of that "sensational and immoral rubbish" she could get her hands on, and some aspects of it indelibly impressed her. Anna Katherine Green had contributed the figure of the nosy old maid to the detective form, and Arthur Conan Doyle had established the stylish and near-superhumanly logical investigator with marked idiosyncrasies, both elements that Dorothy Sayers adapted for her novels. Early in the twentieth century, G. K. Chesterton, whose conservative theological works so delighted Dorothy at Oxford, had based his own detective series on the unequivocal dualism of good and evil.

> By dealing with the unsleeping sentinels who guard the out-posts of society [detective fiction] tends to remind us that we live in an armed camp, making war with a chaotic world, and that the criminals, the children of chaos, are nothing but the traitors within our gates. . . . The agent of social justice [is] the original and poetic figure, while the burglars and footpads are . . . happy in the immemorial respectability of apes and wolves.[11]

Chesterton's metaphor of embattled humanity defended by "poetic sentinels" anchored his "Father Brown" detective series and must have been instantly appealing to Dorothy Sayers, drawn as she was to clearcut heroic conflicts of good and evil like Thermopylae and Roncivaux.

Both Chesterton and E. C. Bentley also humanized their sleuths in response to shifts in British society. Chesterton made his detective a priest to mask his capabilities from the ungodly. Bentley was not content with the mechanical or unrealistically exaggerated prowess of a superhuman sleuth like Holmes. In *Trent's Last Case* (1912), Bentley had presented a completely new sort of detective figure, one who could have flaws and still function successfully in a unified plot.[12] Trent parodies quotations, amuses his associates, and even falls in love – a startling innovation in characterization that Dorothy Sayers later said revolutionized the world of the mystery novel and foreshadowed the work of all of the detective writers of her day, her own included.[13]

As more of her biographical material becomes available, the more evident Dorothy Sayers's early creative attraction to the genre and the first intimations of her major detective become. From authorized access to her correspondence and unpublished manuscripts, James Brabazon believes that the very first flicker of Lord Peter Wimsey occurred to Dorothy around 1920, and she made him a minor character in a draft for the Sexton Blake project she was pursuing with Muriel Jaeger. Dorothy wrote a fictional *Who's Who* sketch for Wimsey, already revealing many of his distinguishing characteristics – the big nose, the Piccadilly flat, the yen for first editions, the aristocratic heritage and the impeccable tailoring. Brabazon feels Dorothy might already have become so intrigued with him that she left off the Blake story and filed Wimsey away for a major role elsewhere.[14]

Dorothy Sayers recalled that she had developed the plot for *Whose Body?*, her first detective novel, from a party game she had played at Oxford.[15] Later, while she was enduring her brief teaching stint at Clapham, a macabre opening came to her: she wrote to her parents on 22 January 1921 that she was envisioning "a fat lady dead in her bath . . . with nothing on but her pince-nez."[16] The next summer, when she was home and bored into starting a novel, Dorothy changed the victim's sex, heightening what Brabazon calls the scene's "instant appealing vulgarity"[17] and setting up a crime that only Lord Peter Wimsey could solve.

Whose Body? disgorges a maddening puzzle for Scotland Yard: a prominent Jewish businessman married to a former county girl, like Dorothy's friend Charis Barnett Frankenburg, disappears just when a naked "Semitic" corpse – not his – materializes in an innocuous architect's bathtub. In her mystery-writing debut, Dorothy L. Sayers could not have made her professional trademark clearer: she announced through Lord Peter Wimsey that the more open one is toward those around him, the more likely he is to deceive them.[18] She earned a great part of her enormous success by following her own advice with remarkable consistency, taking care to play a scrupulously fair game with her audience. She laid bare every clue to Sir Reuben Levy's fate for conscientious readers, spinning out every last thread of motivation for inspection and going so far as to explain her method itself through Wimsey as well, the same method that she maintained throughout her novels. She set up a series of clues, like those scrambled letter-puzzles often used as children's party games, to be sorted and rearranged into an order that makes sense.[19] Dogged persistence can do the job, patiently testing every possible combination until at last the right one appears; this is the conventional method plodded through by ordinary policemen, like Wimsey's painstaking friend Charles Parker of Scotland Yard. The child who takes the party prize, however, is generally not the sober stalwart lad who tries, tries again; most often it is a twitchy little eight- or nine-year-old who suddenly, unerringly, sees the answer and cannot possibly explain why – a bolt of intuition that instantaneously aligns all of the elements into their one proper sequence.

Poets possess that kind of gift, and so did Dorothy Sayers. She endowed Lord Peter Wimsey with it, and many of her other talents and desires besides. Dorothy craved luxuries of mind and body she could never have afforded in 1921, but in her fiction she could easily give them to the aristocratic Lord Peter, making him a part of herself. Though not conventionally handsome, he, like Dorothy, had a flair for clothes and color; his Piccadilly flat glowed in primrose and gold and flame-tones, the colors of an illuminated manuscript, against his black grand piano. He could sublimely play works by Scarlatti, a composer like Mozart, too easy for beginners and too hard for virtuosi; he was as comfortable with French as English, and he thirsted after rare medieval books as incessantly as he did for rare vintages and elegant cuisine. At the start of *Whose Body?*, Lord Peter's mouth veritably waters for a rare folio *Divina Commedia* worth nearly four times his superb valet Bunter's yearly wages[20] – and Bunter was very well paid indeed for the 1920s. Wimsey's high valuation of this book for his Dante collection is vital, because his acquisition of it, mentioned in seven crucial passages of the novel,[21] parallels his search for the murderer, a revealing clue to the principles of craftsmanship and the moral certainties that anchored Dorothy L. Sayers's detective novels from the very start.

According to Barbara Reynolds, Dante's presence is not just a factor in the intellectual atmosphere of 1921, it provides the moral basis for Lord Peter's solution of the crime and the method in which he carries it out.[22] Dante's message in the *Divine Comedy* is uncompromising: the individual must accept the eternal consequences of a choice made by free will. The villain of *Whose Body?*, a scientist animated by intellectual pride, believes that the consciousness of good and evil is a purely physical matter, and acts accordingly; Wimsey, however, musing on the *Divine Comedy* – in which men and women freely choose between good and evil, constants built by the Almighty into His universe – intuitively grasps the solution.

As a medievalist, Dorothy Sayers would have been familiar with the general concept of Dante's *Divine Comedy*, the culminating literary achievement of the Middle Ages, although she said she first read the work when she was over fifty. In the journey that he makes to Paradise, Dante the allegorical traveler must first pass through the inferno, where Dante the poet has arranged the lost souls according to the degree of their rejections of God's love. Those who betray and kill friends through pride, considered by the Western Church the most heinous of the sins and the one underlying all the rest, suffer torment at the very bottom of hell, where their own free choice put them to be damned for all eternity.

The villain of *Whose Body?* chose early on to put his own desire for revenge beyond Christian law. His scientific training and his unerring perception of the victim's own avarice gave him the means for a particularly ghoulish murder of a man who trusted him. The murderer's fine mind found justification for the act in philosophical positions then becoming popular, like Nietzsche's *Beyond Good and Evil*, available in England in 1907,[23] a work which might be taken as advocating the destruction of the conscience, exactly the necessary condition for human evolution[24] that the murderer proclaims with relish in *Whose Body?*.

Just before bringing this proud spirit to bay, Lord Peter Wimsey "was communing with Dante,"[25] where all man's sins and punishments neatly follow divinely ordained law; then, at first intellectually and at last physically, Wimsey duels an opponent whose talents equal his own. Lord Peter wins by sidestepping a fatal injection with a reference to an earlier innoculation, like Eric Whelpton's, that went haywire.[26]

To that point, Wimsey resembles a medieval knight-errant riding gorgeously out to conquer evil. To mask his brilliance, Dorothy L. Sayers did give him a silly facade similar to Bertie Wooster's, a creation of the humorist P. G. Wodehouse, something she later tempered as not befitting the gravity of homicide, but she also endowed Lord Peter with many qualities of the chivalrous English gentleman – courtesy toward women and scrupulosity in keeping his word and playing fair, even with wicked enemies. Wimsey enjoys every moment of his quest as long as it remains a game.

Presumably Lord Peter grew up in the traditional Anglican faith of his forefathers and subscribed to its creed, although Sayers does not overtly discuss his religious belief in this early novel. Dorothy L. Sayers lifted her chevalier out of his medieval tapestry, however, and gave him an entirely modern moral dimension. As a former British officer, Wimsey, like so many of his countrymen, experienced intermittently disabling shell shock, compounded by guilt that arose from his aristocratic sense of responsibility for the men who had suffered and died in his charge. Whatever chivalric black-and-white ideal of warfare he might once have held, he had lost it forever in the trenches. Dorothy Sayers sentenced him ever afterward to view even the murderers he pursued as perplexing mixtures of good and evil – the mystery of wickedness forming the core of their criminal motivations. Mere mortals like himself, Wimsey seems to have felt from the start, ought not to put themselves above the law to judge; they should allow God, not man, to decide human fate. In *Whose Body?* Wimsey risks his life like a medieval knight through a duel, the combat of two well-matched individuals, one on the side of right and the other as clearly in the wrong. Sayers thus prevented Wimsey from falling into the sin of pharaisism, which she had at fifteen declared that Christ himself detested. Bringing killers to justice was one thing for Lord Peter Wimsey; pulling the gallows rope was something he could not knowingly do. He and Dorothy Sayers had to give criminals the freedom of choice that traditional Christianity allows all human souls, and so she had to devise ingenious ways of causing the wicked to trap themselves – mostly, as in *Whose Body?*, through their overweening pride.

By the time Dorothy Sayers finished *Whose Body?* in October 1921, she was in that uncomfortable state that follows most acts of creation – tired, a little disgusted with herself, unsure of what to do next. She had to appeal to her father, whom she called "Tootles," for money to get the novel typed; the process took a long time, and to make her holiday season even bleaker, she received an eviction notice for 5 December.[27] One publisher gave her a glimmer of hope, though, and Muriel Jaeger found her a reasonable three-room flat in Great James Street, Bloomsbury, near her former room. That Christmas Dorothy struck a bargain with her parents; she asked them to support her for the next six months, and if Lord Peter didn't pan out during that time, she would return to teaching.

Given her feelings about that profession and her desire to stay in London, Dorothy was taking a sizable risk with her future. Her major biographers have penetrated the mystery of that winter of 1921–22: another man was rivaling Lord Peter for Dorothy's affections. Brabazon says that unlike Lord Peter Wimsey, John Cournos brought her "little but misery."[28]

Ralph Hone has also sensitively sketched Dorothy Sayers's unhappy love affair with Cournos, a Russian Jew who had emigrated to America as a child, but many of its details were not available until Brabazon received access to eleven letters Dorothy sent Cournos in 1924 and 1925. In 1957, the year that Dorothy died and shortly before his own death, Cournos donated the letters to Harvard's Houghton Library under conditions of extreme secrecy, breached only when Dorothy's son Anthony Fleming and Cournos's stepson Alfred Satterthwaite allowed Brabazon to inspect them for the latter's authorized biography. Until these letters are made public – if ever – Brabazon's is the only account of them available.[29]

Cournos was in Oxford in the spring of 1921, and Dorothy may have met him then, but almost certainly he was a part of her quasi-bohemian life-style in London until October 1922. He was exotic, handsome, impecunious, arrogant, hell-bent on making the world as aware of his destiny as a great literary artist as he was himself. Cournos' *Autobiography*, Brabazon says, shows that he was gifted with "pretentious self-importance and a self-pity of cosmic proportions."[30] Cournos and Dorothy Sayers shared some similarities in their backgrounds and personalities; both had recently been jilted, both loved to shock the bourgeoisie, both were writing books. With his built-in capacity for aggressive self-aggrandisement, Cournos was indeed a man Dorothy Sayers could have fought with, but he does not seem to have been worth what the battle cost her. He left England abruptly in October 1922, not even bothering to send her a postcard,[31] and married the writer Sybil Norton (Helen Kastner Satterthwaite) in 1924. The letters that Dorothy sent him then, Brabazon says, offer a rare, if not unique, view of Dorothy as a vulnerable human being, and help to explain the sometimes rigid offense which she later practiced as her best defense.[32]

Already on 18 January 1922, Dorothy had told her parents that she and Cournos had differed on a "point of practical Christianity"[33] – a euphemism for their opposing views on sexuality. While her letters to Cournos cannot be discussed directly, Dorothy Sayers later put much of herself on more public view through Harriet Vane of *Strong Poison* and three more novels. Harriet was accused of murdering an artist who had insisted, like Cournos, on free love contingent upon contraception, which Harriet and Dorothy both rejected out of religious conviction and personal taste. Then, in life as in Dorothy's fiction, after tormenting his lover shamelessly, the noble artist had opted for bourgeois satisfaction after all, revealing himself as a shameless hypocrite, the one kind of sinner Dorothy Sayers could not forgive. The affair with Cournos dragged on, never consummated and increasingly frustrating, but fortunately for Dorothy her career was finally looking up. Both she and Cournos were thinking about new books, and in April 1922, she acquired an agent, Andrew Dakers, who quickly set about finding a publisher for *Whose Body?*. She had also applied that March for an opening as a copywriter with London's largest advertising agency, S. H. Benson's, a few minutes' walk from Great James Street. After a trial period that May she settled into full-time work at Benson's, where she would stay for the next nine years. Dorothy Sayers must have felt she had hit the jackpot that July when the American firm Boni and Liveright made an offer for *Whose Body?*. She celebrated by cooking the man she thought she wanted a five-course dinner accompanied by vermouth, Burgundy, and Grand Marnier Cordon Rouge.[34]

After it became apparent late that fall that the way to Cournos' heart, assuming he had one, was not through his stomach but through areas her principles forbade, Dorothy looked elsewhere. In today's terms, her biological clock was ticking more and more loudly. She was close to thirty, and two men, both of them intellectuals and egotists, had thrown her over. Around Christmas she wrote her mother, by then possibly unshockable, "I am coming home . . . on Saturday with a man and a motor-cycle."[35] By the next April, Dorothy Sayers was pregnant.

Though close friends and relatives might have suspected, only a very few people knew that John Anthony Fleming, whom Dorothy Sayers "adopted" around 1934, was in fact her biological son, born in Bournemouth 3 January 1924 – disclosed when Janet Hitchman rummaged through legal records for an unauthorized biography published in 1975.[36] Again, Brabazon's account is the fullest currently available, postulating Dorothy's need for a physical relationship and its fulfillment with a man she described as a "poor devil," an out-of-work motor mechanic she came across one weekend. Brabazon calls him simply by the pseudonym "Bill," and describes him as a man of action, claiming that Dorothy would have married him but for his unwillingness to accept the baby. Her pregnancy was an accident that threatened not only their relationship but Dorothy's job and her status with her parents as well.[37] She handled the catastrophe as best she could; as a result of her salary and her love of good food, she had been gaining weight, and she managed to hide her condition, taking two months off from Benson's, ostensibly to work on a new novel, which she in fact did do but under some agonizing emotional stress. Until two days after the child's birth, Dorothy hoped that Bill would accept the child, but he refused. Faced with the wages of what must have seemed "a great sin," she turned to her cousin Ivy Shrimpton for help, arranging to board the child with Ivy at Oxford. She told Ivy that she hoped to take her son back at some later date.[38]

Dorothy Sayers returned to work at Benson's about two weeks later, putting up a brave front and still hoping for a change in Bill's attitude that never came. She finally had to tell him off for good in April 1924. How wretched that year was for her, Brabazon says, shows only in her letters to Cournos, with whom

Dorothy shared an awkward incident: on 4 December she saw Bill in a café with another woman, who accidently dumped a cup of tea in Dorothy's lap, adding insult to a bitter injury. By 22 February even Dorothy Sayers's stamina was faltering; she told Cournos that she was having trouble doing her work, and she was afraid Benson's would fire her. "I haven't even the last resort of doing away with myself, because what would Anthony do then, poor thing?"[39] Anguished as she was, she had to support herself and her son by dreaming up catchy advertising slogans and completing *Clouds of Witness*, her second Wimsey novel, and a handful of short stories. She accomplished all of this by the end of 1925.

Whose Body? was published in Britain by T. Fisher Unwin in October 1923, shortly after release of the American version, and the royalties must have been a help to Dorothy Sayers during her leave from Benson's for the birth of her son. She had begun thinking about a second novel as early as February 1922 during a visit to Dorothy Rowe,[40] but her ill-fated infatuation with Cournos and the disaster with Bill prevented her from completing it for three years, by far the longest period of gestation of any of her novels. At last published in 1926 by Unwin, *Clouds of Witness* represents a turning point both in her personal life and in her literary career. Dorothy Sayers was now thirty-one, and if she had known the American baseball expression "three strikes and out," she might have felt it applied to her attachments to men, since she had endured three bitterly unhappy love affairs brought on by counting the world well lost for men who spurned her. Her second novel, unavoidably influenced by her situation, might also have been an attempt to correct a flaw she found in *Whose Body?*. She had wanted to crossbreed the traditional detective story with the mainstream novel but later judged that her initial attempt had failed: "One cannot write a novel unless one has something to say about life, and I had nothing to say about it, because I knew nothing."[41]

She had a great deal to say about it by the time she wrote *Clouds of Witness*. This novel deals with a devastating sexual passion whose fiery winds whip its victims hither and yon, like the sinners Dante positioned in his upper inferno who yielded to lust. Dorothy Sayers had been living with the results of what

Catholicism, Anglo or Roman, calls sin, situations where she had, as old Thomas of Britain had put it in his *Tristan*, knowingly chosen "novelty" with love affairs against her reason and against her skill in understanding her own moral creed. Dorothy Sayers's own unhappiness seems to have shadowed *Clouds of Witness*: most of its characters are fretful, cantankerous, quarrelsome, belligerent, or downright obnoxious, all symptoms of sexual anxiety, a conclusion attributable to Dr. Freud, himself a popular topic of conversation in 1920s England.

Lord Peter Wimsey faces the possibility of murder in his own family when his brother the Duke of Denver becomes the prime suspect in the death of Denis Cathcart, the slickly handsome fiancé of Wimsey's sister Mary, a case that steams with fleshly fireworks. Mary has taken up with Cathcart to camouflage her infatuation with Goyles, a impecunious, raving Socialist with a motorbike; the Duke has forbidden her to marry Goyles on pain of losing her inheritance. The Duke put himself in harm's way by an assignation with a beauteous farm wife whose husband trembles on the brink of mayhem; Cathcart himself is wrecked by an exquisite pragmatic Viennese courtesan; and even Wimsey's friend, dependable Charles Parker of Scotland Yard, turns ill-tempered when hopelessly smitten by Mary's charms.

Lord Peter himself has undergone a change in *Clouds of Witness*. The giddy chatter that earlier marked him as a spiritual descendent of Bertie Wooster still appears, but it is modulated by Wimsey's increasing emotional stability, even after being set on by dogs, nearly drowned in boggy marshland, shot in the shoulder and ferried across the stormy Atlantic in an open cockpit; his chivalric impulses are also tempered by practicality. Dorothy Sayers had by now learned that whatever does not kill a detective hero must make him stronger.

In terms of her own situation, *Clouds of Witness* might represent Dorothy Sayers's revenge upon the desirable but flawed men who had given her so much misery. The Duke of Denver nearly undid himself by slipping out for a little respite from his domineering duchess Helen, possibly named for Cournos' recently-acquired wife and one of the most hilariously distasteful creatures in Sayers's novels. Lady Mary threw over her money-grubbing Socialist because she minded his being an unmitigated fool more than his being a potential murderer, and Farmer Grimethorpe, who had crushed nearly every spark of his beautiful wife's individuality, met an eminently suitable end under the wheels of a London taxi. Denis Cathcart, after Wimsey the most interesting figure in *Clouds of Witness*, strongly resembles Eric Whelpton; raised like Whelpton in France and ensnared by a glamourous femme fatale, as Dorothy felt Whelpton had been, Cathcart was "hot stuff but absolutely impersonal,"[42] a self-made victim of the very double standard that seemed to give men the upper hand in European society. *Clouds of Witness* allowed Dorothy Sayers to say what she had to say about how passion fatally befogs the intellectual and moral judgment of men and women, and as Brabazon observes, writing it probably "did her good."[43]

So did her work at Benson's. Regimentation had never been palatable to her, and as her 1933 mystery *Murder Must Advertise* shows, she felt comfortable with the madcap camaraderie of the 1920s advertising agency, where everyone was more or less free to do his or her own thing, so long as the deadline was met.

> Everybody is always out of his room. If he isn't chatting with the copy-department, or fooling around the typists, he's in the studio, clamoring for a lay-out, or in the printing . . . or in the press-department . . . or in the vouchers . . . or if he isn't in any of those places, he's . . . slipped out for surreptitious coffee.[44]

She liked her work – her best-known slogan was, "It pays to advertise!" – and she became the chief copywriter for the phenomenally successful J. & J. Colman campaign to increase their sales of mustard. Dorothy unleashed her broad sense of humor with the Mustard Club, headed by Baron de Beef, a hobby raiser of Welsh Rabbits, and including figures like Lord Bacon and Cookham, Lady Hearty and Miss Di Gester. The Mustard Club fun continued for several years and even resulted in a cookbook to which Dorothy and her husband contributed.

Besides her work, Bloomsbury offered Dorothy Sayers a wide variety of amusements. Notorious for liberal thought and "free love," the area was full of young intellectuals and artists. Dorothy had not only bought a motorcycle and through Bill had become a competent motor mechanic, but she had abandoned the viola and the chamber music that she had played in a small orchestra near

Les Roches for a saxophone and *le jazz hot*. She also pursued a variety of hobbies, like crossword puzzles, jigsaws and photography, with indefatigible gusto and incorporated them into her books. Some wild-eyed political factions headquartered themselves near the flat in Great James Street, which she kept until she died, and she lampooned them pungently as the Soviet Club in *Clouds of Witness*, but they could not infiltrate her essentially conservative outlook; Dorothy Sayers's penchant for arguing must have brought on some vigorous debates. However colorful her life-style, there seems no indication that it affected her equally conservative sense of right and wrong. The most heinous sin both then and later for Dorothy Sayers would have meant the intellectual decision to reject the formal dogma of her faith and knowingly accept Evil as Good, something that so far as is known she never committed, although as time went on she was – like most human beings – better able to recognize her own shortcomings, such as the essential greed motivating the institution of advertising in which she was so enthusiastic a participant.

Around August of 1925, Dorothy wrote to Cournos, asking him "to find her a companionable man,"[45] but no one knows whether Cournos did so. Brabazon suggests Dorothy might have met her future husband through Bill, since both men frequented motor racetracks. She might just as well have run into Oswald Atherton Fleming in a pub where advertising people and journalists gathered. They became friendly that fall and were married quietly the next April in the registrar's office in Clerkenwell Road, Holborn, since Fleming was a divorced man. In the eyes of her Church, Dorothy Sayers would be "living in sin" for most of the rest of her life.

Fleming was a Scot, born in the Orkney Islands at the extreme northern tip of Britain, and he was proud of it – so much so that one of his enduring fantasies involved the chance that he might be the fourteenth Earl of Wigton, a title created in the fourteenth century by the son of Robert the Bruce. Fleming liked to be known as "Major," and he preferred "Atherton" instead of his christened second name "Alfred," but Dorothy referred to him simply as "Mac." Twelve years older than Dorothy Sayers, he had served as a cavalryman and correspondent in the Boer War; he was married in 1911 and worked in public relations for car makers at Coventry, especially Daimler, until 1914, when he joined the Royal Army Service Corps. After being gassed and shell-shocked, he unwisely checked himself out of an army hospital at the close of the war, forfeiting his Acting Captain's pension, and when he resumed his journalistic career away from his family, his marriage foundered. From Mac's 1919 book *How to See the Battlefields*, Ralph Hone concludes that the war had "mutilated" Mac's spirit so badly that by 1924 he no longer supported his wife and their two daughters.[46] His wife's divorce on grounds of adultery became final during the summer of 1925, and according to Brabazon, Mac hardly ever paid the stipulated alimony; after their wedding Dorothy Sayers kept up the payments to Mac's former wife until Dorothy herself died.[47]

During the first year of her marriage, Dorothy was working on her third novel, *Unnatural Death*, titled *The Dawson Pedigree* in the United States. This presented the perfect crime case which Lord Peter Wimsey, like many mystery writers and their fans, had dreamed of solving: a murder with no detectible weapon, no clues, and no motive.[48] In both *Whose Body?* and *Clouds of Witness*, Dorothy L. Sayers had had to make her killers confess to untangle her plots, but she never did it again. *Unnatural Death* represents a giant step forward in her technique and provides valuable insights into her professional and personal lives.

Lord Peter's entertaining family is almost entirely absent from *Unnatural Death*, and even the indefatigible Bunter seems muted. In their places Dorothy Sayers introduced Miss Alexandra Katherine Climpson, a middle-aged spinster employed as Lord Peter's eyes and ears. Miss Climpson opens up comic vistas of British manners at levels of society that could only be reached through the natural inquisitiveness and gossip power of old maids, an intelligence-gathering source Wimsey feels had been hitherto completely untapped. Acting on a hunch sparked by a hint from a disgruntled physician, Wimsey sends Miss Climpson to investigate the apparently natural death of a well-to-do elderly woman from cancer; no medical evidence indicates foul play and the logical suspect, her niece, is the deceased's only beneficiary, apparently ruling out a motive. Wimsey cannot resist the challenge.

Dorothy Sayers constructed *Unnatural Death* as a crescendo of horror that begins almost imperceptibly and closes with an explosion of publicity that overshadows Wimbledon.[49] As Wimsey closes in, witness after witness is found mysteriously dead, culminating with a foolish young woman who had lied out of love to protect the murderer. Two-thirds through the novel, Miss Climpson grasps the motive, nothing less than the pride that cast Lucifer from heaven, as Milton put it: "Better to reign in hell than serve in heaven,"[50] but it takes Wimsey's combination of logic and intuition to unmask the killer, the most spine-chilling unnatural criminal Sayers had created to this point.

The importance of this novel to Dorothy Sayers's personal and professional development lies in its unflinching treatment of the unnatural element itself, not merely the gruesome excess of pride that leads to murder but abnormal sexuality, which only a few years earlier would have been an unthinkable topic for a novel. Dorothy Sayers opted for practicality in her business costume, a mannish suit and sensible shoes, and her hair, always a problem after her adolescent illness, behaved best cut short and slicked back; her appearance thus caused superficial observers to leap to erroneous conclusions about possible lesbian tendencies in her personality. If her three deeply felt passions, Whelpton, Cournos, and Bill, and her marriage to Fleming were not proof enough of Dorothy Sayers's unequivocally heterosexual orientation, Miss Climpson's reaction to idolatrous love between persons of the same sex ought to settle the question forever. In many important respects, such as her High Anglican persuasion, Miss Climpson was Dorothy as she might have been had Mac not come along; and with logic, with the self-possession of a completely womanly woman, and with unshakable theological certitude, Miss Climpson voices Dorothy Sayers's conviction that it is both more natural and more proper for opposite sexes to attract and cleave to one another.[51]

In *Unnatural Death* Dorothy Sayers, the devout Anglo-Catholic, also explored the thorny moral issue of what killing does to the killer, for the first time using a kindly country vicar, a literary echo of Henry Sayers and possibly an attempt to make peace with her family. The clergyman helps Lord Peter Wimsey to reconcile his itch for the game of criminal investigation with the unpleasant side effects of guilt it gave him – at best, guilt over the capital punishment of the perpetrator, and at worst, painful recriminations over the deaths of innocent victims, in this case the very maidens a knight-errant ought to have protected. After he confesses his responsibility, a time-honored Catholic ritual here placed in an informal secular context, Peter receives a kind of absolution along with a priestly admonition: "Remember that if we all got justice, you and I wouldn't escape either,"[52] an ethical outlook Dorothy Sayers shared, and one that removes her novels, even the earliest, far from the ordinary run of detective fiction.

For a little while marriage brought Dorothy Sayers domestic satisfaction. She kept her relationship with Mac strictly separate from her coworkers at Benson's, but at this point it seemed solid and companionable, though not overly demonstrative – their usual terms of endearment were "old boy" and "old girl."[53] Mac was doing well as a racing and crime reporter for the *News of the World*, and both he and Dorothy considered "eating as a fine art."[54] Their interests at first seemed to mesh handsomely; Mac loved to cook, concocting and trying out many of the recipes for Dorothy's Mustard Club Recipe Book, and Dorothy went with him to Boulogne when he was reporting on a pair of sensational crimes. He also had a flamboyant man-of-the-world streak that appealed to Dorothy – once, when his Daimler ran low, he fueled it up with whiskey – and an innate decency she needed badly after her various hurts; and Brabazon goes so far as to deduce from Dorothy's later writings on love that Mac "was good in bed."[55]

Just after she and Mac were married, Dorothy Sayers's literary career was mushrooming. In 1926, *Clouds of Witness* had had good reviews and sold well, and *Unnatural Death* was published in July 1927 by Ernest Benn, who had incorporated with Fisher Unwin earlier that year. An up-and-coming employee at Benn's, Victor Gollancz, strongly encouraged Dorothy Sayers while she was writing her first novels, and when Gollancz decided to leave Benn to start his own firm, she wanted very much to turn her work over to him, but Benn refused to release her from her contract for two more novels. She polished them both off in the next two years, at the same time undertaking several projects for Gollancz. She was working on a volume of short Wimsey fiction, started a biography of the early detective novelist Wilkie Collins, which she never completed but worked at sporadically for the rest of her life, and hurled herself into enormous research on the genre of mystery fiction, all time-consuming major projects which she attacked with her usual thoroughness, even though she was holding a full-time job at Benson's.

Britain's economic climate likely strengthened Dorothy Sayers's resolve to make the most of Lord Peter's popularity. At the beginning of the 1920s, widespread inflation had brought wholesale prices to 225 percent of prewar levels,[56] and in 1925, Britain had returned to the gold standard at prewar parity, a move that raised British export prices and impeded production, worsened the nation's balance of payments, and increased unemployment. The economic crisis was exacerbated by the general strike of May 1926 and was echoed in spades by the collapse of the entire German economic system in 1927. By 1928, the year of the noble but unenforceable Kellogg-Briand Treaty which "outlawed war as an instrument of national policy"[57] and the "Flapper Vote" which reduced the voting age for British women from thirty to twenty-one, the British were paying a painful four shillings on the pound income tax with 10 percent of the nation's workers unemployed. Dorothy had to have felt the economic pinch.

The concentration on her work and the need to make money from her books probably intensified the strain which began to appear on Dorothy Sayers's marriage in 1927. Mac had expensive tastes and a backlog of bills; he was beginning to have stomach trouble from his military service, and worse, the nightmares from the trenches were becoming tougher to hold at bay. His work was suffering, and so were his relations with Dorothy. David Higham, who became Dorothy's agent and lifelong friend two years later, felt that she had married Mac in part "because she thought she might cure his drinking – a hopeless task she should never even have thought of"[58] and one that worsened as her income rose and his declined. In addition, there was Anthony. Dorothy had originally hoped that Mac would agree to bringing her son, then a year and a half old, into their home, but a year later she observed in a letter to Ivy that "maternal affection" was not her strongest suit,[59] and she preferred not to bring the child into an already complicated situation. She was probably right. An extremely busy mother unaccustomed to small children and a stepfather with increasing physical and emotional problems were unlikely to have offered a toddler an adequate family life. Guilt over her husband's unhappiness, separation from her child, and her own situation, since her Church considered that by marrying a divorced man she was living in sin, must have played a large role in *The Unpleasantness at the Bellona Club* (1927), one of the bitterest novels Dorothy Sayers wrote.

Stomach trouble, no money or job, an overworked wife, and the income tax: all these pressures weighed down *Bellona Club*'s George Fentiman, just as they were doing to Mac, and Dorothy Sayers incorporated them into a murder case. When George's ancient grandfather is found dead at the Bellona Club, George, shell-shocky and desperate, becomes a major suspect in his death. George's wife, as many wives of alcoholics do, not only endures his unconscionable abuse but tries to cover up his vicissitudes. The domestic bickering rings sadly true: George denounces "hard-mouthed cigarette-smoking females" that want only money and notoriety, "pretending they're geniuses and business women . . . flying off to offices and clubs and parties."[60]

Dorothy Sayers drew Mac harshly here, but she did not spare herself, either. Loving the wrong man had trapped Sheila Fentiman in a kind of self-destruction, just as it had done to Ann Dorland, another suspect in the case, who had wanted passion and had fallen first for an artist and then for a cad who had made a fool of her. Women in those situations understandably might yearn after a knight in shining armor, and Wimsey predictably appears, an impulsive Roland to Charles Parker's careful Oliver.[61] Dorothy Sayers used images from Dante's *Inferno* in this novel much as she did in *Whose Body?* to suggest the depths of human degradation. His disgust at depravity tempts Wimsey to wash his hands of the case and drives him to tell Parker that in sixty years the two of them may be inhabiting circles of hell that involve murderers;[62] but a little later Wimsey refers to Dante again, when he finds the clue that eventually solves the case: despite – or because of – his acquaintance with hell, Dante himself once painted an angel.[63] The genuine artist, Dorothy Sayers believed firmly and wrote in her short story "The Unsolved Puzzle of the Man with No Face," will always be sincere with his art,[64] and she was with hers.

Wimsey saves George for Sheila Fentiman and rescues Ann from being arrested for murder, taking her to a sumptuous Savoy dinner and predicting she will find a "man of the world" who will be "reliable and kind," and proud that hers will be "the leading brain of the two"[65] – a recipe for a marriage between equals, a goal women of intellect like Dorothy Sayers rarely achieve, though they can dream – or what's a heaven for?

Mac lost his job with the *News of the World* around the time that *The Unpleasantness at the Bellona Club* was published in the summer of 1928. He and Dorothy vacationed in Kirkudbrightshire, in the south of Scotland, at Gatehouse of Fleet, which Dorothy Sayers used later as the locale for *The Five Red Herrings*, and Mac's spirits seemed to pick up; he worked on some culinary articles for the *Evening News* and a cookery book for Crosse and Blackwell's, and they added the flat above to Dorothy's in Great James Street that August, providing a little more breathing room that they both needed.[66] The first of several collections called *Great Short Stories of Detection, Mystery, and Horror* that Dorothy edited for Gollancz came out that fall, and her introduction to it remains one of the classic analyses of the mystery genre. Late in the year, twelve of Dorothy's Wimsey short stories appeared as the immensely popular collection *Lord Peter Views the Body*, also from Gollancz. Four of these stories date from 1925–26, while the rest exhibit developments drawn from her study of the theory of the mystery genre and look forward, like "The Unsolved Puzzle of the Man With No Face," to advancements she would make in the genre in the 1930s. "The Adventurous Exploit of the Cave of Ali Baba," claims Ralph Hone, "is as suspenseful as anything Sayers ever wrote."[67]

The Detection Club, one of the lasting preoccupations of Dorothy Sayers's life, also sprang into existence in 1928 from Anthony Berkeley's idea that mystery writers should meet periodically for dinner and shoptalk. Dorothy Sayers was a prime mover in establishing its modus vivendi – rent for the club rooms at 31 Gerrard Street, the address of Dorothy's fictional "Soviet Club," and the club's operating expenses would be paid for by sales of joint projects by its members, like its successful BBC radio serials and its collaborative novels. The club's initiation ritual has the distinctive Sayers touch; the candidate stands before the president, hand on a skull (called "Eric") lit up by a candle fastened inside, and binds himself with Book of Common Prayer-like strictures:

Do you promise that your Detectives shall well and truly detect the Crimes presented to them, using those Wits which it shall please you to bestow upon them, and not placing reliance upon nor making use of Divine Revelation, Feminine Intuition, Mumbo-Jumbo, Jiggery-Pokery, Coincidence, or the Act of God?
And the Candidate must answer, "I do."[68]

By keeping those commandments, Dorothy Sayers achieved a solid following as a mystery author by the time she was thirty-five. With all of the demands on her time, she was understandably irritable with people who wanted to waste it foolishly, but those certainly did not include her family. She was at her father's bedside when he died of pneumonia in September 1928 at Christchurch, and that Christmas she moved her mother and Aunt Mabel into "Sunnyside," a house she bought for them at Witham, about an hour from London. When Mrs. Sayers died of a strangulated hernia the next July, Dorothy and Mac moved to Witham themselves, and Aunt Mabel remained with them as long as she lived, part of a growing household that involved cats, dogs, a parrot, and during the Second World War, even pigs.

Dorothy Sayers was putting her literary house in order, too. Victor Gollancz introduced her to David Higham, who became her agent in August 1929. Higham believed that Dorothy came to him "to get her away from a publisher [Benn] who would now hardly publish her with success," and he said he managed to "rescue her from the advertising racket so that she could write full time, as she wanted to."[69] She also tidied up an end that had been loose since Oxford; finally, in 1929, Benn published *Tristan in Brittany*, in which Sayers used a smooth, high-spirited, prose narrative to fit together her translations of the extant fragments of Thomas's poem that Lord Peter Wimsey had been collating at the British Museum in *Unnatural Death*.[70] In her introduction, she praised Thomas as a "thoughtful and competent psychologist," who scrupulously dissects the thorny problems of morality contained in the fatal passion shared by these most famous lovers of the Western world. Dorothy Sayers stressed the "desperate beauty" in that illicit passion and Thomas's "frank exposure of the squalid accompaniments of unlawful love,"[71] a combination of the best and the worst that human beings can make of themselves, and a foreshadowing of the more profound roles that love and evil would play in the novels that she herself had by now lived enough to write.

Notes

1. Asa Briggs, *A Social History of England* (New York: Viking Press, 1983), p. 258.
2. Wilfred Owen, "Anthem for Doomed Youth," in *British Literature* 2, ed. Hazelton Spencer et al. (Lexington, Mass.: D.C. Heath and Co., 1974), p. 1228.
3. Quoted in Briggs, p. 261.
4. Quoted in Briggs, p. 264.
5. Ibid.
6. Clive Aslet, *The Last Country Houses* (New Haven, Conn.: Yale University Press, 1982), p. 85.
7. Ibid., p. 89.
8. Quoted in Briggs, p. 264.
9. Jessica Mann, *Deadlier Than the Male* (New York: Macmillan, 1981), p. 27.
10. Ibid., p. 40.
11. G. K. Chesterton, quoted in R. D. Stock and Barbara Stock, "The Agents of Evil and Justice in the Novels of Dorothy L. Sayers," in *As Her Whimsey Took Her*, ed. Margaret P. Hannay (Kent, Ohio: Kent State University Press, 1979), p. 14.
12. Dawson Gaillard, *Dorothy L. Sayers* (New York: Frederick Unger, 1981), p. 50.
13. Ibid., p. 73.
14. James Brabazon, *Dorothy L. Sayers: A Biography* (New York: Charles Scribners' Sons, 1981), p. 123.
15. Dorothy L. Sayers, quoted in *The Daily Express* 28 February 1934, quoted in Brabazon, p. 87.
16. Dorothy L. Sayers, Letter to parents 22 January 1921, quoted in Brabazon, p. 87.
17. Brabazon, p. 87.
18. Dorothy L. Sayers, *Whose Body?* (1923; New York: Avon, 1961), p. 46.

19. Ibid., p. 127–28.
20. Ibid., p. 19.
21. Ibid., pp. 10, 18, 65, 115, 144, 160, 170–71.
22. Barbara Reynolds, *The Passionate Intellect* (Kent, Ohio: Kent State University Press, 1989), p. 3.
23. Walter Kaufmann, ed. and trans., *The Basic Writings of Nietzsche* (New York: Modern Library, 1968), pp. 185–86.
24. Sayers, *Whose Body?*, p. 127.
25. Ibid., p. 161.
26. Ibid., p. 168.
27. Brabazon, p. 87.
28. Ibid., p. 88.
29. Brabazon, pp. 89–96.
30. Ibid., p. 89.
31. Ibid., p. 96.
32. Ibid., p. 89.
33. Dorothy L. Sayers, Letter to parents 18 January 1922, quoted in Brabazon, p. 91.
34. Brabazon, pp. 91–92.
35. Dorothy L. Sayers, Letter to parents 18 December 1922, quoted in Brabazon, pp. 96–97.
36. Hanet Hitchman, *Such a Strange Lady: A Biography of Dorothy L. Sayers* (New York: Harper and Row, 1975).
37. Brabazon, pp. 97–105.
38. Ibid., p. 103.
39. Dorothy L. Sayers, Letter to John Cournos 22 February 1925, quoted in Brabazon, p. 105.
40. Dorothy Rowe was teaching at Bournemouth, and there is a possibility that she was aware that Dorothy Sayers gave birth to her son there. See Brabazon, p. 102.
41. Dorothy L. Sayers, "The Art of the Mystery Story," quoted in Hone, p. 41.
42. Dorothy L. Sayers, *Clouds of Witness* (1926; New York: Avon, 1966), p. 124.
43. Brabazon, p. 107.
44. Dorothy L. Sayers, *Murder Must Advertise*, quoted in Alzina Stone Dale, *Maker and Craftsman: The Story of Dorothy L. Sayers* (Grand Rapids, Mich.: William B. Eerdmans Publishing Co., 1978), p. 64.
45. Dorothy L. Sayers, Letter to John Cournos, no date given; quoted in Brabazon, p. 113.
46. Ralph E. Hone, *Dorothy L. Sayers: A Literary Biography* (Kent, Ohio: Kent State University Press, 1979), p. 48.
47. Brabazon, p. 253.
48. Dorothy L. Sayers, *Unnatural Death* (1927; New York: Avon, 1964), p. 83.
49. Ibid., p. 203.

50. John Milton, *Paradise Lost*, Book I, quoted in Sayers, *Unnatural Death*, p. 155.
51. Sayers, *Unnatural Death*, p. 158.
52. Ibid., p. 191.
53. Brabazon, pp. 135, 137.
54. Sayers, *Unnatural Death*, p. 64.
55. Brabazon, p. 116.
56. Walter L. Arnstein, *Britain Yesterday and Today: 1830 to the Present* 5th ed. (Lexington, Mass.: D.C. Heath and Co., 1988), p. 273.
57. Ibid., p. 292.
58. David Higham, *Literary Gent* (New York: Coward, McCann, and Geoghegan, 1978), p. 211.
59. Dorothy L. Sayers, Letter to Ivy Shrimpton 13 May 1927, quoted in Brabazon, p. 141.
60. Dorothy L. Sayers, *The Unpleasantness at the Bellona Club* (1928; New York: Avon, 1963), p. 55.
61. Ibid., p. 63.
62. Ibid., p. 142.
63. Ibid., p. 157.
64. Dorothy L. Sayers, *Lord Peter Views the Body* (1928; New York: Avon, 1969), p. 220.
65. Sayers, *The Unpleasantness*, p. 180.
66. Brabazon, p. 140.
67. Hone, p. 56.
68. Dale, pp. 86–87.
69. Higham, p. 211.
70. Sayers, *Unnatural Death*, p. 38.
71. Dorothy L. Sayers, Introduction to *Tristan in Brittany* (New York: Payson and Clarke, 1929), pp. xxix–xxxi. Thomas's version of the Tristan story "is distinguished by his rationalizing tendency and his remarkable interest in character," and he "makes an eloquent appeal to reason to justify his account as against less sensible variants." Introduction to Thomas of Britain, *The Romance of Tristram and Ysolt* by Roger Sherman Loomis, trans. (New York: Dutton, 1967), p. xxix. The qualities Loomis highlights would have appealed strongly to Dorothy Sayers's own talents and would have helped prepare her to develop her own techniques of fiction.

6 Human Comedies
1929–1936

> Marriage has destroyed the mystery.
> Dorothy L. Sayers, "The Omnibus of Crime"

In the later 1920s, Britain was enjoying a deceptive euphoria at home and abroad. The General Strike of 1926 had cost the labor unions about a third of their financial reserves and the loss of a half million members, and in its wake union leaders adopted a moderate tack in their subsequent negotiations with management.[1] Social reforms, like the Local Government Act of 1929 which shifted the burden of caring for the indigent from property taxes to the National Treasury, were also beginning to redistribute the nation's wealth. Prior to seeking to outlaw war with the idealistic Kellogg-Briand Treaty of 1928, Great Britain's Parliament in 1926 had acknowledged international changes brought about by World War I by establishing self-governing dominions like Canada and Australia as autonomous members of the Commonwealth. John Buchan, whose best-selling adventure stories featured clean-living heroes saving the Empire from Yellow, Black or Brown Perils, declared "Civilization has been saved, and, on the whole, the nations are once more a stable society."[2]

Beneath the cozy surface, however, lurked more sinister economic realities. Great Britain had never really returned to normalcy after World War I. Its foreign investments had slumped, 40 percent of its merchant fleet had been lost, and Britain was rapidly losing international markets to aggressive new competitors like Japan, which was cutting seriously into the British textile trade. In 1929, the United States was supplying 34.4 percent of the world's industrial production, while Germany, even though paying formidable reparations under the Dawes Plan, matched Britain's 10.3 per cent.[3] The balloon burst on Black Friday, 28 October 1929, with the crash of the American stock market; the immediate loss of $26 billion in the value of U.S. securities ripped apart the 1920s' fragile, artificial financial structure and plunged the world into a staggering economic depression.

106

E. M. Forster has remarked that "the Twenties react[ed] after the war and recede[d] from it. The Thirties . . . [were] apprehensive of war and . . . [were] carried toward it."[4] In 1930, in fact, a noose of failed loans began to choke the West; the stoppage of American loans to Germany caused that country to cease its reparations to France and Britain, who then found themselves unable to repay war loans to the United States, and international tensions began to rise. A year later a major European economic crisis drew Britain further into the maelstrom; the Austrian banking system nearly collapsed, spreading the crisis to Germany, and British bank reserves supported by the Bank of England and heretofore as solid as Gibraltar were badly depleted by defaulted loans to continental banks. The ensuing drain on British gold reserves caused a withdrawal of foreign funds and a run on the British pound, forcing Britain to negotiate a $80 million loan from the United States. To meet its terms, the British cut unemployment benefits and devalued the pound from $4.86 to $3.40, draconian measures that brought in the coalition National Government to cope with the financial crisis.[5]

Britain's downhill slide in the 1930s was less drastic than the United States' Great Depression, which was itself intensified by widespread drought and crop failures, but conditions in Britain were trying enough; British exports and iron and steel production each fell by half between 1929 and 1932, and shipbuilding virtually ceased. By December 1930, 2.5 million British workers were unemployed, and by the middle of 1932, as Hitler began his rise to power in Germany, nearly 7 million people out of Britain's total population of 45 million were existing on public welfare.[6]

Dismal economic times breed an appetite for escape. In both Britain and America, average citizens dreamed themselves into the shoes of the rich and famous as a way to avoid the unpleasant here and now. British historian Michael Bentley has observed that the rise of Britain's lower middle class, thirsty for the security of the good old days and eager to sample the privileges of the declining aristocracy, paralleled the growing political power of the urban working class. "In this context Victorian class privilege acquired a classical status, and developed into a collection of atavistic values depicted in the popular culture dominated by P. G. Wodehouse, Noel Coward, Dorothy Sayers, and Agatha

Christie."[7] Losing oneself at the theatre or the movies also helped; by 1939, "four million British cinema seats gave daily access to the romantic escapism of Hollywood,"[8] but retiring alone with a book to one's home, the traditional Englishman's castle, allowed an even less costly means of closing out the miserable reality of joblessness. Along with radio programming, hobbies, and games like Monopoly and contract bridge, detective stories flourished. According to sociologist Asa Briggs, the British home "became more of a centre of private relaxation during the 1920s and 1930s . . . the years of the crossword puzzle, the detective novel, and the 'hobby', which was very much an 'individual thing'."[9]

The changes in the world around her helped Dorothy Sayers to move beyond the boundaries of the 1920s detective story. Although her Wimsey fiction was highly popular and lucrative, it no longer satisfied her artistically, and she was beginning to think about developing the series into a new art form. In 1928, she established the theoretical basis for combining the traditional novel of detection with the comedy of manners in her introductions to three short story collections edited for Gollancz, beginning with *Great Short Stories of Detection, Mystery, and Horror* (published in the United States as *The Omnibus of Crime*).[10]

Many mystery buffs consider Dorothy Sayers's 1928 introduction "the finest single piece of analytical writing about the detective story."[11] She declared that "the art of self-tormenting" by any kind of mystery "made to be solved" was a basic human need that transcended the desire for simple amusement,[12] and she knew very well from personal experience that the common denominator of such pursuits – the reassuring existence of a solution, no matter how difficult the problem – was one of the individual's few consolations in an increasingly uncertain world. Events had shown that the technological innovations of the nineteenth century had increased rather than decreased the dangers of everyday life, and Dorothy Sayers had already fortified the concept of the detective as a knight-errant who protected the weak and brought the wicked to justice; she called him "the true successor of Roland and Lancelot."[13] Loyal Englishwoman that she was, Dorothy Sayers also could not resist pointing out the qualities that had brought the detective novel to its zenith among the Anglo-Saxon races, stressing their devotion to law and order as the basic construction principle of her novels, a tricky exercise in shifting points of view to keep all clues and discoveries as accessible to the reader as to the detective himself.

For Dorothy Sayers, the evolving mystery novel had both artistic status and artistic challenges of its own. Besides the inherent Aristotelian unity of beginning, middle, and end, she felt that its stereotyped characterizations should give way to more human figures, demanding increased creative effort to produce heightened realism. She observed that portraying the murderer as a sympathetic human being required the execution by hanging of that same "real" person, and the taking of a human life could not be carried out lightly – the basis for Lord Peter's growing pangs of conscience. Furthermore, she realized that the demise of prewar certitudes required the detective story to achieve both "a higher level of writing and a more competent delineation of character" than before, in particular requiring that the sleuth should now possess "a tenderer human feeling" under his frivolous or ruthlessly efficient exterior. On the other hand, "tender" most definitely did not involve frivolous romantic interests. Dorothy Sayers scorned "heroes who insist on fooling about after young women" instead of concentrating on solving crimes,[14] although she did cite instances in Collins's and Bentley's works where substantial relationships between detectives and sensible girls furthered the development of character, prefiguring her own creation of Harriet as Wimsey's future wife.[15] The same hard-headed practicality supported her predictions for the genre; she foresaw ingenious new methods of mayhem and murder, sophisticated corpse disposal, and elegant gadgetry to buttress the detective's poniard-keen wits.

Dorothy Sayers closed her first analysis of detective fiction with an image drawn from that private world she took such pains to keep separate from her profession. Marriage to the author's muse, she insisted, would destroy the mystery. Every novel had to employ entirely new devices, or readers would detect the writer's methods rather than the crimes. Her illustration seems to reveal sensitive matters in her own marriage; stressing the use of the detective novel as a catharsis for everyday pressures, Dorothy Sayers declared, "We read tales of domestic unhappiness because . . . that happens to us; but when these things gall too close to the sore, we fly to mystery and adventure because they do not, as a rule, happen to us."[16]

Domestic unhappiness was becoming all too real to Dorothy Sayers. After she left Benson's at the end of 1929, she and Mac moved to the Witham house that she had originally bought for her mother. The next year they acquired the cottage next door and remodeled the two fifteenth-century buildings, which had been joined together by an eighteenth-century facade, into one residence with fireplaces in several rooms and toilets and baths crammed "higgledy-piggledy" into nooks and crannies of the stairs.[17] "Sunnyside" also had large gardens and a sizable green-house. The idea was that Dorothy could work there without interruption and still be close enough to London to attend to her business easily and to keep in contact with her friends in the Detection Club, but there seem to have been drawbacks. As James Brabazon has remarked, a freelance writer is constantly at work,[18] something non-writers generally fail to appreciate, and Dorothy Sayers had little time or inclination to mingle socially in Witham. Writing was her major source of income, and added to her own financial responsibilities were debts Mac had incurred both before and after their marriage; it took her until 1929 to pay them off.[19] Alzina Stone Dale has also commented that Mac did little around the Witham establishment but take phone messages, which he often mislaid;[20] and Dorothy's agent David Higham recalled that late in her life, she told him that Mac had often nagged her to work when he thought she might be slacking off, while at the same time, Higham said, Mac was "comfortably on the bottles" she bought him.[21]

Dorothy Sayers's religious principles precluded divorce, and she did what she could for Mac; their vacations in Scotland helped a little, and she made sure to praise the little cooking he did and the painting he occasionally attempted. In fairness, the isolation from London must have been a hardship for Mac; he was ill and out of work, dependent on his wife for his living. She chose to exclude him from her professional world, where she was rapidly becoming a celebrity, probably in part because of that British middle-class propriety that covered up alcoholism at all costs "from the neighbors."

110

Mac's drinking and his violent temper also meant that bringing Anthony to Witham was out of the question,[22] a situation bound to have caused Dorothy Sayers pain. How much it cost her and how she bore the burden is evident in a letter she wrote in 1943, twenty years after Anthony's birth: "I can't think of any personal misfortunes that have befallen me which were not, in one way or another, my own fault. I don't mean this in the profounder & [sic] more religious sense. I mean that I know jolly well that if anything unpleasant happened in my life I had usually 'asked for it.' "[23] If she was using "religious" here in its broadest theological sense as pertaining to the doctrine of Original sin, it is abundantly clear that Dorothy Sayers had a firm conviction of personal responsibility and the moral consequences of free choice. Such demanding positions generally are of long duration in a person's character, not assumed posthaste in a momentary emotional conversion, and seem the logical reason for her remaining in a difficult marriage; Dorothy Sayers had made her own bed, and she intended to make the best of lying in it.

Knowing we have made our own misfortunes makes them even harder to tolerate, and when it all galled "too close to the sore," Dorothy Sayers flew to her old refuge, mystery fiction, producing some of the most memorable novels of the genre's golden age. The mysteries she wrote in the 1930s fall into two parallel groups; in one, she followed up the theory of constant innovation that she had announced in her 1928 introduction to *Great Short Stories of Detection, Mystery, and Horror*, maintaining the sales she needed to support herself and her family. In the other, she faced and to some extent resolved her personal and artistic problems through fictionalized autobiography, creating Harriet Vane to marry Lord Peter Wimsey and get him out of Dorothy's own life for good.

The more pragmatic group of detective novels Dorothy L. Sayers produced in the early 1930s include *The Documents in the Case* (1930), *The Five Red Herrings* (1931), *Murder Must Advertise* (1933), and *The Nine Tailors* (1934). She matched her newly sensitive depiction of character with shocking technological methods of murder, and the combination pleased her growing audience. All of these novels sold well, ensuring her a comfortable living, even though they were not the novels she wanted most to write.

The Documents in the Case, written in 1929, stands out in Dorothy Sayers's work for several reasons:[24] the entire novel consists of letters; she dared to exclude Lord Peter Wimsey, the heart and soul of her fiction; and for the first time in her career, she chose to collaborate on a detective novel. Her partner in this endeavor was Robert Eustace, the *nom de crime* of Dr. Eustace Barton, a physician who had written a few stories himself and who had furnished technical material to other mystery writers. Barton supplied the plot and the ending of *The Documents in the Case*, both grounded in then brand-new scientific thinking,[25] while Dorothy Sayers used a drily comic style that makes this book much more a novel of manners than any of her previous works had been.

By 1929, both Einstein's special theory of relativity and Freud's psychoanalytical method had filtered into the popular consciousness through newspapers and superficial educational notions with predictably ludicrous misinterpretations, as one of the novel's major characters, the celebrated Professor Hoskyns, points out.[26] Misunderstandings about science abound in *The Documents in the Case*, a collection of statements regarding the suspicious death by mushroom poisoning of George Harrison, a self-taught fungus expert. In her climactic scene, Sayers amalgamated theology, astrophysics, relativity, evolution, genetics, and spectrometry, ingeniously implanting the solution of the mystery into the greater enigma of the origin of life itself.

Dorothy Sayers also greatly expanded the old epistolary form, which generally limits a narrative to a single point of view, by using letters from six different writers, fictional newspaper accounts, and lengthy statements from the two characters who had to cooperate to solve the crime. She unveiled some delicious examples of all-too-true human nature, like the spinster housekeeper Agatha Milsom, diagnosed by her latest Freudian physician as "sex-repressed;" Agatha's chief symptom is that she unceasingly knits socks that never quite fit for men who never really want them. Along with the fun the other characters poke at a neurotic old maid, though, Dorothy Sayers includes enough motivation for Agatha's problems – the postwar shortage of men left thousands of women repressed, after all – to round out the character convincingly.

Dorothy Sayers here magnified the technique of seeing the

principal figures of this novel from several points of view, a process she applauded as revolutionary in E. C. Bentley's *Trent's Last Case*. The murderer strikes most of the other characters as innocuous and likable, and even when he is unmasked by his former friend Munting, the latter, like Lord Peter, has serious qualms about turning the criminal over to the authorities. The man had been Munting's schoolmate and his friend, and even more importantly, he has genuine talent; can Munting take the responsibility for destroying it? Here we see the same moral dilemma that haunts Lord Peter Wimsey in the short story "The Unsolved Puzzle of the Man with No Face" and in several other novels.

Dorothy Sayers could not keep traces of her personal disappointments out of *The Documents in the Case* either. Her bitterness about hypocritical pseudo-artists like John Cournos is clear: "They can't love – they can only fornicate and talk";[27] and the Harrisons' marital difficulties seem to parallel her own problems. Like Mac, Harrison had authored a cookery book, and like Mac, too, he found it impossible to show his wife that he cared for her, which caused Mrs. Harrison to insist that it was no good for him to praise her behind her back if he always "scolded and snubbed" her to her face: "it only makes it worse"[28] – another reason, perhaps, why Dorothy Sayers refused to let Mac mingle with her friends.

Even without Wimsey, *The Documents in the Case* sold well. It became a Book Guild choice for July 1930, and Dorothy wanted to use the earnings to take Mac on a trip to the United States on the *Mauretania* the next May, but the excursion never transpired. They did travel frequently to southern Scotland, adding a parrot with a redoubtable vocabulary to the house at Witham, as well as acquiring the backdrop for *The Five Red Herrings*, published in March 1931.

For all its literary innovations, *The Documents in the Case* could not have completely satisfied Dorothy L. Sayers's public, which was lusting after Lord Peter. *The Five Red Herrings* gave him back to them, but much of the Wimsey entourage they had come to cherish was missing. Miss Alexandra Climpson and Wimsey's eccentric family never appeared at all, and even the unflappable Bunter and Scotland Yard's Charles Parker made shorter appearances than previously. Sayers had told Victor Gollancz that she had wanted to try out the "pure puzzle" mystery,[29] temporarily abandoning character development in favor of train schedules, Galloway idiom, and six hard-to-distinguish suspects, and for many readers *The Five Red Herrings* turned out to be one of her least effective novels.

Besides whetting the appetites of Dorothy Sayers's fans for less herring and more Wimsey, however, this novel does advance the technique of fictional detection. The clue that unravels *The Five Red Herrings* is visible from the outset, allowing Dorothy Sayers to win the mystery writer's ultimate accolade fairly: " 'What a fool I was not to see it!' . . . Precious tribute! How often striven for! How seldom gained!"[30] Furthermore, though Wimsey is caught up in the thrill of the chase and elegantly proves his solution, the crime turns out to have been accidental, and he apologizes.[31] Dorothy Sayers had successfully integrated her theory into stylish practice, allowing both detective and villain more "good streaks" and convincing "human feelings."[32]

While she was working on *The Five Red Herrings*, Dorothy Sayers produced another important essay, "The Present Status of the Mystery Story," published in the November 1930 *London Mercury*. She believed that the genre's tendency toward increasing sophistication would lead to the loss of the common touch and bring about its downfall. Her own rare combination of intellectual brilliance and tough common sense equipped her to commit verbal mayhem on literary pretentiousness: "Without fine writing, common feeling degenerates into common rant . . . [while] fine writing without common feeling . . . mummifies."[33]

Dorothy Sayers also boldly claimed that English mystery writers unabashedly linked powerful phraseology to melodramatic story lines, much as the great tragic dramatists Aeschylus and Webster had done. She believed, in fact, that the greatest mystery writers shared a "touch of the eternal,"[34] identifying the art that she defended, practiced, and advanced with tragedy as one of the oldest and noblest means of plumbing unsolvable puzzles that turn, just as murder mysteries do, on the question of why man chooses to commit evil acts. As she neared forty, Dorothy Sayers was consciously developing her novels, all based on conservative theological principles regardless of the ingenious

114

contemporary modes of mayhem employed, into serious psychological studies that still allowed her readers to enjoy a gleeful escape from their stress-filled times.

Not long after, in her introduction to Gollancz's *Second Series of Great Short Stories of Detection, Mystery, and Horror* (1931), Dorothy Sayers described her field as rapidly changing, with a new "popularity and respectability" that she said came close to alarming its friends.[35] She felt that in a distressed economy the steady sales of detective novels were a sign of health, and she applauded the genre's newly evident respect for the King's English that her own work had helped to further. The mystery novel begins, she claimed, with an inspiration that initially enfolds its creator with the "happy glow of murderous enthusiasm," but cools abruptly when he has to produce a plausible plot and psychological verisimilitude.[36] Detective novels needed more space to do this properly, and she pointed out that publishers were starting to allow 120,000–word books instead of the puny 70,000–word average of the 1920s. (Dorothy's books were expanding in company with her own girth, a result of her love of fine dining.) She admitted that coming trends in fiction would force writers into an entirely new technique, but she was certain someone would invent a new formula to merge detection and psychological analysis. She was, in fact, working on it herself.

The challenge was perhaps the best antidote Dorothy Sayers could have found to her increasingly problematic home life. Since Mac was increasingly housebound, they were together too much, and neither was noted for patience. Dorothy refused to look elsewhere; as she had written to John Cournos in 1925, "absolute and utter faithfulness" was her own brand of fanaticism.[37] Her association with the British Broadcasting Company, which began in the summer of 1930, must have been a godsend, taking her out of the house and providing her an outlet for her long-dormant dramatic urge through radio appearances and a new broadcast detective series, "The Scoop," which she organized late that year, furnishing its opening and closing episodes and performing in it herself with gusto.

Dorothy L. Sayers also provided the impetus for *The Floating Admiral* (1931), a collaborative novel for which thirteen Detection Club members supplied individual chapters and separate solutions

115

to a gruesome murder. Her introduction laid out rules that made this fictional game approach real life; each contributor had to tackle his chapter without knowing the previous authors' solutions, and each had to cope with all of the roadblocks his predecessors had placed in his way.[38] The exercise had helped her achieve a remarkable insight – that pride in their own reasoning powers can completely blind people, preventing them from seeing that their entirely logical solutions may be quite wrong, and someone else's quite right.[39] Just then she was immersed in change ringing to supply background for a new Wimsey novel that would meet the issue of good versus evil more profoundly than she had ever done before, but in the meanwhile she had to provide for Anthony's education and keep good food, one of the few pleasures she and Mac still shared, on the table. She drew on her years at Benson's to finish off quickly her next detective experiment, *Murder Must Advertise*, published early in 1933.

Dorothy Sayers disliked this book. She felt it had been thrust upon her by necessity, and she felt this attempt to wed the kind of serious criticism of life in *The Documents in the Case* with the puzzle technique of *The Five Red Herrings* had flopped. A few years later, she dismissed *Murder Must Advertise* as "not quite successful," though she still felt its basic ideas were sound. She said she had pitted two "cardboard worlds," advertising and the drug scene, against each other, allowing Lord Peter, who represented reality, to appear in them both only in disguise, but she concluded her working out had been "a little too melodramatic" and her "handling rather uneven."[40] Possibly, as Philip Scowcroft has suggested, this may have been due to the difference she sensed between her thorough knowledge of the advertising world, which often takes advantage of its audience through deception, and her lack of experience with the drug scene.

Dorothy Sayers's intimate portrait of Pym's Publicity is often praised as this novel's greatest strength, but the "criticism of life" that she attempted here also hints at the advocacy of Christian morality that dominates her later work. She deliberately set the false worlds of advertising and drugs side by side to point up their common denominator of deceit, offering illusory escape from real-life problems at a cost that devours the soul. As the rich man who had everything a hungry writer in 1921 had wanted, Lord

Peter had never appreciated until he worked at Pym's the "enormous commercial importance" of the lower middle class, who hungered for luxuries and leisure they could never enjoy and who "could be bullied or wheedled" into wasting hard-earned money on momentary and illusory gratification.[41] Peter's social conscience had begun to stir.

Murder Must Advertise also contains a lightly sketched self-portrait of Dorothy Sayers as Miss Meteyard, sometime scholar of Somerville, famous for the "vulgarest limericks ever recited within [Pym's] chaste walls."[42] Like Dorothy, Miss Meteyard had problems with the income tax, a striking rather than a conventionally pretty countenance, and a powerful devotion to the doctrine of fair play that unravels this crime, in which the victim asks for his own catastrophe: when a person starts "to worry about whether he's as good as the next man," Miss Meteyard firmly states, he sets off an "uneasy snobbish feeling and makes himself offensive."[43] With Mac, Dorothy Sayers lived day in, day out with that kind of insecurity, often a major element in alcoholism. She tried to cope with Mac's feelings of inferiority by encouraging his sporadic creative forays, like the *Gourmet's Book of Food and Drink* he published in 1933, but its offhand dedication to Dorothy, "who can make an Omelette,"[44] seems almost grounds for a wife to reach for a blunt instrument.

Dorothy Sayers's working pace had become herculean. Besides her novels and her activities for the Detection Club and the BBC, she wrote ten major critical articles between 1931 and 1934; and she reviewed over 350 detective novels for the *Sunday Times* between 25 June 1933 and 18 August 1935. She contributed to *Ask a Policeman* (1933), another Detection Club collaboration, and in the same year she produced her second collection of short fiction, *Hangman's Holiday*, which includes four Wimsey stories, two "others," and six featuring a new sleuth, Montague Egg, whose job hawking wines and spirits let Dorothy Sayers exercise her comprehensive knowledge in that area. By November 1933, she had also finished the most famous of her mystery experiments involving Lord Peter as a solo artist, *The Nine Tailors*.

A few years later, Dorothy Sayers described *The Nine Tailors* as "a shot at combining detection with poetic romance, and it was, I think, pretty nearly right."[45] For this novel she spent over two

117

years mastering the arcane science of campanology, the ringing of church bells in constantly shifting mathematical sequences, an "English peculiarity"[46] that appealed to her puzzle-loving nature. Experts could find only a few small errors in the change ringing passages of *The Nine Tailors*, and she was made an honorary member of bell ringers' groups and Vice-President of the Campanological Society of Great Britain, achievements that she later confessed made her "sinfully proud."[47] That phrase is significant since she built *The Nine Tailors* on the theological doctrine of sin and punishment, working out the concept that instruments dedicated to the glory of God and wielded innocently in His praise may take human life in obedience to a law whose precepts men, like Job, are incapable of fathoming.

This novel taught Lord Peter Wimsey a stern lesson: that no man can be an island of righteousness when all are stained with the mark of Cain, and Dorothy Sayers's own description of the experimental mystery formula she used in this novel makes the best sense of its form. The key is her lifelong fascination with poetic romance, especially lost causes like Thermopylae and Roncevaux, and particularly with the figure of the noble hero Roland, one of her models for Wimsey himself. She was able to deepen Wimsey's characterization in *The Nine Tailors* by allowing him to practice a medieval steadfastness like Roland's in a world that chooses to be deaf to both his call and his God's.

The Nine Tailors also taught Lord Peter humility; for the first time his deductive powers strike a snag, because he is reluctant to pursue a solution that he senses is morally flawed – in his words, "doin' good that evil may come".[48] Wimsey discovers everything about the murdered man, who was found mysteriously in some-one else's grave, except the name of the man's killer and the means of his death. Frustrated, Wimsey retires to other pursuits only to be recalled to Fenchurch St. Paul to save a damsel in distress. By setting this novel in the flood-prone Fen Country where she grew up, Dorothy Sayers made potential act-of-God disaster shadow the action with the threat of divine retribution. She also managed a few "touches of the eternal," as she called serious writing, which grappled with the mystery of man's sinful nature and the punishment that it earned by using named church bells, not human beings, as agents of divine justice. *The Nine*

118

Tailors climaxes with overtones of the Biblical Flood and the cadences of the *Book of Common Prayer*, wedding its great rhythms to Sayers's melodramatic story: "Gaude, Sabaoth, John, Jericho, Jubilee, Dimity, Batty Thomas and Tailor Paul – awake! make haste! save yourselves! The deep waters have gone over us! They call with the noise of the cataracts!"[49]

Dorothy Sayers sketched herself again in this novel, this time as an orphaned teenager just setting out to Oxford and authorship. Like Dorothy, young Hilary Thorpe had recently lost her parents; Hilary's father had detested tombstones, a clue, perhaps, to the absence of markers on the graves of Mr. and Mrs. Sayers at Christchurch. Peter once more employs his endearing capacity to brace up insecure or troubled young women, as he did for Ann Dorland in *Unnatural Death*, wounded by cads, and Miss Meteyard in *Murder Must Advertise*, mourning the everyday prettiness she would never have. Wimsey can see what these hurt women cannot; just as he predicted a "man of the world" for Ann and helped Miss Meteyard to take consolation in her "good bones," he encourages Hilary, telling her she will be a writer someday because she has "the creative imagination."[50] For the first time in her fiction, though not the last, Dorothy Sayers declares that artistic creativity works from inside out, enabling the artist to see the finished work not as an extension of himself but as an independent creation, a hint at two of her greatest works to come, the autobiographical novel *Gaudy Night* and her theological-aesthetic exploration of human and divine creativity, *The Mind of the Maker*. Dorothy Sayers also looked hard at her own personality through Peter's eyes in *The Nine Tailors*; Hilary's luck would come late in her life rather than early, Peter said, because people would first think she was "dreamy and romantic," and then "really hard and heartless. They'll be quite wrong both times – but they won't ever know it, and *you* [Sayers' italics] won't know it at first, and it'll worry you."[51]

When Dorothy Sayers finished *The Nine Tailors* in November 1933, her doctor ordered her to take a rest. Her pace of writing had been taxing enough, but she also had reached that critical point in a marriage where a woman has to decide whether to leave her husband. She went on a three-week motoring holiday with her old friend Muriel St. Clare Byrne and came to two important conclusions: she would stay with Mac, who had helped her when she needed him, and she informally adopted John Anthony, now ten, asking him to call her "Mother" and to use the name Fleming when he shortly thereafter entered Malvern, a well-known public school.[52]

She had come to a decision about Lord Peter, too; she had simply outgrown him. Even after all her experiments in fictional detection – totally excluding him from *The Documents in the Case*, giving him a "pure puzzle" to solve in *The Five Red Herrings*, attempting a serious criticism of life in *Murder Must Advertise*, and joining detection to poetic romance in *The Nine Tailors* – Lord Peter Wimsey was boring Dorothy Sayers nearly to death.

When Dorothy Sayers began *Strong Poison* in 1930, she later confessed, it was her "infanticidal intention" to marry Peter off and be done with him.[53] She had to stay her hand at first because Peter's popularity ensured a substantial living in a risky economic climate, but she also discovered an artistic difficulty, the problem of finding a suitable way for the autobiographical Harriet Vane to accept him without losing her self-respect. That posed Dorothy Sayers exactly the kind of intellectual challenge she could not resist. She set about performing a major operation on Peter, making him a "complete human being, with a past and a future, with a consistent family and social history, with a complicated psychology and even the rudiments of a religious outlook."[54] The last feature indicated that she now felt her hero needed more than a skin-deep Anglican sensibility to be a "complete human being," and she had to implant "religious rudiments" in him that she knew were convincing – in other words, her own. The surgery was successful, and Peter lived more fully than he ever had before, but Dorothy Sayers had still to cope with the only woman capable of mesmerizing Lord Peter: herself.

Harriet Vane and Dorothy Sayers cannot be equated any more than Hamlet and Shakespeare can, but Harriet shared Dorothy's early hurts, her passion for intellectual honesty, her musketeerish élan. Marrying her to Peter took four long mystery novels which capped Dorothy Sayers's career in the field, *Strong Poison* (1930), *Have His Carcase* (1932), *Gaudy Night* (1935), and *Busman's Honeymoon* (1936). In *Strong Poison*, Dorothy's first novel for Gollancz, Harriet and Peter met but had to part because Harriet refused to marry out of gratitude. Harriet's pride held prospects of marriage still further at bay in *Have His Carcase*, but in *Gaudy Night* Harriet and Peter both shed their prejudices and celebrated a happy ending in the idyllic *Busman's Honeymoon*.

Dorothy Sayers felt that twentieth-century men and women lacked the spiritual security that traditional Christianity had once offered. She wrote in 1931, "with the loss of the Dantesque heaven and hell and the discoveries of the human subconscious and the time-space continuum," the pressures of the unknown had made minds and possibly nerves "more sensitive."[55] Her own conservative religious position and evidently, from her sales, the preferences of her readers favored the notion of punishments for sin and rewards for virtue, and whether she consciously intended it or not, the hell-purgatory-heaven structure of Dante's *Divine Comedy* undergirds those Wimsey novels where Harriet Vane appears. *Strong Poison* and *Have His Carcase* descend from sins of the flesh to the depths of deliberate betrayal wreaked on family or trusting friends; *Gaudy Night* ascends through a spiritual purgatory to an earthly Eden; and *Busman's Honeymoon* offers a glimpse of marital paradise as Dorothy Sayers might have wished she had known it.

As a medievalist, Dorothy Sayers would have been acquainted with the Western Christian tradition founded by St. Gregory the Great in the late sixth century which places pride (*superbia*) at the root of all the other sins – envy, anger, despair, and avarice, sins of the spirit considered more serious than the fleshly failings of gluttony and lust.[56] Dante built on that teaching, creating an elaborate topography for his *Inferno*, with adulterers and gluttons in its upper reaches and traitors embedded in ice with Satan at its bottom. R. D. and Barbara Stock have noted that about 1930, when Dorothy Sayers decided to invest Wimsey with more tender human feelings and basic religious sensibilities, her portrayal of evil became more like Dante's.[57] Sayers herself remarked on the change in 1933; her early villains, she felt, had "brought a kind of zest with them. But some of the new ones seem to have come from a narrower and deeper and more intimate inferno; because we have realized only too well that kingdom of hell is within us."[58]

Strong Poison opens with Harriet in the dock, her fate in limbo. As with Dante and Beatrice, Peter gazed upon her with unquestionable

121

love at first sight: Peter's "heart turned to water."[59] Condemned by her peers for living "in sin" with the radical artist Philip Boyes, Harriet damned herself for letting Boyes make a fool of her. Not long after she had violently broken off their affair, Boyes died of arsenic poisoning, and circumstantial evidence brought Harriet to trial. Peter chivalrously offered her his detecting skill, and, smitten, his aristocratic hand in marriage, assuring her that he made love "rather nicely," but she sardonically rejected his "garden of bright images,"[60] leaving him only the short penitential season of Advent to save her from the gallows.

Like Dorothy Sayers, Harriet had been independent since her early twenties, and afraid of being hurt again, she let her pride cause her to refuse Peter's sincere offer of love. His own pride is just as dangerous, because his stakes are Harriet's life. Early in the book he appears tempted when he tells Miss Climpson that "it must be fun" to think one could control life-and-death matters.[61] Miss Climpson quite correctly observes that Peter is toying with the Creator's prerogative.

A few cracks in those walls of pride begin to appear, however, at the close of *Strong Poison*, after Peter clears Harriet by identifying the real killer, who acted out of simple greed. Peter leaves her, refusing to do the "King Cophetua stunt" of forcing himself on a woman bound to feel grateful to him for saving her life, though he cannot resist horrifying his insufferable sister-in-law Helen, the Duchess of Denver, by announcing during the family Christmas celebration that he intends to marry the former prisoner – if she'll have him.[62]

Have His Carcase plunges Harriet and Peter into much lower depths of the "intimate inferno." Harriet, on a walking holiday to heal her heart, bruised not only by Boyes but from having to reject Wimsey, comes upon a body spreadeagled on a rock, a fresh river of blood steaming in the summer sun, one of the ugliest murder cases Dorothy Sayers created. Set in Wilvercombe, an upper-middle-class watering place packed with older women reduced to "making a public scorn" of themselves in front of the waiters,[63] this novel shows how irreversably fraudulent souls damn themselves through deceit.

Peter hurries to Wilvercombe to help Harriet with the investigation, and for a while they work together effectively, but when he inadvertently tells Harriet he came so that she would not have to send for him, she looks around for "something really savage" to do to him. She lights on the same image that had closed *Strong Poison*, accusing him of humiliating her with his chivalry and like the Old Testament figure King Cophetua, expecting her to fall at his feet in gratitude.[64] Peter's chivalry is real, however. He strikes back, proving himself exactly the man Harriet had always wanted to fight with and demanding the same "common honesty" she had always been seeking. The two of them are finally able to temper their destructive pride by solving the case together; Wimsey's brilliant logic deciphers Harriet's subconsciously observed clue to a sordid betrayal of trust, the worst sin in Dante's *Inferno*. The victim was lured to his death through his forlorn genealogical pretensions, and Wimsey attributes the crime to some "malignant and interfering demon,"[65] an image that Sayers carried further in *Gaudy Night*.

Have His Carcase gave Lord Peter Wimsey the first case that he could not solve alone, while it taught Harriet to abandon enough of her pride to see what genuine chivalry was all about – not the least of those knightly allurements being a powerful physical attraction. While investigating the murder scene, she attentively muses as Peter plunges into the sea: "He strips better than I should have expected."[66] Later, as she watches Peter mastering a skittish mare, the only witness to the crime, Harriet's insight swells into "modified rapture" at his horsemanship; one cannot control a horse, the trademark of the knight, unless he has himself in hand. Upon such presentiments of wedded bliss, Harriet and Peter leave the damned souls of Wilvercombe and much of their own destructive pride behind them.

Between 1930 and 1934 Dorothy Sayers put herself more and more directly into her writing. Besides creating various autobiographical characters for her novels, she started a straightforward autobiography in early 1932, "My Edwardian Childhood," in which, James Brabazon says, she analyzed her particular kind of imagination and distinguished between her concepts of imagination and fantasy.[67] Possibly Dorothy Sayers broke this account off at thirty-three manuscript pages and never published it because she was unwilling or unable to work through her adolescence, a period when she had felt badly misunderstood.

123

About two years later, after her decision to stay with Mac, Dorothy Sayers tried a similar project in "Cat o'Mary," a fictionalized and pseudonymous autobiography that, as Brabazon has proven, derives from "My Edwardian Childhood." He feels she needed to distance herself from the narrative to let her true feelings about herself and her early childhood show, as she did in the handwritten subtitle "The Biography of a Prig" which she added to the manuscript of "Cat o'Mary." "Cat o'Mary" was announced in the *New York Times Book Review* on 14 October 1934, but it was never published. In its two hundred pages, Dorothy Sayers treated her youth through her severe illness at Godolphin, but her notes indicate that the story would then have departed substantially from the facts of her life. Brabazon concludes that either she found the transition from autobiography to fiction too difficult or that once she had coped with the emotions behind the confessional section of this book by writing them down, she lost interest in its heroine.[68]

Dorothy Sayers herself described "Cat o'Mary" as a mainstream novel dealing with a woman Oxford graduate who had been satisfied with her role as a wife and mother until attaining middle age; then, suddenly, she decided her "real vocation and full emotional fulfillment" belonged in intellectual pursuits,[69] a topic that sounds even more relevant today than it must have been in the 1930s. While Dorothy was at work on "Cat o'Mary" in June 1934, however, she received an invitation to propose the Toast of the University at Somerville's annual Gaudy Dinner, and the trip completely changed her creative direction.

Dorothy Sayers's 1937 essay "Gaudy Night" provides invaluable insights into her thinking while she was writing the novel that is widely considered her best. Most importantly, she believed Oxford solved at one stroke all three of the authorial problems she was battling. The only ground where Harriet could meet Peter as an equal was that of the intellect, because only there had Harriet never betrayed her standards. Oxford's intellectual integrity, one constant in an unstable world, would let Dorothy say things she had been wanting to say all of her life. At last, too, she would be able to merge a detective plot with the romantic interest essential to a novel of manners,[70] a "happy ending" that took on Dantean depth in her resulting novel *Gaudy Night*.

Harriet's five-year denial of her strong feelings for Lord Peter Wimsey comes to a head at the start of *Gaudy Night*. For her epigraph, Dorothy Sayers used John Donne's view of Oxford as the Garden of Eden,[71] an echo of the "garden of earthly delights" Peter had promised Harriet when they met in *Strong Poison*, and the goal of *Purgatory*'s seven-story mountain. Harriet Vane, like Dorothy Sayers, is a successful mystery writer, and she becomes drawn into investigating some strange activities at Shrewsbury, the women's college where she had been an undergraduate – an epidemic of poison penmanship that threatens the college's internal stability as well as its position in Oxford's academic community.

Dante's *Purgatory* eradicates the roots, not just the fruits, of sin. In her introduction to her translation of *Purgatory*, Dorothy Sayers claimed that if one is drawn to death's second kingdom at all, "it is by the cords of love."[72] She made love houseclean many souls in *Gaudy Night*; love of Oxford itself changes the values that have been keeping Harriet and Peter apart, and the love of intellectual integrity motivates Shrewsbury's Senior Common Room members, the college's dons and administrators, to maintain the honor of their profession above their personal loyalties.[73]

The sound of Harriet Vane's last name illustrates the pride she has to overcome in *Gaudy Night*. At the outset, she is still glorying in having broken all her old ties and "half the commandments."[74] She watches her old friends at the reunion suffering in and out of matrimony, one of them a once-brilliant scholar married to an indigent farmer – "a Derby winner making shift with a coal cart."[75] The spectacle reinforces Harriet's reluctance to accept a husband who had bought her gratitude. Gratifyingly, rambunctious young Reggie Pomfret uninvited hurls himself at Harriet's feet, and while she cannot consider him seriously as a suitor, she, a shade grimly, at least finds him "no King Cophetua."[76]

To overcome her pride, Harriet turns to her writing, her ostensible excuse for being at Oxford, and the lifeline she had clung to in spite of everything. Peter now gives it new meaning by suggesting she abandon "jig-saw" stories and write "about human beings for a change,"[77] exactly what Dorothy Sayers had decided to do herself. In the process Harriet's lyric voice re-awakens, and she starts a sonnet that Peter finishes for her, their

125

poetic collaboration furnishing each a symbol of their future intimacy. As *Gaudy Night* progresses, Harriet draws continually nearer to Peter, and at last she realizes that her long-held image of him as King Cophetua has been sickeningly false.

Harriet's material and spiritual need to work had been at the bottom of her prideful independence, while Peter's aristocratic breeding had shaped both his strengths and his weaknesses. Harriet struggles alone with the poison pen for thirteen chapters of this novel, and by the time Peter miraculously appears in Oxford, he has acquired new depth. He relentlessly exposes all his frailties to Harriet, his physical conceit, his regret at the debilitation of his caste, his "cursed hankering" after the old values that had spurred Roland at Roncevaux and the Spartans at Thermopylae.[78] After he confesses his faults to Harriet while they punt down Oxford's sacred Isis, Peter is transfigured before her eyes and exhibited to speechless country cousins and shrieking American tourists as the legendary "Wimsey of Balliol," the prototypic English gentleman. Dorothy Sayers had an even more humbling purgation in store for Lord Peter a little later in *Gaudy Night* when she made him suggest that Harriet rework Wilfred, one of her characters who had only been able to "purge himself" by taking his beloved's sins on himself and "wallowing in vicarious suffering,"[79] something Peter admits he himself had been doing in *Strong Poison*.

The last plateau Harriet and Peter face in *Gaudy Night* is the most dangerous because he had to step back and let her risk her own life to capture the criminal, violating all of his chivalric instincts but satisfying his devotion to justice and truth "without a thought of heaven or hell," as he quotes to Harriet, putting all of himself into her hand "like a ripe apple"[80] from the Tree of Knowledge. The earlier Peter Wimsey who had reveled in song and duels and longed for epic rearguard battles had set out to bestow heaven and earth upon his beloved, but as Dorothy Sayers revamped him, he has to settle for equality, giving Harriet Oxford – which he knew was already hers. At the close of *Gaudy Night*, Harriet and Peter climb up to the top of the Radcliffe Camera, looking out over the holy city with renewed vision. They beg each other's forgiveness and agree to meet later at the foot of the stairs at Balliol College for a performance of Bach's heavenly

Concerto for Two Violins, and Harriet's eyes follow Peter as he leaves: "All the kingdoms of the world and the glory of them."[81]

It took Dorothy Sayers from the Somerville Gaudy on 13 June 1934 to 4 November 1935 to see into print the book she said she had always wanted to write. She had finally found in Oxford's ancient ritual of conferring academic degrees the words with which Harriet could accept Peter: "*Placetne, magistra?*" Lord Peter Wimsey asked, mortarboard in hand; and Harriet Vane, his equal in the intellectual integrity that mattered most to Dorothy Sayers, replied simply, "*Placet*" – It pleases.[82]

Gaudy Night also pleased Dorothy Sayers's readers. It sold out its first edition, 17,000 copies, on publication and had sold 40,000 copies in Britain alone by April 1936.[83] The distinguished American classical scholar Edith Hamilton wrote for the majority when she applauded the "ease and grace" with which Dorothy Sayers had meshed the love story with detection, pointing out that Harriet was "a wish-fulfillment, what every scholastic woman wants to be. Brim full of learning and of fame, yet able – and in her thirties too – to work havoc in an undergraduate heart and hold to herself firmly, through year after year of refusals, a rich and noble lover. . . . 'Oh, these are the dreams that visit women's pillows.'"[84]

A few niggling spirits objected to Peter's metamorphosis. J. R. R. Tolkien liked Dorothy Sayers herself, but he said he "could not stand *Gaudy Night*. I followed P. Wimsey from his attractive beginnings so far, by which time I conceived a loathing for him not surpassed by any other character in literature known to me, unless by his Harriet."[85] Others expressed distaste for Harriet as an autobiographical incarnation of Dorothy Sayers, and Q. D. Leavis, whose husband shaped several generations of British critics, expressed outrage on several fronts. Mrs. Leavis asserted that "only D. H. Lawrence . . . could have reviewed these novels [*Gaudy Night* and *Busman's Honeymoon*] adequately;" she assaulted Dorothy Sayers's supposed social and intellectual snobbery, dismissing *Gaudy Night* as "a best-selling bundle of old clothes," and denounced Sayers's "literary glibness and spiritual illiteracy," her treatment of sex, and the factor that probably had most inspired Mrs. Leavis's venom, Sayers's indisputably impressive sales.[86]

127

Not the overwhelming popularity of *Gaudy Night*, nor Mac's worsening condition, nor the symptoms of aging and a sedentary life that Dorothy at forty-one was beginning to show could slow down her literary production.[87] She turned down a $10,000 offer from Metro Goldwyn Mayer to make a film version of *Murder Must Advertise*, but in 1935 she tried a script herself for *The Silent Passenger*, a low-budget Wimsey film whose producer then refused to use any of her work. She declared he was "muck" and swore off the screen forever,[88] going back to one of her first loves, the theatre, to write the dénouement of the Wimsey saga in dramatic form with her friend Muriel St. Clare Byrne. Almost a year to the day after *Gaudy Night* was published, *Busman's Honeymoon* was ready to open at Birmingham. Dorothy Sayers noted that she had maintained her customary exacting standard of detection by presenting every clue in full sight of the audience, and she had also followed up the technical innovation she had achieved in *Gaudy Night* by making the romantic interest an integral part of the play's theme.[89]

In her 1935 essay "Aristotle and Detective Fiction," Dorothy Sayers also compared Aristotle's famous definition of tragedy to her ideal of the mystery novel. She summed up the entire detective craft in the word *paralogismos*, "the art of framing lies in the right way," which should seduce the intelligent reader into telling the lie for himself.[90] She also remarked that both Aristotle and detective writers agree that their books offer a safety valve for "bloodthirsty passions that might otherwise lead us to murder our spouses."[91] By the time *Busman's Honeymoon* was on the stage, she had completed its novel version, published in June 1937.

Since Wimsey was still Wimsey, the paradise that he and Harriet had earned had to involve a murder to solve, but Dorothy Sayers being still herself, *Busman's Honeymoon* includes paradisical amatory specifics that even veiled in French must have provoked Mrs. Leavis into spasms of envious discontent. Driving to "Talboys," their newly-acquired country home, on their wedding night, Harriet apprehensively eyes Peter's slim aristocratic hands on the steering wheel of his Daimler, "holding the keys of hell and heaven." Harriet had had "too much experience to be surprised and too much honesty to pretend not to understand" when he tells her "it'll be all right on the night," and it is; Peter's performance is entirely comme il faut. In a transport of connubial joy, Harriet forever abandons the notion of King Cophetua and acknowledges Peter as "My lord!"[92]

Roused the next morning by unexpected guests, Harriet and Peter join their voices with them in uproarious song, a little like the chorus of the redeemed in Dante's *Paradiso*: "the song, the shouting, the celestial dance . . . spinning like a top,"[93] the same image Dorothy Sayers had used in the sonnet Harriet and Peter had created together in *Gaudy Night*. Their first morning as man and wife is utterly joyous – until Bunter announces that the week-old corpse of Talboys's former owner has been discovered in the cellar.

Peter is strangely loath to begin his old routine of detection again, because he has come to doubt his right to judge other human beings. The postscript to *Gaudy Night*, ostensibly written by his mother's brother Paul Delagardie, shows Peter torn asunder by his intellect and his nerves, beset at the end of every case by "the old nightmares and shell shock again."[94] At the close of the novel, Peter has shed all his protective disguises, weeping in Harriet's arms for the man Peter's sense of responsibility has brought to the gallows. Harriet's common sense brings them both through the dark night of the soul; had he not interfered six years earlier, she reminds him, she herself might well have died. In her 1937 essay "Gaudy Night," Dorothy Sayers described Harriet and Peter as "the two moods of the artistic spirit . . . in two distinct personalities . . . Peter is . . . the interpretative artist, the romantic soul at war with the realistic brain. Harriet, with her lively and inquisitive mind and her soul grounded upon reality, is his complement, the creative artist. . . . Their only hope of repose is in union."[95] In *Busman's Honeymoon*, Dorothy Sayers had made the union of man and woman her metaphor for artistic creation.

Beginning 16 December 1936, *Busman's Honeymoon* ran for nine months in London with mixed reviews, and it has been revived at London's Lyric Hammersmith Theatre as recently as 12 July to 27 August 1988.[96] Responding to popular demand, Dorothy Sayers kept up "the Wimsey industry" a little longer. In May 1935, she produced an entertaining short biography of Lord Peter Wimsey, ostensibly by his aging Lothario uncle Paul Delagardie, since published as a preface to all reprints of the Wimsey novels,[97] and she had five hundred copies of her uproarious *Papers Relating to the Family of Wimsey* printed in 1936 as Christmas presents for her friends. Her entertaining correspondence with C. W. Scott-Giles, an expert on heraldry, also dates from 1936; in 1977, Scott-Giles published *The Wimsey Family*,[98] complete with the same Wimsey crest of three mice and domestic cat crouched to pounce that decorates the tiles on a fireplace in Dorothy's home at Witham.[99] She left one last Wimsey novel unfinished, which she called "Thrones, Dominations," referring to the third and fourth orders of angels in the medieval hierarchy of heaven. Brabazon describes the six existing chapters as contrasting the Wimsey marriage with another couple's, "writing saturated with an awareness of sex and its potency." Uncontrolled passion is bound to wreak havoc, and Dorothy Sayers's notes "include the capitalized word MURDER" about half through the story.[100]

This abandoned Wimsey project contains an important clue to Dorothy Sayers's personal situation in 1936. In it Harriet acknowledges that her work is her emotional outlet and describes her own new project much as Dorothy Sayers herself might have described "Thrones, Dominations": "The new story was going to be a tragedy. Previous books, written while their creator was struggling through a black slough of misery and frustration, had all been intellectual comedies [but now], peering inquisitively over the edge of her own imagination, [she] saw a drama of agonized souls arrange itself with odd and alluring complications."[101]

Dorothy Sayers's mystery fiction had brought her through some difficult circumstances of her own, both pragmatic and emotional. At this point in her life, she was looking toward new challenges involving "agonized souls," the very term indicating the spiritual emphasis and direction she wished her next projects to take, a focus on the human suffering that wickedness can cause.

Events prevented Harriet and Dorothy Sayers from pursuing those "alluring complications," however. Nineteen thirty-six saw important changes for Dorothy and the world in which she lived; Nazi troops occupied the Rhineland, the Spanish Civil War erupted, and King George V of Great Britain died, ending an era. Less than a week after the night in December 1936 when Edward VIII gave up his throne for Mrs. Simpson, *Busman's Honeymoon* opened at London's Comedy Theatre with Dorothy Sayers firmly in charge as a working playwright. For the first time in her life, she hired a secretary and plunged with characteristic zeal into a new element she immediately loved, professional theatre.

She had met all of her old obligations and Mac's besides; the Wimsey novels, translated into as many as eleven languages and selling phenomenally well,[102] would adequately support herself and Mac and educate Anthony; after fifteen years she had been able to pension off Lord Peter with his panache and her intellectual integrity intact. Wimsey's marriage to Harriet had brought to an end the mystery novels Dorothy had felt compelled to write, and her own marriage to Mac had stabilized, though she had lost any romantic illusions she might have had about it. Dorothy Sayers had made herself the mistress of her earthly fate, and now it would please her to please herself.

Notes

1. Walter L. Arnstein, *Britain Yesterday and Today: 1830 to the Present*, 5th ed. (Lexington, Mass.: D. C. Heath and Co., 1988), p. 290.
2. Ibid., p. 293.
3. Asa Briggs, *A Social History of England* (New York: The Viking Press, 1983), p. 268.
4. E. M. Forster, quoted in Briggs, p. 266.
5. Barry Supple, "The Economy: Adjustment, Affluence, Decline," in *The Cambridge Historical Encyclopedia of Great Britain and Ireland*, ed. Christopher Haigh (Cambridge: Cambridge University Press, 1985), p. 322.
6. Arnstein, p. 294.
7. Michael Bentley, "Social Change: Appearance and Reality," in *The Cambridge Historical Encyclopedia*, p. 328.
8. Ibid., p. 330.
9. Briggs, p. 292.
10. Dorothy L. Sayers, "The Omnibus of Crime," quoted from *The Art of the Mystery Story*, ed. Howard Haycraft (New York: Simon and Schuster, 1946). This essay is Sayers's introduction to the First Series of *Great Short Stories of Detection, Mystery and Horror* (London: Gollancz, 1928), published in the United States as the first *Omnibus of Crime* (New York: Payson and Clarke, 1929). The other series are:

Great Short Stories of Detection, Mystery and Horror, Second Series (London: Gollancz, 1931), published in the United States as *The Second Omnibus of Crime* (New York: Coward–McCann, 1932; and *Great Short Stories of Detection, Mystery and Horror, Third Series* (London: Gollancz, 1934), published in the United States as *The Third Omnibus of Crime* (New York: Coward–McCann, 1935). The U.S. *Second Omnibus of Crime* contains fifty–two short stories, while the British edition contains sixty-seven.

11. Ralph E. Hone, *Dorothy L. Sayers: A Literary Biography* (Kent, Ohio: Kent State University Press, 1979), p. 56.

12. Dorothy L. Sayers, "The Omnibus of Crime," p. 72.

13. Ibid., p. 76.

14. Ibid., pp. 102–103.

15. Ibid., p. 103. I am indebted to Philip Scowcroft for this observation.

16. Ibid, pp. 108–109.

17. Alzina Stone Dale, *Maker and Craftsman: The Story of Dorothy L. Sayers* (Grand Rapids, Mich.: William B. Eerdmans Publishing Co., 1978), p. 79.

18. James Brabazon, *Dorothy L. Sayers: A Biography* (New York: Charles Scribners' Sons, 1981), p. 143.

19. Ibid., p. 143.

20. Dale, p. 78.

21. David Higham, *Literary Gent* (New York: Coward, McCann and Geoghegan, 1978), p. 211.

22. Brabazon, p. 145.

23. Dorothy L. Sayers, Letter to Dr. James Welch 20 November 1943, quoted in Hone, p. 46.

24. This novel also has at its core the real–life Bywaters/Thompson case. Real crime in most of Sayers's fiction, however, is "mostly allusive rather than imitative," and she mentioned about twenty well–known British murder cases apposite to her plots, according to Philip Scowcroft in "Real Life Crime," *Sidelights on Sayers* 25, pp. 20–23.

25. Brabazon, p. 150.

26. Dorothy L. Sayers, *The Documents in the Case* (1930; New York: Avon, 1968), p. 202.

27. Ibid., p. 83.

28. Ibid., p. 146.

29. Brabazon, p. 148.

30. Sayers, "The Omnibus of Crime," p. 84.

31. Dorothy L. Sayers, *Five Red Herrings* (1931; New York: Avon, 1968), p. 285.

32. Sayers, "The Omnibus of Crime," p. 103.

33. Dorothy L. Sayers, "The Present Status of the Mystery Story," *London Mercury* 23 (November 1930), p. 47.

34. Ibid., p. 49.

35. Dorothy L. Sayers, Introduction to *Great Short Stories of Detection,*

Mystery and Horror, Second Series, p. 26.
36. Ibid.
37. Dorothy L. Sayers, Letter to John Cournos 13 August 1925, quoted in Brabazon, p. 148.
38. Certain Members of The Detection Club, *The Floating Admiral* (New York: Doubleday, 1931), p. 3 (Sayers's Introduction).
39. Ibid., p. 4.
40. Dorothy L. Sayers, "Gaudy Night," in *The Art of the Mystery Story*, (hereafter "Gaudy Night") pp. 209–10.
41. Dorothy L. Sayers, *Murder Must Advertise* (1933; New York: Avon, 1968), p. 154.
42. Ibid., p. 13.
43. Ibid., p. 143.
44. Hone, p. 67.
45. Sayers, "Gaudy Night," p. 210.
46. Dorothy L. Sayers, *The Nine Tailors* (1934; New York: Harcourt Brace, 1962), p. 16.
47. Hone, p. 68.
48. Sayers, *Nine Tailors*, p. 214.
49. Ibid., p. 272.
50. Ibid., p. 93.
51. Ibid., p. 94.
52. Brabazon, p. 151.
53. Sayers, "Gaudy Night," p. 210.
54. Ibid., p. 211.
55. Dorothy L. Sayers, Introduction to *Great Short Stories of Detection, Mystery, and Horror*, Second Series, p. 26.
56. Karl Vossler, *Mediaeval Culture: An Introduction to Dante and His Times*, vol. 1, trans. William Cranston Lawton (1929; New York: Ungar, 1966), pp. 245–47. Also see Gregory the Great, *Moralia* XXXI, Chapter 45. Vossler indicates that "the Greek Church, less judiciously [than the Western Church] put lust first, instead of pride." Vossler also observes that "since that time [Gregory's] pride has continued to be, for the Western Church, the source of all sinfulness."
57. R. D. Stock and Barbara Stock, "The Agents of Evil and Justice in the Novels of Dorothy L. Sayers," in *As Her Whimsey Took Her*, ed. Margaret P. Hannay (Kent, Ohio: Kent State University Press, 1979), p. 15. Citations from this collection are used by permission of Kent State University Press.
58. Dorothy L. Sayers, Introduction to *Great Short Stories of Detection, Mystery and Horror, Third Series*, p. 20.
59. Dorothy L. Sayers, *Strong Poison* (1930; New York: Avon, 1968), p. 35.
60. Ibid., p. 38.
61. Ibid., p. 42.
62. Ibid., p. 191.
63. Dorothy L. Sayers, *Have His Carcase* (1932; New York: Avon, 1968), p. 42.

64. Ibid., p. 138.
65. Ibid., p. 305.
66. Ibid., p. 286.
67. Brabazon, pp. 13, 207.
68. Ibid., p. xvii.
69. Sayers, "Gaudy Night," p. 212.
70. Ibid., p. 213.
71. Dorothy L. Sayers, *Gaudy Night* (1936; New York: Avon, 1968), title page.
72. Dorothy L. Sayers, *The Divine Comedy 2: Purgatory* (1955; New York: Penguin, 1984), p. 9.
73. Sayers, *Gaudy Night*, pp. 383, 366.
74. Ibid., p. 9.
75. Ibid., p. 45.
76. Ibid., p. 209.
77. Ibid., p. 256.
78. Ibid., p. 238.
79. Ibid., p. 255.
80. Ibid., pp. 293, 358.
81. Ibid., p. 381.
82. Ibid., p. 382.
83. Hone, p. 76.
84. Edith Hamilton, "Gaudeamus Igitur," Review of *Gaudy Night*, *Saturday Review of Literature* 13 (22 February 1936), p. 6.
85. J. R. R. Tolkien, quoted in Humphrey Carpenter, *The Inklings* (Boston: Houghton Mifflin, 1979), p. 109.
86. Q. D. Leavis, "The Case of Miss Dorothy Sayers," review of *Gaudy Night* and *Busman's Honeymoon*, *Scrutiny* 6 (December 1937), p. 335.
87. Hone, p. 79.
88. Brabazon, pp. 154, 155.
89. Dorothy L. Sayers, *Busman's Honeymoon* (1937; New York: Avon, 1968), p. 213.
90. Dorothy L. Sayers, "Aristotle and Detective Fiction," *English: The Magazine of the English Association* 1 (1936), p. 214.
91. Ibid., p. 213.
92. Sayers, *Busman's Honeymoon*, pp. 31, 57.
93. Dorothy L. Sayers, *Introductory Papers on Dante* (London: Methuen, 1954), p. 174.
94. Margaret P. Hannay, "Harriet's Influence on the Characterization of Lord Peter Wimsey," in *As Her Whimsey Took Her*, ed. Margaret P. Hannay (Kent, Ohio: Kent State University Press, 1979), p. 45.
95. Sayers, "Gaudy Night," p. 53.
96. *Busman's Honeymoon* was revived in July–August 1988 at the Lyric Theatre, Hammersmith, with Edward Petherbridge playing Lord Peter Wimsey. Petherbridge also played Wimsey in the award-winning BBC television series of Dorothy L. Sayers's mysteries. The revivals were a great success, arousing considerable public

interest and producing an upsurge in the membership of the Dorothy L. Sayers Society. The 1940 film version of *Busman's Honeymoon*, shown on the BBC in 1988 as well, seems to have been less effective; Robert Montgomery, an American, played Lord Peter unconvincingly. See Sayers Society *Bulletins* 78 and 77.

97. Hone, pp. 70–71; "Biographical Note Communicated by Paul Austin Delagardie."
98. C. W. Scott-Giles, *The Wimsey Family* (London: Gollancz, 1977); Scott-Giles's title is Fitzalan Pursuivant of Arms Extraordinary.
99. Hone, p. 72.
100. Dorothy L. Sayers, "Thrones, Dominations," quoted in Brabazon, p. 157.
101. Dorothy L. Sayers, *Love All* and Dorothy L. Sayers and Muriel St. Clare Byrne, *Busman's Honeymoon* (Kent, Ohio: Kent State University Press, 1984), xx; manuscript in the Wade Collection, Wheaton College, Wheaton, Illinois.
102. Brabazon, p. 158.

7 Her English Wars
1937–1944

> . . . from the existing good and evil we must
> hammer out the positive good.
>
> Dorothy L. Sayers, *Begin Here*

To envious onlookers, a successful writer's life might look simple – she has no real responsibilities; or antisocial – she practices it in solitude, like a vice; or selfish – she has to guard herself jealously against distractions. The writer knows though that the demands of the craft, as anyone who has fought demons for the one right phrase can testify, are a different matter. What appears easy and self-serving is nothing less than the maddening process of looking into oneself and finding truth; occasionally it arrives as a glorious, full-blown insight, but far more often it has to be cajoled, wrestled, hacked out of lonely hours and through a mountain of fatigue. To develop a craft to support oneself, as Dorothy Sayers had to do, and then to shape it into an artistic vocation, as she did in her forties, takes a good deal more than talent and gritty determination. One of the women she respected most, Elizabeth I, said it demanded "eternal patience" – which, Dorothy Sayers would not have forgotten, is a gift of the Holy Ghost. What drew her onward was the reward that she and all good writers have earned, the ecstasy Harriet Vane described in *Gaudy Night*: "When you get the thing dead right and know it's dead right, there's no excitement like it. . . . It makes you feel like God on the Seventh Day – for a bit, anyhow."[1]

That vital comparison of human creators with the Architect of the Universe indicates that people who see only the surface changes in Dorothy L. Sayers's career, like the youngster who amused her so much by claiming she turned from a life of crime to join the Church of England, miss its entire significance. Far from "getting religion" in the late 1930s, when she began to write religious drama, Dorothy Sayers was maintaining a message that she had used consistently from her very first mystery novel, a "hymn to the Master Maker" that she claimed in a musical metaphor had first appeared even earlier in her *Catholic Tales and Christian Songs*.[2] This theme was the sacramental nature of work, creative work being the capacity in which man most nearly reflects his Creator, and it "unifies all of her writings in many genres."[3] No matter how much variety marked Sayers's clever descants on that theme – embellishments like Wimsey's foibles, his fascinating supporting characters, and the superbly horrendous acts of homicide he solves – all her detective fiction, with *Gaudy Night* at its climax, reinforces the opinion Dorothy Sayers seems to have carried through in her own life, that one must love what one must do; otherwise work becomes a torment or a provocation for choosing damnation. Wimsey and Harriet serve their work, which is discovering the truth, and find freedom in it to love one another, a kind of earthly paradise revealed in the last scenes of *Busman's Honeymoon*, where Peter at last can be free to grieve over and be healed of the consequences of his actions. Sayers's villains pervert their talents and their work, using their creative energy for evil purposes, and earn the condemnation they receive. From her earliest literary efforts to her last, Dorothy Sayers equated "good" with traditional Christian concepts as stated in her Catholic creed: that there is judgement and a hell for those who choose to oppose God's will, and forgiveness and life everlasting for those who unavoidably sin but choose repentance. Once she felt she had exhausted the possibilities of the detective genre to convey her theme, she turned to a historical form that would allow her to approach the problem of good and evil more directly, the one that had given her so much fun at Oxford: the theatre.

Just after Dorothy Sayers's old theatre bug had started to bite and *Busman's Honeymoon* had proved a West End success, she received an unusual opportunity. The Canterbury Festival had been initiated in 1935 with T. S. Eliot's *Murder in the Cathedral*, and its 1936 play was *Thomas Cranmer of Canterbury* by Charles Williams, a fellow Anglican working at Oxford University Press whom Dorothy Sayers recently had met. Barbara Reynolds suggests that Williams might have known about the small verse play "The Mocking of Christ" which Sayers had included in *Catholic Tales*,[4] but in any case, at Williams's suggestion, Margaret Babington, the Festival Manager, in October 1936 invited

Dorothy Sayers to write a play for the 1937 Canterbury Festival, a Service of Arts and Crafts. Babington offered her the story of William of Sens, the foreign architect who rebuilt the burned choir of the Cathedral in the twelfth century, as the play's subject.[5]

Four years later Dorothy Sayers claimed that *Gaudy Night*, the novel climaxing her career in detective fiction, and *The Zeal of Thy House*, the play opening her series of Christian dramas, shared the same traditional theme: that man, no matter how great his God-given talents, risks his soul if he dares equate himself with his Creator.[6] In *The Zeal of Thy House*, the Chapter Monks of Canterbury choose William of Sens over native English architects because he astutely wins each of them over with a different ploy. When William looks on the finished choir, he finds his work so good that none but he, "not even God," could have built it;[7] God and his Archangels hear William damn his soul "for the sake of the work,"[8] and when William rises on a crane to set the capstone in its place in the rebuilt choir's central arch, the rope breaks and he falls. Not killed but condemned to live broken in body, William is eventually healed in spirit, able to see his sin and repent:

> The work is sound, Lord God, no rottenness there –
> Only in me.[9]

Constructed like Ibsen's *Master Builder* around the craftsman's pride in his work, *The Zeal of Thy House* also shows that Dorothy Sayers, like Ibsen, believed that the carpenter's hammer both creates and destroys. She wrote this play in blank verse, but she allowed her monks, and even the eleven-foot archangels whose wing feathers she herself delightedly stitched in place, to speak most realistically in the tongues of twentieth-century men rather than in the plummy voices and the pontifical gestures that usually infect both actors and audiences of religious plays with what she deplored as a "fearful creeping paralysis."[10] In doing so, she knocked preconceived notions about the dullness of religious drama flat, making her theology not only move but take wing and fly. As she said in one way or another in almost all of the speeches, essays, plays and books she wrote at this stage in her life, the drama she created was nothing less than the dogma she believed, and it was completely alive, both to her and to most of her listeners and readers.

The way Dorothy Sayers carried out this idea shocked many people, and of course she had been doing so – and enjoying it – for a long time. She also joined zestfully in the colorful camaraderie of the theatre and all of the crafts that contribute to its art. A year after the highly successful Canterbury Festival performances of *The Zeal of Thy House* from 12 to 18 June 1937, she managed the play on the road, first in London during April 1938, and then out to the provinces until the end of the year. She financed the tour by lending her name and Lord Peter Wimsey's to a Horlick's Malted Milk advertising campaign, bringing on denunciations in the *Times* from some of Wimsey's devoted followers. She brushed them off with a tart reply, letting the world know she and Wimsey had had to work in advertising before.[11]

Dorothy Sayers was also keeping up her relations with members of the M.A.S., which she now wryly suggested might also stand for "middle-aged spread." Marjorie Barber, who was teaching in London and lived with Muriel St. Clare Byrne in a terraced house in St. John's Wood, had urged Dorothy to undertake the play *Busman's Honeymoon*, and in the summers of 1937 and 1938 she and Dorothy took time off to visit Venice. Out of those vacations came *Love All*, Dorothy L. Sayers's last foray into stage comedy.

According to her son Anthony Fleming, *Busman's Honeymoon* and *Love All* together form the missing link between Dorothy Sayers's popular detective fiction and her broader activities as a respected woman of letters,[12] and he believed that she wrote *Love All* in 1938–39 between her two vacations in Venice. Dorothy Sayers herself said she wrote it "just for fun," as a healthy change of pace from religious drama. Barbara Reynolds has also suggested that Marjorie Barber might have "in a sense" collaborated on the play, supplying Italian dialogue and a witty and discerning first reading for her old friend's work.[13] In any case, it opened on 9 April 1940, the day Hitler invaded Norway, and played about three weeks at the tiny Torch Theatre in Knightsbridge. The original title, changed because of another play then running,[14] was *Cat's Cradle*, which harks back to "Cat o'Mary" and hints at an autobiographical context. Anthony Fleming refused, however, to allow Alzina Stone Dale, editor of the first published version of this play (1984), to refer in her preface to his mother's marriage or to facts presented in James Brabazon's authorized Sayers biography, or to himself, although *Love All* contains the character of a child caught between a father who wants his wife to be a traditional, self-effacing homemaker and a mother who is pursuing a successful career as a dramatist.[15]

Love All sparkles with the wit and comic timing Dorothy Sayers had polished by writing *Busman's Honeymoon*, and had World War II not disrupted the London theatre scene, along with almost everything else, *Love All* might have made much more of a commercial splash than it did. *Love All* also voices a vitally modern message about men's and women's careers and marriage. Like any woman's, and indeed like any man's, Dorothy Sayers's opinions were affected by her own emotions and experience, but she consistently based the general conclusions she reached on her own rigorous logic.

If Dr. Freud had asked his famous question of the female characters of *Love All* – Godfrey Daybrook's estranged wife, his mistress, and his secretary – each would have answered: "I want to work – to be a real person again . . . to be alive."[16] Furthermore, they do so through a female mutual aid society that helps them ignore the patronizing, childish, and often selfish males blocking the way in their contemporary British society. "Every great man," comments Godfrey's mistress Lydia, "has had a woman behind him"; but Janet, Godfrey's playwright wife to whom Dorothy Sayers gave some of her own opinions and characteristics, observes astringently, "And every great woman has had some man or other in front of her, tripping her up."[17]

Alzina Stone Dale feels that the theme of *Love All*, a woman's right to put her work above her love, has kept it from being revived,[18] but perhaps the play's time may be coming after all, now that societies and individuals are beginning to awaken to the notion that work should benefit not only the consuming body but the sustaining soul of him – and her – who performs it. If that ideal ever becomes a general belief, womankind will owe a vote of thanks to Dorothy L. Sayers, who not only incorporated it into her popular literature but forcefully exposed in speeches and essays what she considered the British evil of unfairness to women, notably in "Are Women Human?" produced for an unnamed "Women's Society" in 1938, and its sequel, "The Human-not-Quite-Human."[19]

When she undertook to address complex questions of human and superhuman behavior, the most arresting feature of Dorothy Sayers's writing is its clearheaded practicality. Like the academic women who had made a success of Somerville College despite Oxford's male preconceptions, she insisted that "aggressive feminism might do more harm than good";[20] instead, even before war forced Britain to put its women to work in hitherto unheard of numbers, Dorothy Sayers argued that the world could not afford to keep on wasting the talents of half its population, and she sensibly advocated giving the job to the person, male or female, who could do it best. She had no time for putting women into men's jobs simply to say "a woman has done it – yah!,"[21] a position with which white-knuckled airline passengers of today might concur upon hearing of possibly loosened training regulations in order that token females might work as flight controllers or pilots. Dorothy Sayers felt that a woman's rights should be no different than a man's: the chance to have a stimulating occupation, the freedom to pursue pleasures, and the sufficiency of an emotional outlet;[22] and she wholeheartedly agreed with D. H. Lawrence's "shattering glimpse of the obvious" evil in relations between the sexes – a man's unwillingness to accept a woman as "a real human being of the opposite sex."[23]

No one has yet managed to hammer a positive good out of that particularly vexing issue of human relations. In capitalist societies working mothers still face most of the housework and assume the chief responsibility for the children at the end of the day, as do their sisters under Communism, who shoulder the additional burdens of long shopping lines and the lack of labor-saving machinery. Shortly before World War II broke out, Dorothy Sayers's situation was probably even worse. She was putting in devastatingly long hours just to keep her household running and Mac reasonably contented; she often had to do the cooking herself and cope with frequent turnovers of housemaids and secretaries, and the frustration at not being able to work without interruption could result in periods of what she called

141

"disintegration." According to a typical 1939 day's schedule she sent to Muriel St. Clare Byrne, from 8:30 in the morning until 5:50 in the afternoon, Dorothy had exactly ninety minutes to conduct her literary affairs and correspondence.[24] Mac apparently was stoking the domestic fires of discontent, since she used an unhappy marriage as a pungent illustration of Envy in her 1941 essay "The Other Six Deadly Sins": "If my wife is so abandoned as to enjoy . . . anything . . . which I do not appreciate, I will so nag and insult her that she will no longer be able to indulge these tastes with a mind at ease."[25] No matter how angry Dorothy Sayers might have been about women's lot in general and her own in particular, she firmly upheld the solid positive principle that women's work, like men's, should have a sacramental value, and she emphatically celebrated the one Man out of all men who could accept women as He found them: Jesus Christ.

The subject of Jesus Christ's dual nature as God and as man preoccupied Dorothy Sayers during 1938. Along with all of her other commitments, the BBC had asked her to undertake an hour-long Christmas play based on His birth. *He That Should Come*, produced by Val Gielgud, is uncompromisingly realistic, set in an inn at Bethlehem which is packed with an enormous variety of characters – a brusque centurion, philosophical kings, Joseph of Arimathea, strangely impelled to promise a rich gift to Mary's Son if they should meet again – to carry out Dorothy Sayers's purpose, revealing the staggering ironies of human history when its Lord came all unrecognized into it. The same uncompromising insistence on theological truth as the Christian creeds state it – that Christ was not only God but a real man dealing with everyday problems of humanity – underscores four speeches and articles Dorothy Sayers wrote that year counterpointing *He That Should Come*. In "The Greatest Drama Ever Staged," "The Triumph of Easter," "Strong Meat," and "The Dogma Is the Drama,"[26] she announced that the most exciting drama possible is the good news that the same Almighty God who made the world chose to die and rise for love of man.

Dorothy Sayers's faith was securely rooted in her traditional Anglican belief, but the way she professed it in her dramas and her speeches tended to flabbergast Christians who liked their religion watered down. She could never have stomached either a meek and mild sacrificial lamb as her Saviour or a celestial milquetoast as her Heavenly Father. The Jesus Christ Dorothy Sayers found in the Gospels was something like her ideal detective: Christ courageously rescued wayward women and relentlessly scourged moneychangers in the Temple. He was a "dangerous firebrand"[27] that Rome and the Jews were bound to suppress. While she believed "the only completely insoluble mystery" in the universe was why God should have created anything, she was also certain that the creative artist was the only being who might guess at its solution[28] and that the one unforgivable sin, the ultimate demonstration of man's lethal pride, was the refusal to acknowledge that sin existed. Dorothy Sayers called this the sin against the Holy Ghost. To defend one's faith best, she fervently declared, one should attack,[29] and this meant doing as God did through Christ in His life and death on earth and as He continues to do in the eternal present of belief: to accept the whole past and by doing so, change its meaning; to make victories out of mankind's sins; to turn evil into good.[30]

For those who cared to look around as 1938 drew to a close, the world furnished abundant raw material for Christians who wanted to try to change evil to good. Nazi Germany had begun to mobilize, and only six months after British Prime Minister Neville Chamberlain returned from Munich in September promising "peace in our time," Hitler's forces had occupied the Sudetenland and invaded Czechoslovakia, convincing even Chamberlain and the opposition Labour Party that Britain must gird itself for war. War songs like "Lili Marlene" became popular in Britain; in early 1939, a sharp rise in membership of the British Communist Party reflected a middle-class concern about Fascism; and that May the British Society of Authors, Playwrights and Composers circulated a questionnaire to identify its membership's wartime abilities.

Dorothy Sayers was already fighting. In "The Dictatorship of Words," her address of 5 January 1939 as the incoming president of the Modern Language Association, she had already denounced the Nazi use of propaganda in its conquests, and she forcefully opposed the notion of "a muzzled Press" at home which would delude its own public through distortions or suppression of the facts.[31] She had also accepted an invitation to write a second play for the Canterbury Festival, and for that apprehensive June she chose the old story of Faust, who sold his soul to the Devil for infinite knowledge. She felt she had to prevent the devil from walking away with the play, as he tends to do in most works where he appears, while at the same time she had to grapple with the "question of all questions": what is the nature of Evil, and how does it fit into God's Universe?[32]

Dorothy Sayers believed that each generation replies in terms of its own spiritual experience and needs. The Faust that she created while her world inched its way toward another mammoth conflagration is a painfully modern phenomenon, the talented reformer who would toss away everything, even his immortal soul, in one grand gesture to cure all humanity's sufferings. If putting himself on the same level as the Saviour were not proof enough of her Faust's fatal pride, Dorothy Sayers had him abandon himself to despair, denying God's unlimited power to forgive, when he learned that his human efforts could never save his world.[33] Demons drag Marlowe's Elizabethan Faust screaming to hell, and the Eternal Feminine leads Goethe's Faust to heaven; but Dorothy Sayers gave her twentieth-century Faust a choice that suited his sin: the neither blessed nor damned limbo of disbelief or the eternal torment of hell itself. Faust chooses the latter alternative because "He [God] is there also,"[34] indicating Dorothy Sayers's affirmation that even the worst sinner could seek his Lord.

The Devil to Pay did not enjoy the success that *The Zeal of Thy House* had, but it did play in London for four weeks while the storm over Europe continued to gather. Britain's first peacetime conscription had begun in May of 1939, and Winston Churchill, then an independent Conservative who had denounced Chamberlain's Munich settlement as "a total and unmitigated defeat,"[35] now called for a furious pace of rearmament; but Churchill's call was in no way met by the policies of the Chamberlain government, which allowed the Luftwaffe to maintain an air superiority Britain soon would regret. On 24 August the Hitler-Stalin Nonaggression Pact secretly delivered most of Eastern Europe to the Soviet Union, and on 1 September Hitler's Panzers swept down on Poland. Now that its leaders saw the kind of devil it was going to have to pay, Britain could not bargain; the old chivalry no longer stirred British hearts as it had in 1914, but the British sense of fair play and keeping to one's sworn word brought them into war again, with "an absolute conviction that Hitler's Germany could be stopped only by force of arms."[36]

So-called experts led the British public to believe that the declaration of war on 3 September would bring on two months of sustained air attacks with an estimated 120,000 killed and injured, so the British government set about mass evacuations of women and children from London, amounting to ten times the size of the initial Expeditionary Force Britain sent to France. Blackouts were enforced, the theaters and cinemas were shut down, and the BBC put "into a strait-jacket." The Ministry of Information, a bureaucratic innovation, tried ineffectually to appeal to England's sense of history[37] in a patronizing fashion particularly repugnant to Dorothy Sayers – in an appointed advisory capacity, she even submitted a plan for reorganizing the whole Ministry, which they ignored.[38] Her feelings about the Ministry became so vehement that in "The Wimsey Papers," eleven morale-boosting articles she wrote for *The Spectator* from 17 November 1939 to 26 January 1940, she gave them the most loathsome employee she could think of, Lord Peter's domineering sister-in-law Helen. Dorothy Sayers felt the "Ministry of Instruction and Morale" was "as good a spot as any to intern the nation's trouble-makers" like the Duchess of Denver, whose three secretaries were paid, as Peter's mother gleefully informed Harriet, "by a grateful country to endure her."[39]

Dorothy Sayers's opinion of the Ministry of Information had been lowered by her brief encounter with them in the autumn of 1939, terminated by mutual consent. They found her "difficult and loquacious," while with typical forthrightness, she said that she had tried to get them "to exercise a little sense," but that nothing could be accomplished until the Ministry "carried out a ruthless purge of parasites."[40] She was undoubtedly right, but no bureaucratic agency would have harbored such a clear-eyed fumigator as Dorothy Sayers. Brabazon notes that her parting of the ways with this arm of His Majesty's government was "a considerable blow" to her,[41] but on the other hand, she had her own private war effort to maintain that fall. She must have been very proud that Anthony had won a scholarship to

Malvern College, but Mac's physical condition, like his emotional state, was growing more precarious all the time. On 9 September, Victor Gollancz asked Dorothy Sayers to consider writing a Christmas message to the nation, and she seized the chance to step back from her own problems and view the conflict not merely in terms of individual or national inconvenience, but in the context of the struggle of good against evil that had occupied her thinking and writing for so long. In a book-length essay, *Begin Here*, she laid out a blueprint for her country to build good out of the ultimate evil of war.

Ralph Hone describes Dorothy Sayers's reaction to the national emergency of late 1939 as "imperiousness" with "a new testiness' in her speeches and writings,[42] indications of her bull-dog determination to make every single British man and woman act not only to save themselves but to build a better world. Her exhortations in *Begin Here* do sound peremptory, but she was defending England, everything she held dearest, with as forceful an attack as she could muster because she sensed more clearly than many of her contemporaries that soon her country would stand alone, fighting not only for the life of Western civilization but for its very soul.

Even though Dorothy Sayers had to write *Begin Here* in what she called "indecent haste," she hoped that it would inspire individuals to creative action "towards the restoration of Europe."[43] Six years before Hiroshima and Nagasaki, she could still believe that war was not an ultimate catastrophe, because it tests the foundations of culture and destroys old habits and mistakes to clear the way for a new beginning, which she insisted had to be based upon a Christian understanding of work as an image of divine creativity. In the six sections of *Begin Here*, she touched on nearly every kind of evil she thought was assaulting the modern world – economic abuses, educational failures, per-versions of language, the debasement of the press, corruption in government, the horrors of Communist and Fascist totalitarian-ism, and even the despair of the middle-aged over their lost youth. The solutions she suggests, like the religious dramas which many in her audiences found refreshing and some too bold for comfort, come straight from her view of Christian dogma.

Dorothy Sayers firmly believed that the evil of the past could not be erased; it had to be grasped firmly now and shaped into a future good. If the war wiped out mass entertainment – which she dismissed as "dope" – then people would have to learn to amuse themselves, putting their God-given mental capacities, which she insisted should increase, not decrease, as one ages, to creative work that feeds both body and soul. She felt that the Western concept of human nature had steadily degenerated from the Middle Ages, when the Church had taught that man's spirit and body, in an earthly imitation of Christ, were equally good. The great creative individuals, and she cited Dante and Christ as examples, threatened totalitarian states because creators sustained the common men's spirits, and Dorothy Sayers said that if a culture lost the great ones, it stood to lose everything.[44] She reserved a ferocious contempt for those who denied that all men had a right to use their minds creatively, declaring that "it is to flatter a generation of mental sluggards that the lickspittles of public life make a virtue of imbecility."[45]

Begin Here shows Dorothy Sayers at her most porcupinish, and she must have realized it; she later felt that the book would be best forgotten.[46] Noble as the notion of laboring for the sheer joy of creation may be, not many can achieve it or afford it. But as James Brabazon has pointed out, Dorothy Sayers had a wide romantic streak in her personality,[47] and like Athos, her favorite musketeer, she was entirely willing to endure temporary discomfort for a cause that had captured her heart.

World War II was going to have to be the British "people's war," and Dorothy Sayers was prepared. In *Begin Here* she had unequivocally stated that the individual, not the government, was going to have to take the responsibility for winning this war, and she was already practicing what she preached during the "phony war," that uneasy winter of 1939–40 when British and French divisions sat behind the static Maginot Line that protected France's border with Germany, but not Belgium's. At the outset Allied strategy called for starving Germany into submission by economic blockade alone, and Neville Chamberlain went so far as to question whether Germany, being occupied with digesting Poland, intended to attack the West at all.[48] Others, like Dorothy Sayers, more realistically devoted themselves immediately to the war cause. She undertook a great deal of traveling, speaking to factory workers about ideas from *Begin Here*, principally "the great economic obsession," her belief that Fascists, Marxists and capitalists were godlessly standing in the way of "creative man," the individual transfigured by work that had genuine meaning. The Devil could hardly have found work for her idle hands either, since besides her writing and speaking and domestic chores, she was sewing for herself and constantly knitting socks and sweaters for seamen on the British trawler she had adopted as a part of her war effort, the H. M. T. Varanis.[49]

Dorothy Sayers resurrected Lord Peter Wimsey and his associates for the "Wimsey Papers," causing her popular characters to make amusing suggestions on coping with wartime inconveniences, her private "ministry of information." Harriet is at Talboys practicing emergency evacuations, Miss Climpson and the Cattery are gathering information on the Home Front, and Peter's nephew the Viscount St. George is flying Spitfires, the last gasp of chivalrous individual combat in the twentieth century. Even if the sacrifices of war nearly bled it out of existence, there was an England that would always belong to Dorothy Sayers in spirit, and she summed it up in Peter's older brother Gerald, the Duke of Denver, who swaps street argot with a horde of evacuated London urchins relocated to one wing of Duke's Denver. The Duke also indefatigibly plants oaks – the English aristocrat, even overbred and drained by taxes, sees to it that "what the land requires, the land shall have, so long as he is alive to serve it."[50] She felt that the Ministry of Information had taken a "rude and contemptuous tone" in dealing with British citizens, and she wrote to Sir Richard Maconachie, who had contacted her on their behalf, that the Ministry's anti-rumor campaign had left her "with the feeling that I am a scoundrel and a treacherous coward, though perhaps slightly less so then [sic] the greengrocer and the woman next door, of whom the very worst may be expected." She felt it was far better to "encourage, encourage, encourage, and *never* [Sayers's italics] give a man a bad opinion of himself."[51]

The last of the Wimsey Papers, 26 January 1940, strikes a more somber note; from a secret mission for the Foreign Office "somewhere abroad," Peter writes to Harriet,

> There is something you must tell the people . . . this is a battle of a new kind, and it is they who have to fight it, and they must

do it themselves and alone . . . they must lead themselves. This is a war against submission to leadership, and we might easily win it in the field and yet lose it in our own country. . . . The new kind of leaders are not like the old, and the common people are not protected from *them* as they were from *us* [Sayers's italics]. . . . [The people's] salvation is in themselves and in each separate man and woman among them. . . . It is the only thing that matters.[52]

Evidently Dorothy Sayers's opinions were unpopular with someone in authority, either at *The Spectator* or in the government, for this Wimsey Paper was headed by an announcement that the episodes would appear thenceforth at irregular intervals, and in fact they ceased with that issue.

She had more profound matters demanding her attention. That February, Dr. James Welch, the BBC's Director of Religious Broadcasting, asked her to consider a series of plays on the life of Christ for the Children's Hour. It was Dorothy Sayers's kind of project; she could put her fascination with the interrelation of history and the Bible into plays where she could treat Christ's life realistically, with modern speech. She also asked and received Dr. Welch's sanction for using Christ Himself as a character, something British stage convention had not allowed since the Middle Ages.[53] By the evidence of her fiction and available letters, Dorothy Sayers was the sort of person who offered children the same respect she would give to sensible adults, and she intended to do the same thing in these plays. Through some of the darkest days of World War II, until October 1942, it took a major row with the BBC, battles with the Lord's Day Observance Society and the Protestant Truth Society, and months of grueling work to finish the twelve episodes of *The Man Born to Be King*, but in the end Dorothy Sayers did it her way, and the series became one of her greatest achievements.

During the spring of 1940 she was also working on a revival of *The Zeal of Thy House* for Canterbury, eventually cancelled, and getting her stage comedy *Love All*, written in 1937–38, ready to open in London. On 9 April, the day of its première, the phony war suddenly became horrifyingly real. The Soviet Union had attacked small Finland, which had put up a fight, and with Hitler's blessing had gobbled up Latvia, Estonia, and Lithuania.

The German Navy assaulted Copenhagen, Denmark, and all of Norway's major ports with the intention of preventing Allied intervention in Scandinavia and securing neutral Sweden's iron ore for the Third Reich. With the same kind of coordination among air, sea, and land forces that had made the Blitzkrieg so devastating in Poland, the Nazis brought Denmark to surrender in five hours and Norway in sixty days. The Royal Navy and the Norwegians managed to sink or cripple half of Hitler's destroyers and three out of eight Nazi cruisers, but the Luftwaffe forced the British Expeditionary Force to withdraw, abandoning Norway to Nazi occupation and the quislings.

The disaster in Norway proved the last straw for the House of Commons. Leo Amery, a Conservative member of parliament who had once been Chamberlains' cabinet colleague, spoke for the majority in the debate preceding a vote of confidence and quoted Oliver Cromwell's words to the Long Parliament, telling the would-be architects of "peace at any price," "In the name of God, go."[54] On 10 May when the Blitzkrieg descended on Holland, Belgium, and France, Chamberlain resigned and George VI asked Winston Churchill, then sixty-five, Chamberlain's First Lord of the Admiralty, to form a wartime government; three days later, Churchill offered his countrymen nothing but "blood, toil, tears, and sweat." Churchill "mobilized the English language and sent it into battle"[55] with a glorious success that Dorothy Sayers wholeheartedly attributed to Churchill's being a man of letters; his ringing speeches were among England's strongest weapons during the summer of 1940. Holland fell in five days, Belgium in three weeks; and by early June Hitler's Panzers had flanked the Maginot Line and were rumbling along the road to Paris. On 25 June, France capitulated, acquiescing to the Nazi takeover of the French Navy and the German occupation of three-fifths of the country at France's expense, including the entire Atlantic Coast. In May and early June, 338,000 Allied troops, 224,000 of them British, had to be rescued from the beaches at Dunkirk by an impromptu British flotilla of naval vessels, private craft, and fishing boats – in Churchill's words, "a colossal military disaster."[56] England stood alone against Nazi Germany, poised confidently for invasion across the Channel. Now, Dorothy Sayers wrote in a stirring poem, this was "the war that England knows"[57] defending itself against great odds.

During this deadly spring Dorothy Sayers took on her most important challenge to date as a literary artist and as a Christian. She began corresponding in April with E. V. Rieu, who had published several of her essays as pamphlets for Methuen, about the projected "Bridgeheads" series of books to help Britain cope with the reality of war. Muriel St. Clare Byrne, who was working on the series volume *Privilege and Responsibility*, and Helen Simpson, another friend of Dorothy's, were to share the editorship of the Bridgeheads series with her. Dorothy L. Sayers's *The Mind of the Maker*, published in July 1941, was the first in the series, addressing the work of the creative artist as the reflection of Divine Creation, and it is generally accepted as her theological masterpiece.

No matter how demanding her work might be, Dorothy Sayers seems never to have restricted herself to only one project at a time. While she was at work on *The Mind of the Maker* from the spring of 1940 to early 1941 and writing the episodes of *The Man Born to Be King*, she also produced a number of important speeches and articles having to do with religious belief and practice and the sacramental nature of work, all in the context of Englishness. Since she was an intensely involved writer and a woman with more than she should have had to do at home, it seems no wonder that many of her opinions were couched in terms as spiny as the African brush-tailed porcupines she adopted in April of 1940, part of a plan by which citizens could contribute to the upkeep of animals at the financially troubled London Zoo.[58] Her choice of beast, like the sizable cactus collection she kept in her Witham greenhouse, reflected her affinity for creatures that kept their tender inner beings covered with formidable offensive weaponry – and she perhaps poked a little fun at herself as well.

Dorothy Sayers delivered "Creed or Chaos?"[59] her most important speech of 1940, for an Anglican Church Festival on 4 May at Derby, a week before Winston Churchill took the reins of a shaken nation soon to be fighting for its life. "Creed or Chaos?" was rebroadcast the following 11 and 18 August, as the Battle of Britain began in earnest. Her title leaves no doubt that she saw the war as a clear-cut life-and-death choice between

151

Christianity and pagan dogma, which she felt in the hands of Nazi Germany and the Soviet Union alike was nothing less than the prideful sin against the Holy Ghost, "energetically practising evil in the firm conviction that it is good."[60] She based her call for "active and positive effort to wrench a real good" out of that evil on the Christian creeds, the Church's practical response to heretical opinions, examining seven key positions of Christian teaching: that the identification of God the Creator with Christ the Redeemer means that Christianity is the only religion which allows a value to evil and suffering; that the human soul resembles Christ in choosing creativity and suffering over happiness, and that sin does not pay simply because it is wrong and can be amended with the help of God; that the entire universe is the embodiment of God's creative energy and thus man's physical being cannot be evil in itself; and that man's creative impulse should be channeled into work that allows him to imitate his Maker, in accordance with the laws God set over the universe. Defying God's laws "in the name of religious toleration," Dorothy Sayers said, had brought "utter chaos," threatening to bring on "the flight from reason" and "the death of hope," but she believed the Church might yet seize the opportunity to rebuild the nation on the firm footing of its traditional doctrine.[61]

She was addressing England, of course, and its salvation through its English Church. England needed all the support, spiritual and otherwise, that it could muster. Not since 1066 had the threat of double-pronged invasion from Normandy and Norway been as potent as it seemed in the summer of 1940. Hitler expected Britain to capitulate quickly, but Churchill defiantly declared, "we shall never surrender,"[62] and Britain gallantly responded. Two hundred fifty thousand Britons enlisted in the Home Guard in one twenty-four-hour period; rationing of butter, sugar and bacon began; and Churchill took steps he had foreseen as First Lord of the Admiralty, ordering the British Navy to destroy the French fleets at Oran in Algeria and Dakar in French West Africa, fortifying the Suez Canal against Italian Libya, and occupying Iceland to safeguard North Atlantic shipping. In response, Hitler tried to gain air superiority over the Channel for Operation Sea-Lion, the German invasion, by opening the Battle of Britain in full force that August, sending as many as 1800 bombers and Messerschmitt-109 fighter escorts a day to assault British factories, ports and airstrips. "Never in the field of human conflict," Churchill claimed, "was so much owed by so many to so few."[63] Seriously outnumbered, Royal Air Force Hurricane and Spitfire pilots shot down two German planes for each of theirs downed. Late that month unescorted British bombers impudently struck back at Berlin, and Hitler, enraged, commanded the Luftwaffe to destroy London. Between 7 September and the end of the year, the "Blitz" night-bombing offensive cost the city 13,339 killed and 17,937 wounded, countless buildings destroyed and families shattered; but as Churchill said, London could take it. Dorothy Sayers wrote to Anthony that Spain in 1588 and France in 1815 "broke themselves upon England," and she had every expectation that Germany should do the same thing.[64]

In "The Mysterious English,"[65] a speech she gave in London during the Blitz, Dorothy Sayers told Hitler and the world what they could expect of her nation. She used "mystery" here in its near-religious sense, to explain why against all reason a small, beleaguered nation should defend itself so ferociously. England, she claimed, drew its strength from its "mongrel" breeding, a healthy mixture of many racial stocks. Its language – and Dorothy Sayers was one of its ablest practitioners – derived its glory as "the most various, rich and expressive instrument of human speech since Pericles"[66] from its double roots in Latin and Anglo-Saxon. English patience could endure for a long time, she said, but when it broke at last, it would strike swiftly, thoroughly, and without warning, and Englishmen would fight best when they defended their home. A Spitfire pilot had told her that seeing the enemy's bombs dropping on his own country "made all the difference." The name Britain, Dorothy Sayers said, stirs the Englishman's pride, but the name of England "stirs his heart":[67] let the intruder beware.

The mongrel defending his own doorstep, however, received some harsh blows that fall. Coventry had to be sacrificed to keep the knowledge that the British had broken the Nazis' Ultra Code from leaking out, and U-boat wolfpacks ravaged British shipping during the winter of 1940–41. That January the Lend-Lease Agreement Churchill signed with the United States brought some desperately needed American help, but the terms John Maynard

Keynes negotiated proved in the long run too expensive, causing Britain virtually to cease being an exporting nation. By the climax of the Blitz on 10 May 1941, British civilian losses stood at 43,000 dead and 51,000 injured; thus when Hitler broke his agreement with Stalin and invaded the Soviet Union on 22 June, many a Britisher must have heaved a sigh of relief to have German attention diverted, at least for a little while.

Dorothy Sayers fired several important salvos in her own arena of the "English war," the practical applications of theology, during the first few months of 1941. She was the only woman among ten speakers invited to the Archbishop of York's Conference on the role of Christian faith and principles as guides to action during the war. The Conference was held at Malvern College in January, coincidentally the school Anthony was attending, and its various participants represented widely diverse doctrines and positions. Dorothy Sayers addressed "The Church's Responsibility," reiterating her previous statements that all human activity should be directed at producing good in imitation of the Almighty, the better to worship Him; and that man must choose between following the Gospel, trying one's best to make good out of evil, or reconciling oneself only to the letter of the law, passively giving up to indolence or, like Germany, actively giving over to evil.[68]

In February, after a bad bout of flu, she attacked the lukewarm in faith in a BBC broadcast, "The Religion behind the Nation," stressing that a nation wishing to preserve its Christian ethics but unwilling to exercise them boldly is heading for disaster, and she spoke at Brighton on 8 March 1941 on "The Vocation of Work," one of her chief preoccupations. She also published "The Church in the New Age" in March, calling for Christianity incorruptibly to oppose the spirit of that or any other age,[69] and in April 1941, her essay "Forgiveness and the Enemy"[70] blasted religious hypocrisy, especially the "priggish," forgiving Christian who smugly assures his enemy he will pray for him – thus arousing the murderous urge that Lord Byron claimed had incited Cain to kill Abel. Asked by the *Fortnightly* editor that March for a Christian justification for "undying hatred" of the enemy, Sayers produced it by using irrefutable logic: the sins of Nazi Germany were unforgivable precisely because the sinners didn't believe they were guilty. In June, she also aired six ten-minute radio talks on God the Son, probably dress rehearsals for *The Mind of the Maker*, which appeared in July. Dorothy Sayers never hesitated to offer her opinions, particularly on such touchy topics as politics and religion; many proved unpopular, several were attacked and savagely denounced, but none were illogical or boring. *The Mind of the Maker* itself met with resounding approval, the *Church Times* declaring that "theology in Miss Sayers's hand is more exciting than crime."[71]

Dorothy Sayers was approaching fifty while she was working on *The Mind of the Maker* – time, she felt, for her to "give sustained thought" to her vocation as a literary artist.[72] Her general intention in the *Bridgeheads* series was to give Britons a "constructive purpose" they could live and die for,[73] and she believed this could be nothing less than work in its sacramental sense as a reflection of Divine Creation. She justified her position by using the creative process of the writer, something she knew intimately, to illustrate one of Christianity's most puzzling and abstract teachings, the doctrine of the Trinity. In the process, as James Brabazon has acutely observed, she accomplished something truly remarkable: she was able to draw man and God closer to one another.[74]

When provoked, Dorothy Sayers could wield the English language like a barbed lance, and willful sloppiness roused her to fury. In her preface to *The Mind of the Maker* she denounces "the slatternly habit of illiterate reading" which she felt was responsible for ignorance or misconceptions about Christianity's official dogma as stated in its accepted creeds.[75] She also insists that she is simply presenting the truth about the nature of the creative mind as she has learned it from the teachings of the church. Once she defined her terms in the first section of the book, however, no writer could make her points more precisely, with more respect for her readers' intelligence or with less inflation of her own formidable achievements in drama and fiction. The author of *The Mind of the Maker* is very much the brilliant woman who had a reputation for arrogance, yet who respected ordinary Englishmen and women far more than their own Ministry of Information did. She was "kindness itself" to fellow church workers,[76] actors, and anyone else who sincerely sought after truth.

155

Basic to *The Mind of the Maker* is the one attribute of God which the Book of Genesis indicates that humanity shares, the ability to create. In expanding upon the final speech written for St. Michael the Archangel in *The Zeal of Thy House*, Dorothy Sayers saw the creative process in writing as triune, each element corresponding to the working of One Person of the Trinity:

God the Father	God the Son	God the Holy Spirit
:	:	:
the Creative Idea	the Creative Energy	the Creative Power

In terms of the creation of a book, the writer's "idea" is an entity in his mind that allows him to recognize and use the right word, phrase, character, twist of plot, and so forth, so that the finished work has a unity in itself. The "energy" is the whole process that produces the book in tangible form. The "power" is the means by which the author reads his own book, speaks to others, and engenders their response.[77] The three are inseparable, and none can exist without the others; and although in human (that is, imperfect) creations, one element may overshadow the other two and produce an unbalanced piece of literature, the Creator's work is perfect, although humanity can never glimpse it as completed.

Even though *The Mind of the Maker* is a theoretical work resting solidly upon Christianity's established dogma, Dorothy Sayers still put the essence of herself into it, and a few examples easily demonstrate that it is a gold mine of insights into her attitudes toward her own work. The Divine Author, like His mortal reflections, she says, can be expressed only in a great synthesis of His individual works, which is more than the sum of its individual parts – hence her well-publicized and entirely justifiable distaste for inquiries from persons who confused her characters with herself or tried to dredge her own personality out of her books. In Chapter VI of *The Mind of the Maker*, "The Energy Incarnate in Self-Expression," she declares the writing of autobiography dangerous, since it demands either foolish disregard of risk or the kind of supernatural courage Christ had but ordinary human beings can only revere from afar, perhaps a hint to her abandonment of "My Edwardian Childhood" and "Cat o'Mary." Chapter VII, "Maker of All Things – Maker of Ill Things," contains a germinal discussion of Evil in the universe, where Dorothy Sayers concludes that humanity can redeem evil and make it good either by laughing at it or using it for instructive purposes. The true creative imagination, directed outward, she insisted in Chapter IX, "The Love of the Creature," is the antidote to self-absorptive fantasy, which focuses inwardly, and her pungent illustration of the difference ought to be tattooed on the foreheads of all educationalists turned loose to "enhance the creativity" of innocent children. Genuinely creative youngsters, Dorothy Sayers firmly believed, tell objective stories impossible to confuse with ordinary daydreams, while "dreamy little liars grow up . . . into feeble little half-baked poets."[78] A glance at many autobiographical first novels today goes far toward proving her point.

The Mind of the Maker stands alone in Dorothy L. Sayers's distinguished body of writing for its brilliant motivating idea, the synthesis of Christian doctrine and human creativity; its insights into artistic activity, the work that gives meaning to human lives; and the power of its meticulously crafted message, that man, through that work, can overcome evil and turn it into good. That she wrote it at all testifies to her determination to define her own vocation; that it is exquisitely crafted bears witness to the maturity and self-discipline of her talent; and that it came in the midst of Dorothy Sayers's wars – her nation's armed conflict with Hitler, her own battles with the press and the BBC, domestic upheavals with Mac – makes *The Mind of the Maker* seem a downright miracle. In this case, certainly, "the law of nature . . . [was] not destroyed but fulfilled."[79]

On 23 October 1941, Dorothy Sayers delivered an address at Westminster, "The Other Six Deadly Sins,"[80] in which she tackled the unpleasant human habit of disobeying God's law. She refused to accept lust as the keystone of depravity that her contemporary society considered it, instead pointing out that the sins of wrath, gluttony, covetousness, envy, and sloth (in the descending order of wickedness Church tradition had maintained since the sixth century) share lust's dependence on pride, the root of every human failing. She considered pride itself as the sin of the noble mind which desires, like her Faust in *The Devil to Pay*, to remove all human suffering, very much the sin of her own time and the heart of the false doctrine of progress, which she believed was sapping the strength of Western civilization.

According to James Brabazon, Dorothy Sayers's letters to Muriel St. Clare Byrne reveal that life at home was becoming day by day more trying. Mac's hostility and mockery exacerbated all the irritations of the war for Dorothy Sayers, like the blackout, the rationing, the need to keep chickens and pigs for food, and housing an evacuee boy from London for two years.[81] All of this may have contributed to her mood when her twelve-part radio drama, *The Man Born to Be King*, struck serious snags during the winter of 1941–42, the nadir of World War II for Britain and its Allies. Accounts of the difficulties over the presentation of *The Man Born to Be King* agree that Dorothy Sayers had laid out her approach from the outset with perfect candor,[82] aiming at a realistic presentation of Christ. Initially, the series of twelve forty-five minute radio plays was to have been aired on the Children's Hour, but Val Gielgud, whom she respected and liked, had become head of radio drama, and Dorothy Sayers was to have worked with a new producer, Derek McCulloch, who was for many years the presenter of the BBC Children's Hour. In November, what appear to have been reasonable suggestions from McCulloch's assistant producer, May E. Jenkin, about adapting certain speeches in the first script to the capacities of children met with Dorothy Sayers's vehement opposition and ignited her ultimatum: Val Gielgud or else.[83]

The war was pressuring even Dorothy Sayers's ability to concentrate; the night that Japan bombed Pearl Harbor, the Luftwaffe dropped incendiaries across Witham, and she had to dive for safety, her manuscript on the Creative Mind under one arm and her half-finished script on John the Baptist under the other.[84] A longer-lasting conflagration ensued at a press conference on 11 December when she outlined her methods and read a few excerpts of dialogue at the request of a reporter; before the first script had been aired, self-appointed guardians of public decency undertook to defame her work as "irreverent," "blasphemous," "vulgar," and "scandalous," and the melee was on. Dorothy Sayers relished the thought of having the Lord's Day Observance Society and the Protestant Truth Society publicize her series,[85] but she was adamant that her authority had to be

158

absolute as regarded the writing, that the actors should be chosen
for their dramatic ability, not their piety, and that Gielgud had to
be in charge, or she would abandon the project. At last the BBC
surrendered unconditionally, moving her series to Gielgud's department so that he could take over as director. For all her
dictatorial posturing, when all was said and done, Dorothy
Sayers produced a meticulously accurate historical view of the life
of Christ which at the same time was theologically sound and
made excellent theater. The plays began in December 1941 and
ran until October 1942; their reception was overwhelmingly
positive – even Mac declared they'd "got a good Christ"[86] – and
the series has been frequently rebroadcast since, most recently
from January to March 1975.[87]

In her introduction to the published version of *The Man Born to
Be King*, Dorothy Sayers called Christ's human life and death
"the greatest tragic irony in fact or fiction"[88] because the people
of His time literally knew not what they did. She took the unpre-
cedented job of realistically presenting His Manhood so seriously
that she abandoned the phraseology of the King James Version,
which she felt had become familiar enough to be largely ignored,
and returned to the original Greek, retranslating to infuse the
story with new life. She relied most heavily on the Gospel written
by Christ's beloved disciple John, since that saint, the only
eyewitness to many of the events of Christ's life, also provides the
clearest chronology of its events, and she noted that she had not
referred to much exegetical literature, preferring to rely on ca-
nonical Scripture as her authority. Though she admitted her
inadequacies as a "detective novelist" in daring to re-create the
life of her Lord, she could honestly state, "I am a writer and I
know my trade."[89] Her refusal to crucify Him again by watering
down His story gives her work an incontrovertible integrity and
makes for irresistible theater.

As corollaries to *The Man Born to Be King*, Dorothy Sayers gave
six radio talks on God the Son during 1942, and on 13 February
at Reading she delivered her first postscript to *The Mind of the
Maker*, "The Creative Mind," in which she prophetically called
for scientists to "come to terms with the humanities," since each
had to use language to set free the products of the imagination;[90]
and she warned that words had to be used carefully, since they

159

were instruments of power. She spoke at Eastbourne on 23 April, suggesting in "Why Work?" that the nation preserve the positive good of thrift that the war had enforced and that work itself be considered the thing a person lives to do, his offering of himself to God, a position similar to Jacques Maritain's neothomist advocacy of Christian involvement in secular affairs.[91]

By October 1942, when the broadcasts of *The Man Born to Be King* were completed, what Dorothy Sayers was living to do was apparent: she had brought to life once more the world where Christ had walked. She adapted the speech of all the characters to their personalities – Matthew, a brash little Jewish tax collector, speaks cockney with a dash of Hollywoodese; the centurion Proclus, the rough yet tender soldier's idiom of Mac at his best; the simplicity and sorrow of the Mother of God, with a touch of Irish on her tongue; Jesus Himself, who brought fire and sword as well as forgiveness and redemption, with a voice "that can do anything."[92]

In her invaluable introduction and explanatory notes to the published play cycle, Dorothy Sayers observed that the central enigma she had to solve was Judas's motive, and she concluded that he had betrayed his Lord out of pride, the sin basic to all the rest. She made Judas a former follower of John the Baptist and an idealistic intellectual, like Sayers's Faust, eager to save his world, certain that he knew the best way, and smoulderingly jealous of his right to lead. Judas's pride leads him to see his own worst failings in others; he is gulled into believing that Christ is selling out the principles that had attracted Judas to Him. Dorothy Sayers makes Judas descend step-by-step toward the center of hell,[93] ending in the ultimate manifestation of pride, suicidal despair, and denying the Omnipotence of God by believing that no Divine Victim has the power to wash away his human guilt.

The figure of Christ in *The Man Born to Be King* may well be Dorothy L. Sayers's greatest literary creation. She was able to get around the old British law preventing the appearance of Christ on stage because in the radio play He would only be heard, not seen. In the sense she used this device in *The Mind of the Maker*, the idea that gave birth to this play cycle allowed her to choose unerringly the exact words and tones, the best sound effects, pauses and even the last paralyzing silence at Calvary that utterly convince her hearers He "was made man." In His arrest in the Garden, for instance, the crisis of the entire work, Christ's humanity, is shattering; He asks His captors, "Let go my hands a moment," to heal the soldier's ear that Peter struck:[94] the amazing paradox of Almighty God limited, and yet not limited, by human form.

The bitter moments in Gethsemane were the climax of Jesus's human tragedy, but Dorothy Sayers made the last three plays of *The Man Born to Be King* exceed the dénouement of a tragic fall. This Hero is Divine, and the gradual revelation of the Risen Christ turns His followers from their mortal world and toward the Kingdom of Heaven, which may only be attained by the exercise of free choice, that is, through childlike faith and willing sacrifice. Dorothy Sayers saw that Thomas's simple "My Lord and My God!" far exceeds the Aristotelian *anagnoresis* that leads to *peripateia*; Thomas's works mark the stupendous revelation of a catharsis of pity and terror beyond all human capacity. For the best reasons possible, Dorothy Sayers called Christ's story a Divine Comedy.[95]

While *The Man Born to Be King* was being aired, the war had widened to cover the globe. For the British and their Allies, in 1941 and early 1942 one disaster had followed another from the destruction of the House of Commons in May 1941, to Japan's sneak attack that December at Pearl Harbor and Japanese victories at Singapore and the Philippines, the 1942 loss of 656 British ships – 3.5 million tons of shipping – in the North Atlantic, and the Nazi conquest of the parts of the Soviet Union that produced sixty percent of its coal and nearly half of its grain.[96] British bombing raids on Germany brought on an appalling reprisal when the Nazis destroyed many of England's most historic cities. Not until the late summer of 1942 did "The Grand Alliance" begin to turn the tide with United States Navy victories at the Coral Sea and Midway, the hard-won Battle of Guadalcanal from August 1942 until January 1943, the pivotal British defeat of Hitler's "Desert Fox," Field Marshal Erwin Rommel, at El Alamein in October, and the monumental Soviet defense of Stalingrad which culminated in February 1943. Nazi Germany was by no means finished; the gas chambers had begun Hitler's grim "final solution" to "the Jewish question," and Nazi scientists

161

were at work on the V-2, the first long-range missile, but still Britain could breathe a little more easily in what Churchill called "the end of the beginning."[97]

"Lord, I Thank Thee," Dorothy Sayers wrote in November 1943, titling a poem she used on her Christmas cards that year which catalogued all the things she didn't care for that the war was preventing – foreign travel, reading newspaper ads, and being misquoted by the press, who were now too short of paper to do so.[98] As usual, she was making the best of a difficult situation with unquenchable humor. She named all the female pigs she raised at Witham "Fatima" and the males "Francis Bacon"; she maintained a cat maternity room open to all the town's felines, and she would save their kittens from drowning by distributing them to her favorite restaurants as mousers. "Aunt Sayers" even once gleefully took her friend Marjorie Barber's dog Bunter to tea at Fortnum's in the heart of London's West End.[99]

Dorothy Sayers was fifty years old in June 1943, and she had a right to need a rest. The pace of her literary production, to say nothing of her theatrical efforts and her wartime activities, had been harrowing. As diversion after *The Man Born to Be King*, she had written one last Wimsey story in 1942, "Talboys," a tale involving a village flower show rivalry in which one of Lord Peter's sons is accused of theft, but it was not published until thirty years later, well after her death.[100] James Brabazon has remarked, too, that as the war went on, it lost much of its romantic appeal for Dorothy Sayers. The chivalric individual combat of Spitfire pilots in the Battle of Britain had given way to the grimy endurance of such annoyances as buzz-bombs, rationing, and Yanks "over-paid, over-sexed, and over here," and Dorothy Sayers's writing changed as well. After "The Gulf Stream and the Channel" and "They Tried to Be Good,"[101] essays celebrating the idiosyncracies and the consciousness of responsibility that had brought Britain to the pinnacle of Empire and the depths of war, she abruptly began to write unrhymed poetry with the look and feel of Eliot's "Waste Land" but with a mellowed, even gentled, spirit quite new to her literary expression. In September 1943, the newly elevated Archbishop of Canterbury, William Temple, who had admired Dorothy Sayers's work for a long time, offered her a rare honor, the Lambeth

Degree of Doctor of Divinity, and had she accepted, she would have been the first woman in history to have received it. Brabazon makes three guesses about her refusal: her unwillingness to become involved with ecclesiastical machinery; her consciousness of personal sinfulness, because her marriage to Mac, a divorced man, could not be recognized by her Church; and the possibility of the truth about Anthony's parentage being unearthed by an inquisitive reporter, which might have destroyed her credibility as a spokesman for conservative Christianity.[102] Even so, the offer must have gratified her deeply.

For the next few months, Dorothy Sayers fulfilled the recommendation for middle age that she had made in her 1938 essay "Strong Meat" – to approach life with the zest of an energetic child. She tackled a curious combination of literary and religious topics, working briefly on a nonreligious play "full of swords and treason"[103] drawn from Jean Froissart, the fourteenth-century French chronicler of western Europe, but she never completed it. She was elected a vice-president of the English Association on 29 May 1943, a mark of the respect that academics felt toward her, and she invested several months in an article for a projected symposium on "The Future of the Jews," only to have her work rejected because it approached Christ as the mystical center of human history and declared that the Jews' sufferings were the result of their refusal to accept Him as their Messiah. She also abandoned an attempt at a verse drama on Admiral Darlan, a former head of the French Vichy government who in 1942 defied Marshal Pétain and brought North and West Africa to the side of the Allies. The work she did at this time that most reveals her softer side was "Target Area," published in *Fortnightly* for March 1944, a tribute to the music teacher she had known at Godolphin, Fräulein Fehmer, who had returned to Germany and become a Nazi; as Ralph Hone has pointed out, the thought that British bombs might destroy the strong mind and hands that had so unforgettably re-created Chopin's music brought Dorothy Sayers "the awareness of the intricacies of human relationships."[104] She eventually located Fräulein Fehmer in Frankfurt and sent her food and clothing until her old teacher died in 1948.

None of these projects, however, satisfied Dorothy Sayers for long. The war finally seemed to be approaching its close with the

Allied invasion of Normandy on D-Day, 6 June 1944, even though Hitler subsequently assaulted England with rocket-propelled pilotless aircraft that struck at random, adding an element of brutal happenstance to the hazards of war. That August Dorothy Sayers was still absorbed with the conflict of good and evil, and she was consciously or unconsciously looking for a new positive good to hammer out of it when she picked up a book she said she had never read before; it was the Temple Edition of Dante's *Inferno*, and her inner world would never be the same again.

Notes

1. Dorothy L. Sayers, *Gaudy Night* (1936; New York, Avon, 1968), p. 149.
2. Dorothy L. Sayers, *The Mind of the Maker* (London: Methuen, 1989), p. 207.
3. Margaret P. Hannay, Introduction to *As Her Whimsey Took Her* (Kent, Ohio: Kent State University Press, 1979), p. xi.
4. Barbara Reynolds, *The Passionate Intellect* (Kent, Ohio: Kent State University Press, 1989), p. 9.
5. James Brabazon, *Dorothy L. Sayers: A Biography* (New York: Charles Scribners' Sons, 1981), p. 143.
6. Sayers, *The Mind of the Maker*, p. 207; quoted in Ralph E. Hone, *Dorothy L. Sayers: A Literary Biography* (Kent, Ohio: Kent University Press, 1979), p. 85.
7. Dorothy L. Sayers, *The Zeal of Thy House*, in *Four Sacred Plays* (London: Gollancz, 1948), p. 68.
8. Ibid., p. 34.
9. Ibid., p. 99.
10. Dorothy L. Sayers, "Divine Comedy," in *Unpopular Opinions* (New York: Harcourt, Brace and Co., 1947), p. 19.
11. Alzina Stone Dale, *Maker and Craftsman: The Story of Dorothy L. Sayers* (Grand Rapids, Mich.: William B. Eerdmans Publishing Co., 1978), p. 105.
12. Anthony Fleming, Introduction to Dorothy L. Sayers, *Love All* and Dorothy L. Sayers and Muriel St. Clare Byrne, *Busman's Honeymoon*, ed. Alzina Stone Dale, 2nd ed. (Kent, Ohio: Kent State University Press, 1985), p. xv.

13. Alzina Stone Dale's Preface to the Second Edition of *Love All*, p. xi. See also Barbara Reynolds, review article [of Dale's edition], "I Wrote It Just for Fun," *Seven* 6, pp. 88–89.
14. Ibid., p. x.
15. Ibid.
16. Ibid., p. 197.
17. Ibid., p. 185.
18. Dale's Preface, ibid., p. xxxii.
19. Dorothy L. Sayers, *Are Women Human?* (Grand Rapids, Mich.: William B. Eerdmans Publishing Co., 1971); also contains "The Human-Not-Quite-Human," written during World War II.
20. Ibid., p. 17.
21. Ibid., p. 23.
22. Ibid., p. 32.
23. D. H. Lawrence, quoted in ibid., p. 33.
24. Brabazon, pp. 181–82.
25. Dorothy L. Sayers, "The Other Six Deadly Sins," in *Creed or Chaos?* (New York: Harcourt, Brace and Co., 1949), p. 77.
26. Dorothy L. Sayers, "The Greatest Drama Ever Staged," "The Triumph of Easter," "Strong Meat," and "The Dogma is the Drama," in *Creed or Chaos?*, pp. 3–7, 8–13, 14–19, and 20–24.
27. Dorothy L. Sayers, "Greatest Drama Ever Staged," in *Creed or Chaos?*, p. 5.
28. Dorothy L. Sayers, "Triumph of Easter," in *Creed or Chaos?*, p. 10.
29. Ibid., p. 8.
30. "Strong Meat," p. 17; "Triumph of Easter," p. 11.
31. Dorothy L. Sayers, "The Dictatorship of Words," *The Times*, 6 January 1939, p. 7.
32. Dorothy L. Sayers, *The Devil to Pay*, in *Four Sacred Plays*, pp. 110–11.
33. Ibid., p. 113.
34. Ibid., p. 208.
35. Winston Churchill, quoted in Walter L. Arnstein, *Britain Yesterday and Today: 1830 to the Present*, 5th ed. (Lexington, Mass.: D.C. Heath and Co., 1988), p. 316.
36. Arnstein, p. 318.
37. Asa Briggs, *A Social History of England* (New York: The Viking Press, 1983), p. 268.
38. Brabazon, p. 175.
39. Dorothy L. Sayers, "Wimsey Papers," *The Spectator* 163 (17 November 1939), p. 672.
40. Dorothy L. Sayers, Letter to Mrs. MacLoughlin 27 September 1939, quoted in Brabazon, p. 176.
41. Brabazon, p. 176.
42. Hone, p. 100.
43. Dorothy L. Sayers, *Begin Here: A War-Time Essay* (London: Gollancz, 1940), unpaginated Preface.

44. Ibid., p. 121.
45. Ibid., p. 123.
46. Brabazon, p. 178.
47. Ibid.
48. Arnstein, p. 320.
49. Brabazon, p. 180.
50. Sayers, "Wimsey Paper" IV, *The Spectator* 163 (8 December 1939), p. 809.
51. Dorothy L. Sayers, Letter to Sir Richard Maconachie 13 July 1940, quoted in Hone, pp. 116–17.
52. Sayers, "Wimsey Paper" XI, *The Spectator* 164 (26 January 1940), p. 105.
53. Hone, p. 102.
54. Leo Amory, quoted in Arnstein, p. 321.
55. Winston Churchill and John F. Kennedy, quoted in Arnstein, pp. 322–23.
56. Churchill, quoted in Arnstein, p. 324.
57. Dorothy L. Sayers, "The English War," quoted in Brabazon, p. 187.
58. Hone, p. 113.
59. Sayers, "Creed or Chaos?," in *Creed or Chaos?*, pp. 25–45.
60. Ibid., p. 27.
61. Ibid., p. 29.
62. Winston Churchill, quoted in Arnstein, p. 324.
63. Churchill, quoted in ibid., p. 326.
64. Dorothy L. Sayers, Letter to Anthony Fleming 23 June 1940, quoted in Brabazon, p. 187.
65. Dorothy L. Sayers, "The Mysterious English," in *Unpopular Opinions* (New York: Harcourt, Brace and Co., 1947), pp. 78–96.
66. Ibid., p. 80.
67. Ibid., p. 94.
68. See a fuller discussion of this address in Hone, pp. 119–21.
69. Ibid., p. 122.
70. Dorothy L. Sayers, "Forgiveness and the Enemy," in *Unpopular Opinions*, pp. 8–13.
71. Hone, p. 128.
72. Dorothy L. Sayers, Letter to Dr. James Welch 2 January 1941, quoted in Hone, p. 125. In *Writing a Woman's Life* (New York: Norton, 1988), p. 49, Carolyn G. Heilbrun suggests that women of an earlier age – that is, before the middle of the twentieth century – could expel themselves absolutely from society by committing a social, usually a sexual, sin . . . life crises that have been identified as patterns in male lives often occur at a later age in women." In Heilbrun's view, Sayers's hiding of Anthony's parentage would be motivated by the necessity to conceal that sin. Similarly, Heilbrun also observes that fifty is a milestone in creativity for many women: "To allow oneself at fifty the expression of one's feminism is an

experience for which there is no male counterpart, at least for white men in the Western world." (p. 124) Leaving "feminism" as the 1980s sees it aside, perhaps Sayers's achievement with *The Mind of the Maker* at fifty to some extent balanced in her mind her concealment of her motherhood.

73. Brabazon, p. 278. The entire Statement of Aims for the *Bridgeheads* series is supplied in Brabazon's Appendix and is well worth studying.

74. Ibid., p. 205. Dorothy Sayers used a passage from the Russian philosopher Nicholas Berdyaev, her contemporary, as one of her epigraphs to *The Mind of the Maker*: "In the case of man, that which he creates is more expressive of him than that which he begets. The image of the artist and the poet is imprinted more clearly on her works than on his children." In several of her works Sayers cited Berdyaev, who decried man's dehumanization by modern technology and believed man's fulfillment to be in the free, creative act. The intellectual contribution made by Berdyaev's work on Sayers's writings has not as yet been studied in depth.

75. Dorothy L. Sayers, *The Mind of the Maker* (London: Methuen, 1941), p. ix.

76. Helena Saunders, Letter to Editor, *Mythlore* 54 (Summer 1988), p. 60.

77. Sayers, *Mind of the Maker*, pp. 29–31.

78. Ibid., p. 113.

79. Ibid., p. 67.

80. Sayers, "The Other Six Deadly Sins," in *Creed or Chaos?*

81. Brabazon, p. 209.

82. See Hone, pp. 102–12, and Brabazon, pp. 191–206.

83. Brabazon, p. 195.

84. Hone, p. 110.

85. Ibid., p. 103.

86. Ibid., p. 111.

87. Robert B. Harmon and Margaret A. Burger, *An Annotated Guide to the Works of Dorothy L. Sayers* (New York: Garland Publishing Co., 1977), p. 135.

88. Dorothy L. Sayers, *The Man Born to Be King* (New York: Harper, 1943), p. 5.

89. Ibid., p. 21.

90. Hone, p. 133.

91. Dorothy L. Sayers, "Why Work?" in *Creed or Chaos?*, pp. 46–62.

92. Sayers, *Man Born to Be King*, p. 51.

93. Ibid., p. 254.

94. Ibid., p. 248.

95. Ibid., p. 11.

96. Arnstein, p. 331.

97. Winston Churchill, quoted in ibid., p. 333.

98. Dale, p. 129.

99. Ibid., p. 125.
100. Dorothy L. Sayers, "Talboys," in *Lord Peter* (New York: Avon, 1972), pp. 431–53.
101. Sayers, "The Gulf Stream and the Channel," and "They Tried to be Good," in *Unpopular Opinions*, pp. 69–77 and 118–28.
102. Brabazon, p. 215.
103. Hone, p. 136.
104. Ibid., p. 139.

8 A Devouring Passion
1944–1957

> A great poem . . . is yours and mine.
> Dorothy L. Sayers, "Dante's Imagery:
> I. Symbolic"

Analyzing any period of literature from the vantage point of only one or two generations can prove a risky business, and missing the forest of Britain's fine early twentieth-century writers for the towering oaks of Lawrence, Joyce, and Eliot threatens to become a literary commonplace. Ever since these giants changed literature forever, poor imitations of their work have been proliferating and tend to make it all too easy to forget that those writers, whose works are now considered twentieth-century classics, were experimenters in their day, producing sometimes brilliant, but almost always shocking exceptions to the norms of serious British literature prior to World War II.

At the turn of the century "no country had more good novelists than Great Britain."[1] Although Victorian reticence often diluted realistic descriptions of passion and Victorian values often demanded moral lessons, to the Victorians the phrase "good novelists" meant craftsmen like Dickens, Scott, Stevenson, Kipling, or Trollope, writers capable above everything else of riveting their readers' attention with stories virtually impossible to put down. The loosening of standards and the enormous disillusion left in the wake of World War I brought new realism and new values to British writing; some artists of the vanguard, like Lawrence, Joyce, and Eliot, tried out once-forbidden subjects, exotic forms, and bravura techniques, but others remained in the mainstream, convinced that a story was worthless if it did not maintain the reader's interest. Moreover, for a story to captivate its audience at a time when civilization as they knew it seemed to be coming apart at the seams, it had to contain a positive message rather than one which might speed up the disintegration.

In the late 1930s, Dorothy Sayers had come into contact with members of a group of writers, all male and mostly Oxford dons, who shared her conservative religious views, her rigorous scholarly standards, and her devotion to the Middle Ages. "The Inklings" met informally once or twice a week to hear and discuss one another's works in progress; Dorothy Sayers was not a member and probably no woman could have been, given the group's entrenched attitudes about the female sex. For most of his life C. S. Lewis, around whom the Inklings had begun to gather about ten years earlier, considered a married male friend just as lost as a dead one.[2] Ironically, Lewis's own marriage in 1956 caused J. R. R. Tolkien, the most widely publicized Inkling, to feel "betrayed," causing a rupture in their close friendship.[3] Dorothy Sayers did carry on a spirited correspondence about theological and literary issues with Lewis, who had praised *The Mind of the Maker* highly in a review for *Theology*,[4] but her greatest inspiration, the impetus for reading Dante, came from Charles Williams, who joined the Inklings after he moved from London to Oxford in 1939.

In 1925, Lewis had become a Fellow of Magdalen, one of Oxford's loveliest colleges, and Tolkien a Fellow of Merton, one of its most venerable. Both men were involved in a dispute over whether the syllabus of Oxford's Honour School of English Language and Literature should include material written after 1830, which Lewis felt students could just as well read in their bathtubs, or whether the course should require only the more strenuous Anglo-Saxon and medieval studies and philology.[5] Tolkien persuaded Lewis of the latter view, which prevailed until after Lewis left Oxford for Cambridge in 1954.

The name "Inklings" suited Lewis's group because all were involved somehow with writing. It also suggests the Old Norse "Yngling," the name for a member of the ancient royal Scandinavian dynasty which claimed descent from the fertility god Yng (Freyr), reflecting the fascination with Northern mythology that Tolkien, Lewis and several other members had held since boyhood. As early as 1926, in fact, Tolkien had actually set about teaching Old Norse to his friends, who at that time called themselves "the Coal-biters." James Brabazon observes that the Inklings also seemed to have shared a feeling that each in his own way had glimpsed God's plan for the universe,[6] an indication of individual religious convictions which were inseparable from their literary pursuits.

In 1939, both Tolkien and Lewis defended their faith against a notion Tolkien in particular abominated, the belief that reading great literature could improve a student's character as well as his knowledge. This view was less prevalent at Oxford than at Cambridge, "the other place" where the immensely influential literary critic F. R. Leavis maintained that "culture" should be recognized as "the basis for a humane society," though Leavis "did not believe this culture should be based on any one objective standard, least of all Christianity."[7] In his essay "On Fairy-Stories," Tolkien, a devout Roman Catholic, insisted that man produces stories as "a sub-creator." He believed that the smaller joys that an artist creates provide a glimpse of "the greatest and most complete conceivable eucatastrophe,"[8] the story of Christ. Tolkien's position parallels the position on the Trinity Dorothy Sayers worked out in *The Mind of the Maker* two years later. In "Christianity and Literature," Lewis, who had achieved his Anglican Christian belief through a protracted intellectual struggle, placed Leavis and I. A. Richards, another renowned critic, in the "tradition of educated infidelity" that Lewis accused the Victorian critic Matthew Arnold of beginning. Arnold's tradition itself, Lewis said, was a "phase in that general rebellion against God which began in the eighteenth century," and he dismissed Leavis's subjective critical method as "trying to lift yourself by your own coat collar." Lewis flatly declared, "Unless we return to the crude and nursery-like belief in objective values, we perish."[9]

Leavis and Richards were proponents of what Lewis later parodied as "whymperinges of the raskellie auctors in these latter daies, as the Eliots, Poundes, Lawrences, Audens and the like,"[10] and Lewis and Tolkien were doing scholarly battle with Leavis and Richards when Charles Williams arrived in Oxford. Though gifted with a burning intellect, Williams was the least tradition-ally academic of the three best-known Inklings; his lecture style was nine. Both C. S. Lewis and Dorothy L. Sayers followed Williams in calling Beatrice "the divine Godbearer," that is, the image which brought God to Dante.[28] Williams termed Dante's his death in 1945, but even during his lifetime his work received far less attention than Tolkien's immensely popular fantasy

171

novels *The Hobbit* and *The Lord of the Rings* and Lewis's best-selling children's series *The Chronicles of Narnia,* productions which brought Tolkien and Lewis worldwide fame and considerable academic envy. Williams considered "the union of the intellect and the imagination as the highest means of reaching religious truth,"[11] and he and his work captured Dorothy Sayers's imagination so thoroughly that she acknowledged the influence of his thinking not only on her last major work, the translation of Dante's *Divine Comedy,* but on nearly everything else she wrote in the last thirteen years of her life. Barbara Reynolds, in a position to know, declares that "all Dorothy Sayers' work on Dante" arose from her exchange of correspondence with Williams from 16 August 1944 to 9 May 1945.[12]

Charles Williams was a Londoner, an Anglican, and a poet. Chronically short of money, he had to leave University College, London, after two years to support himself,[13] and he took a job as a proofreader for the London office of the Oxford University Press in 1908, where he eventually became an editor. Although he probably considered himself a poet first of all, Williams wrote reviews, historical biographies, and novels to augment his income, and by 1930, he also was lecturing on literature in London's Evening Institutes, where he had developed a devoted, mainly female, following. He apparently was one of those hypnotic lecturers who communicated primarily through emotion, ritually chanting quotations to enrapture his audience with his own love of a wide range of literature. He also counseled his students about their personal difficulties, and Humphrey Carpenter, the Inklings' biographer, notes that Williams' students might easily have gone home "feeling that this was what it would have been like to meet Dante himself."[14] Even Williams's most sympathetic commentators consider much of his prose obscure, and few readers can decipher the esoteric symbolic system of his poetry, like his Arthurian sequences *Taliesin through Logres* and *The Region of the Summer Stars.* Those who knew him personally recall him with kindness, but many readers concur with Martin Seymour-Smith that behind all Williams's work "there seems to be something thoroughly unpleasant."[15] Carpenter feels that Williams enjoyed the thought of inflicting pain.[16]

Williams had in fact been assigned to proofread Oxford's

reissued Cary translation of the *Divine Comedy* in 1910, just after he had written a long sonnet sequence to his fiancée developing the Christian notion that earthly love should bring lovers closer to God, although Williams's own religious belief was not at all conventional. He was fascinated by magic and in 1917 had been initiated into the Order of the Golden Dawn,[17] an occult but probably harmless Rosicrucian sect to which William Butler Yeats also belonged. Williams subsequently left the Order, but the supernatural, especially white and black magic, played a growing part in his writings, demonstrating, Carpenter believes, that Williams had "something more than a calm intellectual interest" in the subject.[18] Williams's detective novels, beginning with *War in Heaven* (1930), contain supernatural elements, and Williams rated his fictional characters most highly if they committed themselves wholesale to the occult, an attitude many readers find hard to swallow. On the other hand, T. S. Eliot, one of Williams's admirers, praised Williams's heightening of the normal world with his perception of the supernatural.[19]

In 1936, C. S. Lewis read Williams's novel *The Place of the Lion*, in which Platonic archetypes materialize in rural Hertfordshire. Lewis called it a "good preparation for Lent," since it clarified for him the special sin of intellectual pride to which academics are especially susceptible. At the same time, Williams was reading Lewis's *Allegory of Love*, amazed, he said, at Lewis's praise of Dante's "noble fusion of sexual and religious experience."[20] The two met shortly after, and when the war caused his publishing firm to relocate their London office to Oxford in 1939, Williams became a full-fledged Inkling through Lewis, much to the chagrin of Tolkien, who felt Williams had displaced him in Lewis's friendship. Lewis was also instrumental in having Williams appointed as a lecturer in the English School, where his courses on Milton, Wordsworth, and the eighteenth century drew full houses. At last, Williams's unorthodox study of Dante, *The Figure of Beatrice* (1943), brought him "something for which he had waited a long time: public recognition,"[21] and his followers became more numerous and more fervent than ever before. One of them was Dorothy Sayers.

Dorothy Sayers had met Williams in the mid-1930s. He had been delighted with *The Nine Tailors*, and around 1936, he had suggested she write the 1937 Centerbury Festival Play.[22] After it was produced, Williams made such a boisterous declaration of his pleasure with *The Zeal of Thy House* at Simpson's, the august London restaurant, that he embarrassed even Dorothy. They kept in touch, and in late 1943 or early 1944, she visited him at Oxford, coming as a successful author to advise Williams on being published. Twenty-four hours later, his landlady Anne Spaulding remarked, Dorothy Sayers "was his disciple, sitting at his feet."[23] Williams soon discovered that Sayers's enthusiasms could be overwhelming, and he wrote to his wife, who had stayed in London, "I like the old dear, but she's rather heavy going . . . but what can one do?"[24]

At that time, Dorothy Sayers later wrote, she "still knew Dante chiefly by repute." She read Williams's *Figure of Beatrice*, which had appeared in the summer of 1943, "not because it was about Dante, but because it was by Charles Williams."[25] In *The Figure of Beatrice* Williams traced the complex meaning that Beatrice Portinari had had for Dante, and by doing so Williams gave Dorothy Sayers gifts that only one extraordinary thinker can give another: a new perspective on the theological problem central to all of her work, the question of good and evil, and the inspiration of pursuing it in a dimension both familiar and newly challenging to her, the translation of a medieval masterpiece.

Beatrice Portinari had spent her short life in thirteenth-century Florence, where Dante Alighieri, who was to be Florence's most famous poet, saw her a few times, adored her from afar, and made her live forever in his work. She first appeared in *La Vita Nuova*, a cycle of courtly love poems with prose commentary expressing Dante's idolization of Beatrice, written when he was twenty-six, not long after her death. Later, in the *Convivio*, a philosophical text, he tried to put Beatrice out of his thoughts and succeeded only in hurling himself into twelve years of the dark night of the soul. Williams believed that the *Vita Nuova* and the *Convivio* were both essential to the understanding of the image of Beatrice that animates Dante's masterpiece *The Divine Comedy*, his poetic account of an allegorical journey through Hell and Purgatory to Paradise. Dante could write it, Williams felt and Dorothy Sayers agreed, because he had lived it.

Williams's *Figure of Beatrice* is difficult reading for many

174

readers. Williams's style is often complex to the point of impenetrability, and he seems to have lacked the forceful common sense and the ability to state abstract concepts in refreshingly clear, concrete examples which characterize everything Dorothy Sayers wrote. Despite such drawbacks, however, *The Figure of Beatrice* offers essential insights into Dante's work, and they harmonized remarkably well with Dorothy Sayers's religious and literary principles, as Barbara Reynolds has unshakably proven in her lucid discussion of Williams's beliefs and the influence they had on Dorothy Sayers, *The Passionate Intellect*. In his introduction to *The Figure of Beatrice*, Williams postulated two paths to God, the more familiar Way of Negation which renounces all images but that of God himself, and its opposite and complement, the Way of Affirmation, which approaches the Almighty through all of the images the Way of Negation renounces. Barbara Reynolds observes that the Affirmative Way was "the more typically incarnational" and "central to Catholic teaching in the Middle Ages."[26] Williams found the maxim of the Way of Affirmation in the Athanasian Creed, the same *Quicunque Vult* that had shaped Dorothy's concept of the Incarnation. Since she had first become intrigued with the Athanasian Creed in her teens, Dorothy Sayers had willingly embraced its articles of faith. Now, after moving beyond her detective-story explorations of the good and evil in human hearts to more overtly theological works, her belief seems to have become so thoroughly a part of her heart, her soul, and in particular her formidable intellect that she affirmed it in all of her subsequent work: "Not by conversion of the Godhead into Flesh, but by taking of the Manhood into God."[27] Williams's awkward but evocative phrase for this spiritual process is "in-Godding." Christ's Incarnation meant that mankind might also join with the Divine through him, but the Church, Williams said, had had to wait for Dante to show in art how one soul could approach its ordained end. He claimed the soul did so through the affirmation of all images, every one of which Dante related to the figure of Beatrice, with whom the whole "in-Godding" had begun for him: the physical image of a girl Dante first saw at a party when he was nine. Both C. S. Lewis and Dorothy L. Sayers followed Williams in calling Beatrice "the divine Godbearer," that is, the image which brought God to Dante.[28] Williams termed Dante's

175

personal experience of Beatrice "romantic love" for three reasons. First, for Williams the term best described a definite personal and passionate sexual love; second, it encompassed more than sexual love; and finally, the study of Dante's record of his love allowed the discrimination between spurious and real Romanticism, which was for Williams the manner of receiving experience.[29]

Williams's definition of "image" as he believed Dante used it also became an integral part of Dorothy Sayers's approach to the *Divine Comedy*. First, the image in this sense was of something objectively outside of Dante: Beatrice was a real person, not the poet's invention. Second, her physical shape stood for "things beyond itself": the beautiful little girl represented Florentine nobility; the goodness that Dante immediately sensed in her made her stand for virtue, and so forth; but Williams insisted she remained the girl Beatrice to the very end – that is, even the vision of the Almighty upon which the *Comedy* concludes still includes the identity of the original Beatrice, whose encounter with Dante inspired the "noble awe and noble curiosity" which brought his work to life.[30]

Williams's entire approach in *The Figure of Beatrice* resembles a religious mystery clothed in a work of literary art, a phenomenon Dorothy Sayers explored as a corollary to *The Mind of the Maker* in her 1944 essay "Towards a Christian Aesthetic." She suggested that the idea of Art as creation is Christianity's only important contribution to the philosophy of the beautiful. She focused on the word "image" as descriptive of the artist's task in its New Testament sense of the Son as the "express image" of God, Who is "unimaginable" except through the Son Who is His Image.

Not long before she died Dorothy Sayers explained the difference between Williams's mind and her own. She felt he was, at least to some extent, "a practicing mystic," one of those rare souls who believes in realities accessible by subjective experience but beyond the physical senses. She knew that she herself was not a mystic, but she felt her intellect allowed her to apprehend what Williams could "grasp directly."[31] This distinction illuminates a seeming paradox in her life and work. She claimed in a letter to a friend on 16 August 1944 that she had never read Dante, and that since she was comparing his work to Milton's, she had better avoid being condemned to the circle of the hypocrites by "really reading Dante"[32] – yet from her earliest published work onwards, she had frequently invoked his name. In her first mystery, *Whose Body?*, she had presented Lord Peter Wimsey as a collector of rare copies of Dante's work, mentioning Dante by name no less than nine times, most crucially as the spark which ignites Peter's decision to take responsibility for trapping the criminal and bringing about his death.[33] At critical moments in *The Unpleasantness at the Bellona Club*, she indirectly described the *Inferno* and observes that Dante once painted an angel,[34] and as has been shown, she shaped the progress of Peter's love affair with Harriet into the pattern of hell, purgation, and heaven. Furthermore, Dorothy Sayers had described Christ's Incarnation as a "Divine Comedy"[35] and treated it as exactly that in *The Man Born to Be King*. She was too thorough a scholar and too precise a writer to use words of such power accidentally or lightly, and furthermore, understanding Williams's *Figure of Beatrice*, as she had done, without knowing something of Dante and his writings would seem to have been unlikely. An Oxford student of medieval literature might be supposed to have had some exposure through reading and lectures to the greatest author of the Middle Ages, and she might even have read certain passages of the *Commedia* earlier, but Dorothy Sayers also believed that each great piece of literature should be first read at its own best age – not necessarily when one is young.[36] Dorothy Sayers's "really reading Dante" in 1944 might be compared to Keats's first reading of Chapman's Homer: although he had experienced it before in other versions, he felt that in Chapman's translation he was "reading" the epic for the first time. In any case, whatever Dorothy Sayers had known of Dante before, Charles Williams opened her eyes, and all at once she saw.

Once Dorothy Sayers began the *Divine Comedy* she could not put it down. In her first letter to Williams after reading Dante she exclaimed, "What a writer! God's body and bones, what a writer!"[37] She came to the *Divine Comedy* almost from the start through the Italian language version, with the Temple Classics facing-page prose version for assistance,[38] and she found Dante the "most incomparable story-teller who ever set pen to paper."[39] She was smitten for many of the same reasons that *The Three*

Musketeers captured her imagination at thirteen, though there obviously can be no comparison of the merit of the two works. She found the *Divine Comedy* funny, romantic, splendidly adventurous – the record of one man's descent into a hell he had chosen for himself and his rise to a better world. Readers can believe in it absolutely because they know they have been there themselves.[40]

Dorothy Sayers poured out her passion for the *Divine Comedy* in long letters to Williams, and he hoped to publish them as a means of bringing the public closer to Dante's work, but he died before he could do so. Portions of the correspondence, comprised of eleven letters from Williams and nineteen from Dorothy Sayers, are discussed in detail in Barbara Reynold's *The Passionate Intellect: Dorothy L. Sayers' Encounter with Dante.*[41] Dorothy Sayers's first essay on Dante, discussing his enormous technical achievements as a storyteller, " . . . And Telling You a Story," led off *Essays Presented to Charles Williams*, originally planned by C. S. Lewis as a festschrift but turned into a memorial volume after Williams's unexpected death 15 May 1945. The title of her contribution emphasizes what mattered most to Dorothy Sayers: Dante's phenomenal ability to create an entire universe of living, breathing beings who typify the sins and virtues which inhabit every member of the human race, binding the universe together in the framework of the most exciting journey a Christian soul could possibly make, its progress toward salvation.

Rereading the *Comedy* was not enough. By Christmas of 1944, Dorothy Sayers had begun to translate it. As Ralph Hone has pointed out, everything she had done earlier had helped prepare her: her knowledge of Latin, which enabled her to learn medieval Italian in only a few weeks; her devotion to the Middle Ages and her command of several genres of literature; her voluminous reading and her knowledge of theology.[42] In March of the next year, Dorothy's friend Muriel St. Clare Byrne told E. V. Rieu, who had published *The Mind of the Maker*, that Dorothy was translating the *Inferno*; Rieu was now the editor of Penguin Classics, and he badly wanted a new English Dante. After seeing a sample of her work, he offered Dorothy Sayers a contract on 8 April 1945, requesting the *Inferno* by 1 January 1946, *Purgatory* a year later, and *Paradise* on 1 January 1948.[43] The Sayers translation of the *Inferno* did not appear until 1949, *Purgatory* in 1955, and *Paradise*, completed by Barbara Reynolds after Dorothy Sayers's death, in 1962; but in early 1945 Dorothy Sayers's last great literary journey was on its way. She dedicated her work to Charles Williams, "The Dead Master of the Affirmations."

Because the smaller projects Dorothy Sayers worked on while she was translating the *Inferno* during the last year of World War II all relate to the problem of evil, they shed important light on the thinking that underlay her version of the *Divine Comedy*. Her context involved Williams's theory of the affirmation of images, a step toward the "in-Godding" of man, and romantic love as one mode of that process.[44] Sayers's "The Terrible Ode," an important essay not published until 1965, eight years after her death, probably dates from 1944.[45] It reveals both her skill at demolishing a critic who had not done his homework and a side of her intimate personal life that otherwise might only be guessed at. An Italian scholar, Giovanni Papini, had claimed that Dante had demonstrated pathological sexual cruelty in two works, the ode "*Aspro parlar*," part of the *Pietra* group that Dante wrote before the *Convivio* and presumably addressed to "the Lady at the Window" (not Beatrice),[46] and in Canto XXXII of the *Inferno*. Dorothy Sayers agreed that the "*Aspro parlar*" deals with physical passion, but she proved through close reading and irrefutable reference to the medieval literary mode of courtly love that the poem describes a healthy, if vigorous, attitude toward sex: the poet suffers because the girl he loves rejects him, and he shows what pleasure he might bring her if only she would accept his entreaties.[47]

Dorothy Sayers used the latter point as her springboard for a brief, pungent explanation of "bedworthiness," the theory behind her portrayal of the sexual attraction between Lord Peter and Harriet which had so inflamed Mrs. Leavis – that both men and women have the right to sexual satisfaction; that the man should know it is his duty to provide it for them both; and that he should have no doubt, given a willing partner, of his ability to do so.[48] Brabazon judiciously observes that this passage demonstrates Dorothy Sayers's entirely heterosexual preference, putting to rest any questions her utilitarian business costume might have raised for those who tend to judge such matters on externals.[49]

At the end of her essay "The Terrible Ode," Dorothy Sayers also insisted that each earthly relation, not just the sexual one, offers the possibilities for both good and evil; the result each person experiences for eternity depends on which direction the human will selects.[50] That overwhelming choice, and the unsettling fact that the necessity of making it generally arrives when one least expects it, is the subject of "The Faust Legend and the Idea of the Devil," a lecture she gave 22 February 1945 to the English Goethe Society.

Dorothy Sayers's basic position regarding the father of lies had not changed since *The Devil to Pay*, but here she examines the concepts of evil shown by previous writers – Marlowe, Milton, Goethe, and (with humility) herself, stressing how the handling of Faust's human choice illustrates the spirit of each author's times; the war put an end to performances of her play, she noted wryly, because Britons had ignored the possibility that Germany might deliberately choose to pursue evil.[51] She went a step further, however, and closed upon Dante's horrifying view of the devil as "idiot and slobbering horror"[52] – universal evil as it really is in all times and at all places, stripped of the superficial glamour that incites mankind to sin.

In May 1944 as the war drew to its close, Dorothy Sayers approached the question of evil from the standpoint of redemption in a play commissioned for Lichfield Cathedral's 750th anniversary in 1946. She had been thinking about the problems of justice, forgiveness, and the suffering of the innocent, but not until she read an important but difficult passage in Dante's *Paradiso* did she come to her theme, stated in the title *The Just Vengeance*. In Dante's work, Christ, as man, suffered an entirely just punishment for man's sins; but as God, his agony was as completely unjust. Dorothy Sayers, with some knowledge at first hand of suffering, added the Pauline element, that Christians in His image must willingly share in His suffering to share in His Redemption,[53] an act of atonement for sin. Under the influence of her passion for Dante as Williams had brought her to him, she claimed this play was her finest achievement. Some commentators disagree, believing exactly the contrary – that *The Just Vengeance* is Sayers's weakest work. Brabazon, who has considerable experience with the theater as an actor, playwright, and producer, believes that her attempt to graft Charles Williams's mystical theories onto dramatic technique, merging the supernatural with the realistic world, was impossible to present successfully on the stage.[54] In her much more extensive discussion of *The Just Vengeance*, however, Barbara Reynolds observes that those involved with the actual production (Brabazon did not see it staged) indicated that the play perfectly suited its times. The actor who played Christ in this play, Raf de la Torre, is said to have believed that the play had changed his life.[55]

The protagonist of *The Just Vengeance* is a fatally wounded R. A. F. pilot encountering a series of Biblical and modern personages moments before he meets his Maker. Dorothy Sayers seems to have intended to demonstrate two involved theological concepts, the act of Atonement from God's point of view and Williams's notion of "coinherence," in which suffering has a positive redemptive function when it is shared or willingly taken on by another. She also incorporated many allusions to Dante's work into the dialogue, which some readers feel makes *The Just Vengeance* difficult to follow and to absorb. It was Dorothy Sayers's first attempt at presenting to her contemporary public Dante's theological concept that man chooses his own destiny; her audience at Lichfield numbered over 10,000, and Barbara Reynolds records that long afterwards Sayers told her that it was her best work.[56]

Once the war was over, Britain could begin to return to some degree of normalcy. Dorothy Sayers went to Lichfield in May 1946 to produce *The Just Vengeance*, and that August at the invitation of the Chairman of the Society for Italian Studies, Dr. George Purkis, head of Modern Languages at the Colchester Royal Grammar School,[57] she began the association with the Summer School of the Society of Italian Studies, Cambridge, which lasted until her death.[58] Dr. Barbara Reynolds, a scholar of Italian letters who was at that time the group's honorary secretary, became Dorothy Sayers's close friend. Dorothy Sayers's first lecture for the Summer School was "The Eighth Bolgia,"[59] a discussion of Canto XXVI, which from a literary point of view Dorothy Sayers considered the finest section of the *Inferno*. Actually, the eighth Bolgia is two-thirds down the penultimate circle of the Inferno, where "the Sins of the Wolf" are punished. Like

Shakespeare after him, Dante knew his audience would need a respite from horror so that what followed might be the more intense, and so he inserted the story of the last voyage of the wily Greek hero Ulysses among the "Councilors of Fraud." Dante relates how Ulysses, after wandering the Mediterranean following the Trojan War, had passed into the Southern Hemisphere and glimpsed the Mountain of Purgatory, but he could never reach it. In Dante's Christian context, Ulysses condemned himself by conquering Troy by deceit rather than by honorable feats of arms, and as an old man he perished for foolishly choosing to wander instead of attending to his duties at Ithaca. How different Dante's view is, Dorothy Sayers could not resist observing, from Tennyson's Victorian exaltation of Ulysses as modern progress at any cost.[60]

Although Dorothy Sayers consistently championed Dante's traditional Christian values, in her 1946 address to the Aquinas Society, "The Divine Poet and the Angelic Doctor,"[61] she set forth her strong belief in the synthesis of ideas as a condition for intellectual and spiritual growth. Dante had begun his studies of Aquinas's philosophy just after Beatrice's death at the end of the thirteenth century, a time, Dorothy Sayers noted, when the Church considered Aquinas a dangerous "modern" who was integrating a pagan philosophical system into Christian dogma. She stated the problem in Williams's terms. The Church, she said, had to choose either the Way of Negation, denying the worth of pagan explorations of natural reason – the thinking of Plato, Aristotle, Virgil, to name only a few great minds of Classicism – or the Way of Affirmation, a reconciliation of pagan and Christian thought enabling Dante to develop his rock-solid structure of the three realms the soul faced after death. Over and over, Dorothy Sayers stressed that God condemns no one to hell; the sinner chooses it for himself. In Dante's poem, God sends human reason in the person of Virgil to guide the soul through the infernal regions, but at the City of Dis, the point of demarcation between upper and lower hell, which respectively punish sins of incontinence and sins of violence and fraud, the soul that is accomplished only by rational humanism cannot pass. God-sent Grace must help it make the choice to go on and face itself, just as it needs God's help to scale the Mountain of Purgatory.

Dorothy Sayers underscored Dante's concept of the crucial point at which Grace must help the soul in its descent through its own hidden depths in her essay "The City of Dis,"[62] where she revealed that while working on the notes for her translation of the *Inferno*, several pieces of a gigantic puzzle had suddenly fallen into place: the entire landscape of hell, she saw, was real and contemporary, visible "by looking into one's self."[63] Moreover, the City of Dis was the infernal image of corrupted human cities, the evil inversion of the City of God that stretches throughout eternity,[64] fiendishly easy to enter – all one has to do is lose the good of the human intellect. She concluded that viewing the City of Dis made a vital comment on present society. When Britain and Europe, aided by the United States, were beginning to reconstruct their bombed-out cities, Sayers insisted that spiritual renewal depended on learning from the mistakes of the past: "the road to restoration and the Earthly Paradise lies . . . through the understanding of Hell."[65]

Dorothy Sayers believed that Dante's unparalleled "understanding of Hell" arose from his powerful faculty of engaging the imagination through visual imagery. In two of her most vivid lectures, "Dante's Imagery: I. Symbolic" and "II. Pictorial," delivered at the 1947 Summer School for Italian Studies, she closely explored the imagery of the *Divine Comedy*, in the process debunking popular critics who ferret out sexual innuendo from every concave or convex surface. She followed Williams in insisting that Dante uses the openly sexual symbol to indicate an element greater than itself in which the sexual meaning still exists.[66] She also found Dante an "exceptionally normal" man, without the urge to glorify or debase the sexual relation itself or women as a group.[67] So far no Inkling reaction to her position has come to light.

The next summer in "The Meaning of Heaven and Hell" Dorothy Sayers again treated the overall plan of the *Divine Comedy* by showing how the significance of the two opposing realms as understood by Christians of Dante's time was exhibited through his intensely visual imagery.[68] Dante constantly enjoins his readers to "look!" and in this essay, as in all of her work, Dorothy Sayers practiced exactly what she said thorough scholarship and solid teaching ought to do: helping sincere people to see things they might otherwise miss and equipping them thus to think for themselves. She got down to educational specifics on how to accomplish this in "The Lost Tools of Learning" (1947), a proposal for a system of education for nine- to sixteen-year-olds based on the medieval trivium, the study of grammar, dialectic, and rhetoric. While her solution might seem utopian – the thought of graduates of today's teacher-training institutions coping with, to say nothing of teaching elementary logic stuns the imagination – Dorothy Sayers's basic position remains valid: that while so-called literacy rates have risen, people's understanding of what they read, speak, and write has plummeted, leaving them prey to deceptions of language like propaganda, false advertising, and illogical news reporting, pitifully unable to separate fact from fiction or to approach new areas with the confidence and equipment needed to learn them.

The *Hell* that Dorothy Sayers completed in May 1948 agrees with her assessment of the inadequacies of modern education, and it seems even more useful in the late 1980s than it was a generation ago. She bluntly stated in her introduction that "no translation could ever be Dante,"[69] but she intended to make his work accessible to as many readers as she could. She followed Maurice Hewlitt's advice of "*terza rima* or nothing"[70] and used Dante's interlocking verse pattern, where the first line of a group of three lines rhymes with the third, the second with the first and third lines of the next group of three, and so on, a formidable task in English because of the language's relative lack of rhyming words, as compared to the Italian. Dorothy Sayers felt that using this rhyme scheme produced speed, rhythms, and force similar enough to the original to justify the difficulty, and she concentrated on it so intensely that Brabazon says her thoughts started to take shape in *terza rima*.[71] She threw dialect, colloquialisms, almost the entire range of English, into her work, and she kept Dante's humor and humility uppermost. When his writing was at its most sublime, though, she humbly declared that the translator had better give up any attempt to equal a poet of Dante's stature.[72]

Sayers' equipped her *Hell* with indispensible adjuncts: appendices treating Dante's Ptolemaic universe, a chronology of events, a discussion of the earthquake which accompanied Christ's death on the Cross; a glossary of proper names, a list of helpful second-ary reading, brief portraits of "the Greater Images" of the work, and illustrative diagrams drawn by Dorothy Sayers's old friend C. W. Scott-Giles, who had designed the Wimsey Coat of Arms. Best of all, she knew when to quit, refusing to overwhelm her readers with the staggering amount of research that encrusts modern Dante studies. Her crystalline introduction surveys European medieval history and the personal circumstances which Dante transformed into his poetry, in the perspective of her profound conviction that the *Divine Comedy* had a special perti-nence to the survivors of World War II, when the thirst for power had unleashed vast new incarnations of the problem of evil.

During the four years that Dorothy Sayers toiled through *Hell*, great changes had come over Britain and the world. Three hundred and fifty thousand British servicemen and women, 60,000 civilians, and 30,000 merchant seamen had died in World War II.[73] The West's great symbol of defiance against totali-tarianism, Winston Churchill, was voted resoundingly from office, victim of a tidal wave of resentment against the Conserva-tive Party for causing both prewar unemployment and the war itself. In his 1946 "Iron Curtain" speech, Churchill warned the world about the growing Soviet menace to democracy, but Bri-tain chose to look inward, toward improvements in living condi-tions for all its citizens, an attitude typified in the 1941 movie *Dawn Patrol*, when one Home Guardsman told his friend, "We found out in this war how we're all neighbours, and we aren't going to forget it when it's all over."[74] British social reforms had already started with the Education Act of 1944, the British Arts Council, and the National Health Service, which was inaugur-ated in 1946. In 1947, the year that India gained its indepen-dence, the nationalization of Britain's basic industries began, first coal and soon iron and steel, oil, gas and electricity, trans-portation, and telecommunications.[75] Dorothy Sayers's Britain was turning into what her old friend Dr. William Temple, Arch-bishop of Canterbury, called "the welfare state."[76]

Dorothy Sayers's home life became more exhausting when her husband's blood pressure, a condition at that time virtually untreatable, flared up in the spring of 1945. Since their prewar holidays in Scotland, Mac had been depressed and had seldom

185

gotten farther from their house at Witham than the local pubs. Despite the problems his drinking caused, Dorothy Sayers was genuinely attached to him, and watching his emotional and physical deterioration must have been hard for her to bear. In 1946, when Anthony applied for a passport and accidentally discovered that Dorothy Sayers was his real mother, the already uncomfortable situation may well have become more trying. Dorothy Sayers used a painful domestic conflict as an example in her essay "The Meaning of Heaven and Hell": a sick husband is consumed by jealousy, and his wife's outside interests cause him to accuse her of infidelity. Her attempts to cater to him only end in complaints that she is forcing him to feel guilty over her martyrdom, and although he may feel twinges of remorse, he takes a lethal pride in his horrendous disposition. In short, "he is not genuinely sorry; he only enjoys making a scene."[77] Such a scene might have ensued when Dorothy had to turn down a prized invitation to a Royal Garden Party in July 1947 because of Mac's condition, an example of the kind of stress she was under at Witham in those days.

Mac was in and out of hospital with a variety of ailments between 1947 and his death from a stroke in 1950, and Dorothy Sayers cherished her outside contacts as an outlet from domestic pressures. Besides juggling her many literary projects, from *The Divine Comedy* to the privately printed translation of Dante's *Pietra* poems she gave her friends at Christmas 1946, she also led in revitalizing the Detection Club. She had a succession of secretaries to help keep up with her enormous correspondence, and she even made a brief sortie into anti-Liberal politics in 1947. She was working on "Where Do We Go from Here?" a production for the BBC *Mystery Playhouse* series in early 1948,[78] and that year she also undertook a German translation of *The Man Born to Be King*. The next spring she plunged with typical verve into a revival of *The Zeal of Thy House*. The Bishop of Colchester approached her in June 1949 to write his Cathedral's 1951 Festival play, and while all of this was going on, she was crusading courageously against the debasement of the English language.

Since the outbreak of World War II, Dorothy Sayers had also been involved with St. Anne's House, an experiment in bringing Anglo-Catholicism to "thinking pagans" in downtown London.[79]

St. Anne's Church had been blown up in 1942, but its clergy house became the center for missionary activities run by two Anglican priests, Fr. Gilbert Shaw and Fr. Patrick McLaughlin.[80] Dorothy Sayers had been corresponding with McLaughlin since the Malvern Conference of 1941, and she took part in the initial series of lectures at St. Anne's, 1943, on "Christian Faith and Contemporary Culture," in the company of T. S. Eliot, Dr. James Welch, a veteran of the BBC's production of *The Man Born to be King*, and Lady Rhondda, Dorothy's fellow Somervillian. James Brabazon made Dorothy Sayers's acquaintance during those lectures and claims the contact changed the course of his life.[81] Her work at St. Anne's may not have changed her overall direction which remained committed to conservative Anglo-Catholicism and to Dante, but it surely complicated Dorothy Sayers's day-to-day existence; she became a member of St. Anne's Advisory Council in 1944 and its Chairman not long afterwards. Merely keeping the organization afloat meant a struggle for the rest of her life.

Well into her fifties, Dorothy Sayers refused to rest on her considerable laurels. Her intense pace demonstrated in concrete productivity her spiritual dedication to a strong work ethic as a positive Christian good, not the necessary evil most of the human race resents it for being. She accurately predicted that victory in the Second World War would mean a "confused, exhausted and impoverished world," but far from advocating a hopelessly ideal-istic abandonment of the technology which seemed to have wrought such havoc, she firmly defended making friends with this mammon of potential wickedness in order to bring it into har-mony with mankind's God-given nature.[82]

Equating the spiritual concept of hell to World War II would be an inexcusable oversimplification, one Dorothy Sayers would never have made, but the mindless devastation of bombing raids and the unspeakable outrage of the Holocaust seem to manifest the willful choice of evil which condemns men to the inferno. As she worked on *Purgatory* between 1948 and 1954, Dorothy Sayers also felt that the postwar world held the potential of positive spiritual benefits that could be realized by regenerating society and individuals alike through the Christian sense of work. The New Testament story of Mary and Martha had intrigued her for a long time. The compulsive housewife Martha is too busy to sit at Jesus's feet and listen to His teaching, but her sister Mary is attentive, and He praises her: a lesson in the advantages of religious contemplation over worldly distractions. The heroine of "Cat o'Mary," Dorothy Sayers's 1934 fictionalized autobiography, was caught up as self-centeredly as a cat in the life of the intellect, but after her personal crisis that year, Sayers seems to have developed a deeper satisfaction in her work, just as Harriet Vane achieved a new level of craftsmanship after she and Peter had purified themselves of their destructive pride through the three hundred-odd pages of *Gaudy Night*. Martha's active witness of faith was more suited to Dorothy Sayers's personality and type of creativity than Mary's contemplation, a Way of Negation shutting out the world's distractions. In her work, Dorothy Sayers had confirmed her belief in the affirmative necessity for Christ's Incarnation many times, and it had been strengthened by her wholehearted acceptance of Charles Williams's positive Way of Affirmation and Dante's exemplification of it in the *Divine Comedy*, particularly the realm of purgatory, where with the help of God souls must work out their own salvation.

If modern people, even Catholics, consider purgatory at all, most think of it as a finite version of hell, full of pitchforks and torment, lasting until relatives or paid clerics secure the departed's release through "indulgences," the practice that helped provoke Protestantism into being. This gloomy prospect is nothing like the airy, serene, and above all transitory realm Dante drew from the Greek religious tradition, still current in Italy in his time, which emphasized the constructive, rather than the retributive, aspect of the soul's purification. In her 1948 Summer School lecture, "The Meaning of Purgatory," Dorothy Sayers claimed *Purgatory* was the least often read and quoted section of the *Divine Comedy*, yet the most beloved to those who did know it; after tracing the doctrine of purgation, she stressed that the indulgence theory of good works, so prone to human abuses, emerged well after Dante's time.[83] The souls he shows in purgatory are overjoyed at being there, not just because they are escaping the pains of hell but because they are eager to join their suffering to Christ's and achieve salvation. This is work that affirms, work with the most profound meaning possible, compared to the ceaseless, useless activity that to Dorothy Sayers was one of the chief torments of hell. One of the recurrent themes of her many essays on Dante is that the individual gets in the next life exactly what he has chosen here on earth, and the souls in purgatory instinctively know when they are cleansed of each sin that bars them from God. They proceed upward by stages on the Mountain of Purgation until they reach its summit, the Earthly Paradise, exactly the point where mankind began.[84]

Dorothy Sayers also incorporated many observations about postwar culture into the lectures and essays she produced while she was translating *Purgatory*. In "Dante's Virgil" (also 1948),[85] she commented that Western civilization seemed to be holding on desperately to human wisdom, which Dante represents in Virgil, the best that man can do for himself, helpless at the gates of the horrific City of Dis, waiting for God's messenger to clear the way to self-knowledge. Virgil – liberal humanism – like Neville Chamberlain cannot cope with minds that have irrationally chosen wickedness. As Virgil and Dante approach the final circle of purgatory, Statius, representing Christian humanism, joins them, and man, now accompanied by both his human and God-assisted capabilities, awaits Beatrice, the vehicle of God's glory.

After the war liberal British humanists were trying to improve the lot of average citizens, but the dreary postwar austerity program necessary to deal with the costs of war initially caused strains in everyday living. Some help was on the horizon; the U.S. Marshall Plan, begun in 1948, was pouring $17 billion worth of aid into Europe; and Britain started to ease controls on food and raw materials, to begin a vast program of socialized medicine, and to issue British passports to all Commonwealth citizens. The Labour government also instituted tough wage restraints and the next year devalued the pound by 30.5 percent. All of these measures failed to control inflation or make widespread improvements in Britain's economic climate, a spreading malaise that even polluted popular taste and church attendance. "Chain store modernism, all veneer and varnish stain, [was] . . . replacing the old mahogany; multi-coloured plastic and chrome biscuit barrels and bird-cages [came] . . . in." Thirty percent of the population went to the cinema at least once a week, but only

12 percent attended Sunday services.[86] Conservative thinkers like T. S. Eliot and Dorothy Sayers saw these changes as futile as Virgil's attempts to pass the City of Dis by himself, because they lacked God's grace as well as the God-given sense of what is beautiful.

Her sense of humor helped Dorothy Sayers face it all, much as Dante had confronted grave reverses in his fortunes. In "The Comedy of the *Comedy*" (1949), she discussed Dante's two kinds of comic expression with keen perception. She saw the entire *Divine Comedy* as pervaded by a subtle and gentle self-deprecation, as though Dante was smiling indulgently at all men and most of all himself among them, beings from whom so little could be expected. However, she also observed the ferocious gusts of satire that Dante unleashed in his Hell, raging at the bitterest might-have-beens of all, the lost of mankind's noble potential.[87] This essay includes passages from her letters to Williams, some of Sayers's liveliest writing, a perfect antidote to the unfortunate general opinion, growing more prevalent with the decay of educational standards, that the *Divine Comedy* is unreadable, in Dorothy Sayers's words, full of "awful Sublimity and unmitigated Grimth."[88]

Nineteen fifty brought Dorothy Sayers some bleak days as well as some good ones. Her reputation as a serious theological writer had burgeoned, and in the spring she sat for a portrait by Sir William Hurchison that later hung in the Glasgow Royal Institute of Fine Arts. On 24 May she went to Durham to receive her first and only honorary Doctorate of Letters, a well-earned satisfaction that must have helped her over Mac's death on 9 June. The breach between Mac and his brother Edgar that had begun when he married Dorothy was healed shortly before his death, when Ann, Mac's daughter from his first marriage, engineered their reunion. All human disputes have at least two sides, but contrary to accounts from Mac's children, Dorothy Sayers seems to have tried to ease the tension. According to Brabazon, Edgar told his niece shortly after Mac's death that the "voluntary allowance" Dorothy had been paying to Mac's first wife for almost twenty-five years would continue, information that Ann Fleming chose not to include in biographical statements about her father.[89] Dorothy Sayers gave Mac the best tribute she could,

190

too; Mac after all had dabbled at painting, photography, and writing, and he had known what was beautiful when he saw it. Ralph Hone notes that only Dorothy Sayers could have placed the word "artist" for Mac's occupation on his death certificate;[90] in spite of the strains of their life together, it was a generous and handsome gesture.

Mac was cremated at Ipswich, and a friend saw to scattering his ashes in the Scottish town of his ancestors. Dorothy Sayers took up her busy life again; she lectured on Dante at the Summer School in August, and shortly afterwards took her first holiday since the war, driving to Stratford to see some Shakespearean plays with Muriel St. Clare Byrne. A few months later she had another death to face; when Ivy Shrimpton died in February 1951, Dorothy Sayers asked her son Anthony, twenty-seven and recently established in a London investment firm, to take care of Ivy's modest estate, bequeathed to Dorothy, who immediately turned it over to Anthony.[91] At that time she was deep in production plans for a new play, *The Emperor Constantine*, to be performed at the Colchester Cathedral Festival. Even for Dorothy Sayers, this was an immensely ambitious project, and she had to lay *Purgatory* aside to devote herself to it, straining everyone's endurance – the cast's and the crew's, the audience's, and eventually her own in the process.

The Emperor Constantine is Dorothy Sayers's last and longest play, performed 3 to 14 July 1951. She loved amateur theater and she was blessed with both experience and plenty of enthusiasm, but James Brabazon, familiar with stagecraft, categorically states that this play would have pressured even a well-funded professional company; it requires twenty-five scene changes, more than ninety actors in period costume, and close to four hours of playing time.[92] Its subtitle, "A Chronicle,"[93] underscores the thirty-year reign of Constantine the Great as a watershed in religious history, including the adoption of the religion by the Roman Empire and the Council of Nicaea in A.D. 325 which once and for all determined the doctrine of the Trinity that Christians must accept. Dorothy Sayers linked the play to Colchester through Constantine's mother Helena, reputed to have located the True Cross in Jerusalem. According to one tradition, Helena was the daughter of the old British chieftain Coel of

Colchester, whose "fiddlers three" Sayers managed to include convincingly in Act I. After the disappointing reception of *The Just Vengeance*, she brought the characters of *The Emperor Constantine* to life with the strong story line and the colloquial dialogue which she had used so successfully in *The Man Born to Be King*.

The highlight of *The Emperor Constantine* is its council scene, facing off Arius, the heretic bishop who backed the concept that the Father preceded the Son, denying Christ's equality in the Trinity, against Athanasius, who argued that the Son's begetting was "of eternity," thus making Christ "of one substance with the Father." Dorothy Sayers used this section as the core of *Christ's Emperor*, a shortened form of *The Emperor Constantine*, which she herself directed on 5 to 26 February 1952 at St. Thomas's Church in Regent Street, London.[94] Both plays reiterate important elements of her traditional Christian stance which appear strongly in her translation of the *Divine Comedy* and in her essays on Dante: the excruciating difficulty one faces in being saved by someone whom one has injured; and the impossibility of undoing evil, which can only be purged and redeemed.[95]

The watchword of purgatory, she wrote in her 1950 essay "The Cornice of Sloth," is "make haste! Work while the daylight lasts!"[96] Having attended – and then some – to her Colchester commitment, Dorothy Sayers returned to the *Purgatory* translation, interspersing the work with more Dante lectures and a raft of smaller projects. She tried out a story, untitled and unpublished, in which a modern British officer is inexplicably blasted back to the fourteenth century and meets Dante. Barbara Reynolds finds the officer is a "thinly veiled persona of Dorothy Sayers herself."[97] In 1951, Dorothy Sayers created another encounter between Dante and a contemporary figure for her lecture "Dante's Cosmos," given for the Royal Institution. According to Dr. Reynolds, Dante had become as familiar to Dorothy Sayers as an intimate friend.[98] She also attempted two fictionalized treatments of Dante's relationship with his daughter Bice (Beatrice), a BBC play, and an unfinished novel that Dr. Reynolds feels is Dorothy Sayers's closest attempt at conveying "the Beatrician vision," a mystical experience in which the world is momentarily transfigured by the presence of one's beloved. Dante, the father Bice adores, becomes for her the inspiration that Beatrice

Portinari was for him, an earthly reflection of the glory that will be revealed to saved souls in heaven.[99]

In less exalted moments, Dorothy Sayers also spearheaded *No Flowers by Request*, a new collective novel to support the Detection Club (she contributed its first episode), and she produced a charming 1953 Advent calendar for children, "The Days of Christ's Coming," that proved so successful she did two more: "The Story of Adam and Christ" for Easter 1954 and "The Story of Noah's Ark" for the next Christmas. Two others, "The Story of Easter" and "The Enchanted Garden," were never published.[100] Her gift for mock-scholarly satire was alive and could deliver a swifter kick than ever; her outrageously funny "Pantheon Papers" appeared in *Punch* from 2 November 1953 to 20 January 1954,[101] slashing away in her best rambunctious style at godlessness and hypocrisy and at those who wanted to stifle religion with "unmitigated Grimth": St. Lukewarm, for example, the patron of railroad caterers, found his martyrdom among the cannibals, but even after prolonged stewing he proved too stringy and juiceless for consumption.[102]

All of this was fun and Dorothy Sayers had earned it, but just as she was settling into the last stages of her work on *Purgatory*, she suffered two jolts to her religious sensibilities. Early in 1954, Kathleen Nott, a vociferous proponent of the scientific method, published *The Emperor's Clothes*,[103] a ferocious denunciation of orthodox religious writers like T. S. Eliot, C. S. Lewis, Graham Greene, and perhaps most of all Dorothy Sayers, for what Nott described as gullibility in believing and defending what they had not seen. A knight of the Middle Ages would not consider jousting with someone not his equal, and for some time Dorothy Sayers and her friends refused to pick up the scruffy gauntlet Nott had thrown down. Brabazon, however, chronicles another attack, sparked by Nott's, that Dorothy Sayers had to take more seriously because it was more personal and better founded. John Wren-Lewis, an associate of Dorothy Sayers's at St. Anne's, read the Nott book and on Maundy Thursday 1954 in the vestry of St. Anne's, he accused Dorothy Sayers and the others of caring only for the dogma of Christianity – the law, rather than its spirit – and of offering nothing but the Creed – all that Dorothy Sayers herself had ever found necessary for belief – to those "thinking pagans" to whom St. Anne's was supposed to minister. The next day, Good Friday, Dorothy Sayers replied to Wren-Lewis at length, and a substantial correspondence ensued. Her side of it has mostly disappeared,[104] although Brabazon provides a condensed version of her Good Friday letter, concluding that in it she acknowledged her inability to experience any "inner light" or spiritual rebirth and her realization that her intellectual approach to her religion was outdated.[105] A much more thorough discussion of the matter appears in E. L. Mascall's article, "What Happened to Dorothy L. Sayers That Good Friday?" Mascall bases his interpretation upon his memories of the matter and his reading of the entire Good Friday letter, which Anthony Fleming allowed Mascall to see. Mascall believes that rather than losing confidence in the Creeds, Dorothy Sayers emerged by 18 June 1954 entirely unshaken in her faith.[106] St. Anne's organized a debate between Kathleen Nott on one side and Dorothy Sayers and C. S. Lewis on the other, but only Sayers showed up on 27 October 1954. She presented her views with her customary vigor, and the statement in which she systematically demolished the logic, the diction, and the syntax of Nott's attack was later published – with some comments of Nott's that seem very pale indeed by comparison.[107]

The *Purgatory* she completed the next September bears no traces of spiritual turmoil. The translation seems to flow even more smoothly than the *Inferno* had; the purifying atmosphere is warm, even tender, and the expository "sermons" which alternate with vivid, courteous actions strike no shoals of impenetrable theological language. Sayers's masterful introduction includes many of the cogent points she had raised in her earlier essays on purgatory, and again she supplies exactly what the reader needs to understand the book and, blessedly, no more. The principle of order in purgatory, she had already said, was a return to the good things God had provided in the Garden of Eden, but she also knew that that Paradise was only earthly; six of the heavens of *Paradise* would be inhabited by those souls devoted to the active life, and the seventh and last by the contemplatives.[108]

By the time *Purgatory* was ready for the publishers, Dorothy Sayers had been working on Dante for ten years. The effort she had put into *Hell* and *Purgatory* had banked, though hardly dampened, her initial rapture over Dante, and she felt she needed a change of pace before starting *Paradise*, which she thought would be "the toughest nut" of the *Divine Comedy*.[109] E. V. Rieu understood her position, and offered her a contract for a Penguin Classics translation of the eleventh-century French epic poem *La Chanson de Roland*, with which she had last worked at Somerville. Chivalry, one of her first loves, was still irresistible to her, and she spent the next two years on her *Song of Roland*, happily tracing out the rules of Carolingian battle and the equipage of war-horses and the glory of a lost cause in an epic form that itself was passing away, like the genuinely feudal system that was also beginning to disintegrate when the poem took written shape. In another of her admirable introductions, Dorothy Sayers made it clear beyond all question that she saw the essential conflict of the poem as a simple clash of Christian against heathen, good versus evil, in a society dominated by warfare – exactly the sort of straightforward battle she liked best.

In the mid-1950s, precious few issues could be defined so distinctly. Old certainties were giving way to new doubts; Britain's eclipse as a world power became apparent in the Suez Crisis of 1956; Soviet troops invaded Hungary, shocking the West by fulfilling Churchill's prophecy, while incomprehensible howls announced that angry young men now had to be reckoned as a part of Britain's national consciousness. In the face of all this Dorothy Sayers said she was too old to change.[110] Her *Introductory Papers on Dante*, seven essays dating from 1947 to the early 1950s, appeared in 1954 with a preface by Barbara Reynolds, who knew her friend admirably well: Miss Sayers, she wrote, did not "pull her punches."[111] Sayers's *Further Papers on Dante*, published in 1957, strongly confirmed that view.

Over eleven years Dorothy Sayers had grown very close to Barbara Reynolds and her family, and by the time that *Purgatory* was complete, she was enjoying overnight visits to their home at Cambridge, where she seems to have gotten along much better with Dr. Reynolds's children than her often-quoted public statements about not caring for youngsters would appear to indicate. Dorothy Sayers probably had protested too much; as a stout and dignified older lady not given to romping in the first place, she was decidedly not the cuddly grandmother type, and she most

195

likely preferred children to be seen and not heard, as they had done in her day, but her children's books show that she could communicate with children easily and well, being one of those rare and admirable people who refuse to condescend to them or put them in their places.

Barbara Reynolds chose to be baptized as an adult, and on 13 December 1957, a Friday, Dorothy Sayers went to Cambridge to be a witness (she preferred the Prayer Book term "godmother") at the ceremony, held appropriately at the little Round Templar Church of the Holy Sepulchre, a reminder of the Crusades, just across from where Barbara Reynolds and her family lived. She recalls that even though Dorothy Sayers was by that time a heavy woman, she knelt for a little while on the stone floor to pray.[112] Barbara Reynolds also feels that their symbolic relationship that day delighted Dorothy Sayers, because it allowed her to show the "immense friendliness" beneath her sometimes forbidding exterior[113] and to enjoy being a cherished member of a family for a little while again.[114] A sadder memory also stirred that afternoon; Ralph Hone has described how, while shopping with Dorothy Sayers, Barbara Reynolds happened to mention her children's teacher Mrs. Eric Whelpton. "The name came stabbing back across the years"[115] and Dorothy Sayers had to turn her face away.

The following Monday she went to London to shop for Christmas presents. She returned to Witham the next evening, turned on the lights, put her hat and coat on her bed, and fell dead at the foot of her stairs, victim of a massive heart attack brought on at least in part by heavy smoking, the good food she loved, and a largely sedentary life. Her secretary found her the next morning, and Muriel St. Clare Byrne, who was her literary executor, had to set about dealing with her estate, which according to Brabazon was worth about £35,000 then, and possibly four times that today.[116] There was also the shock of learning that Anthony was Dorothy Sayers's son, a secret that Muriel and Anthony restricted to Dorothy Sayers's closest friends until it was unearthed by Janet Hitchman in 1973.

Dorothy Sayers was cremated on 23 December 1957, and her ashes were laid to rest under the floor of St. Anne's Tower, where a plaque to her memory was later dedicated by the Dorothy L. Sayers Society: "The only Christian work is work well done."[117]

Six robed bishops attended her memorial service at St. Margaret's Church, next to Westminster Abbey, on 15 January 1958, and C. S. Lewis contributed the panegyric, in which he compared his friendship with Dorothy Sayers to "a bracing high wind," an apt description, as Alzina Stone Dale has noted, "of the coming of the Holy Ghost at Pentecost."[118]

Her sudden death left much of Dorothy Sayers's work undone. She had agreed to write an article for Val Gielgud on translating *The Song of Roland*, and she had been in the midst of another crisis at St. Anne's, from which Fr. Patrick McLaughlin had resigned early in 1957.[119] Barbara Reynolds believes that had she lived, Dorothy Sayers would have undertaken a book called "The Burning Bush," a reference to God's pact with mankind in the Old Testament; she would attempt to show how poets like Dante toss their creative messages alive and vibrant across the centuries.[120] A major problem, however, was presented at her death by Dorothy Sayers's unfinished translation of Dante's *Paradise*; only twenty cantos were completed, with no introductory material, notes or commentaries. At the request of Sayers's executors, Barbara Reynolds took it over, though she describes her initial reaction as "horrified."[121] Several others of Dorothy's friends pitched in to help where they could, and when it appeared in 1962, *Paradise* fulfilled Dorothy Sayers's bright promise of a *Divine Comedy* which not only scholars but ordinary thoughtful readers could savor. Her *Paradise* affirms God's plan for mankind as her lord and master Dante saw it, its goal a heaven all persons of faith could share if they but choose to, where humble redeemed souls revel in "the song, the shouting, the celestial dance . . . the laughter of the rejoicing universe."[122]

Notes

1. Martin Seymour-Smith, *The New Guide to Modern World Literature*, 3rd ed. (New York: Peter Bedrick Books, 1985), p. 211.
2. Humphrey Carpenter, *The Inklings*, First Ballantine Books ed.

(1978; rpt. New York: Ballantine Books, 1981), p. 179.

3. Ibid., p. 268. So far as can be ascertained, none of the Inklings had any homosexual leanings.

4. Ralph E. Hone, *Dorothy L. Sayers: A Literary Biography* (Kent, Ohio: Kent State University Press, 1979), p. 128. Lewis in fact borrowed the central analogy of, on the one side, God and His creation, and on the other, the writer and his book, from Sayers's *The Mind of the Maker* for Chapter 12 of Lewis's own book *Miracles*, 1947. Joe R. Christopher, *C. S. Lewis* (Boston: Twayne, 1987), p. 75.

5. Carpenter, pp. 25, 27.

6. James Brabazon, *Dorothy L. Sayers: A Biography* (New York: Charles Scribners' Sons, 1981), p. 235.

7. Carpenter, p. 25.

8. J. R. R. Tolkien, "On Fairy-Stories," in *The Tolkien Reader* (1964; rpt. New York: Ballantine Books, 1966), pp. 60, 88.

9. Carpenter, pp. 69–70.

10. Ibid., p. 209.

11. Barbara Reynolds, *The Passionate Intellect*, p. 175; This quotation is taken from R. J. Reilly's *Romantic Religion*, p. 152. Dr. Reynolds notes that Patrick McLaughlin disagrees with Reilly.

12. Barbara Reynolds, *The Passionate Intellect* (Kent, Ohio: Kent State University Press, 1989), pp. 16–17.

13. Carpenter, p. 83.

14. In a note, Dr. Reynolds explains that the late Patrick McLaughlin clarified an important point of Church history for her: that the two greatest exponents of the Affirmative Way who brought it to its fullest expression, Thomas Aquinas and Dante, each wrote "at a time when the Negative Way in fact became dominant" (*The Passionate Intellect*, pp. 254–55, note 6).

15. Carpenter, pp. 78–79.

16. Seymour-Smith, p. 238.

17. Carpenter, p. 86.

18. Ibid., p. 86.

19. Ibid., p. 90.

20. Ibid., p. 105.

21. Ibid., p. 108.

22. Ibid., p. 206.

23. Brabazon, pp. 160, 225.

24. Carpenter, p. 208.

25. Ibid.

26. Dorothy L. Sayers, " . . . And Telling You a Story," pp. 1–2, quoted in Hone, p. 146.

27. The Athanasian Creed (*Quicunque Vult*), quoted in Charles Williams, *The Figure of Beatrice* (1943; rpt. New York: Farrar, Straus & Cudahy, 1961), p. 9.

28. In her notes to *Purgatory*, Dorothy Sayers suggests that Statius did not see Beatrice herself in the Garden of Eden, only his own

private Godbearing image. See pp. 327–28 of Sayers's translation of *Purgatory*, cited in Joe R. Christopher, *C. S. Lewis*, p. 108.

29. Ibid., p. 14.
30. Ibid., pp. 7–8.
31. Dorothy L. Sayers, Letter to Prof. G. L. Bickerstith 12 June 1957, quoted in Brabazon, p. 225.
32. Dorothy L. Sayers, Letter to Charles Williams 14 August 1944, quoted in Brabazon, p. 227.
33. Dorothy L. Sayers, *Whose Body?* (1923; rpt. New York: Avon, 1961), pp. 10, 18, 66, 115, 145, 160, 170, 171. The crucial decision appears on p. 160. See also Chapter 5, above.
34. Dorothy L. Sayers, *The Unpleasantness at the Bellona Club* (1928; rpt. New York: Avon, 1963), pp. 142, 143, 157.
35. Dorothy L. Sayers, "Divine Comedy," in *Unpopular Opinions* (New York: Harcourt, Brace and Co., 1947), p. 19.
36. Dorothy L. Sayers, Introduction to *Further Papers on Dante* (London: Methuen, 1957), p. vii.
37. Dorothy L. Sayers, Letter to Charles Williams 26 September 1944. Also see Brabazon, p. 229.
38. Reynolds, p. 19.
39. Dorothy L. Sayers, " . . . And Telling You a Story," in *Essays Presented to Charles Williams* (Oxford: Oxford University Press, 1947), p. 1.
40. Sayers, " . . . And Telling You a Story," in *Further Papers on Dante*, pp. 3, 9.
41. Brabazon, p. 229.
42. Hone, p. 147.
43. Brabazon, p. 234.
44. Williams, *The Figure of Beatrice*, p. 16.
45. Dorothy L. Sayers, "The 'Terrible' Ode," *Nottingham Mediaeval Studies* 9 (1965), pp. 43–54. In footnote 1, p. 42, Sayers cites Papini's *Dante Vivo*, target of her attack, as published in Florence in 1933, and in the text of the same page she indicates that Papini's book had been published for more than ten years.
46. Dorothy L. Sayers's translations of the *Pietra* group appear in an appendix to *The Passionate Intellect*. Barbara Reynolds also discusses Sayers's reaction to Dante's "terrible" ode "*Così nel mio parlar . . .*" on pp. 39–40 of this book.
47. Sayers, "The 'Terrible' Ode," p. 50.
48. Ibid., p. 47.
49. Brabazon, p. 231.
50. Sayers, "The 'Terrible' Ode," p. 50.
51. Dorothy L. Sayers, "The Faust Legend and the Idea of the Devil," in *The Poetry of Search and the Poetry of Statement* (London: Victor Gollancz Ltd., 1963), p. 239.
52. Ibid., p. 240.
53. Reynolds, p. 87.

54. Brabazon, p. 237; also see Hone, pp. 161–62.
55. See Reynolds, *The Passionate Intellect*, p. 92 and p. 247, note 13. The comment from Raf de la Torre came to Dr. Reynolds through Norah Lambourne, set designer for *The Just Vengeance* and a friend and professional associate of Dorothy Sayers since *The Zeal of Thy House*.
56. Ibid., p. 97.
57. Ibid., p. 54.
58. Dorothy Sayers lectured in 1946 and 1947 in the Hall of Jesus College, Cambridge. A good description of this College and other Cambridge sites that are related to Dorothy Sayers and her work is found in "A Tour of Cambridge on Foot," a guide available from the Dorothy L. Sayers Society.
59. Dorothy L. Sayers, "The Eighth Bolgia," in *Further Papers on Dante*, pp. 102–18.
60. Ibid., p. 116.
61. Dorothy L. Sayers, "The Divine Poet and the Angelic Doctor," in *Further Papers on Dante*, pp. 38–52.
62. Dorothy L. Sayers, "The City of Dis," in *Introductory Papers on Dante* (New York: Harper and Co., 1954), pp. 127–50.
63. Ibid., p. 128.
64. Ibid., p. 131.
65. Ibid., p. 149.
66. Dorothy L. Sayers, "Dante's Imagery: I. Symbolic," in *Introductory Papers on Dante*, p. 18.
67. Dorothy L. Sayers, "Dante's Imagery: II. Pictoral," in *Introductory Papers on Dante*, p. 40.
68. Dorothy L. Sayers, "The Meaning of Heaven and Hell," in *Introductory Papers on Dante*, p. 46. Barbara Reynolds indicates that people who saw *The Just Vengeance* found its greatest impact to be visual (see p. 95).
69. Dorothy L. Sayers, Introduction to *The Comedy of Dante Alighieri the Florentine: Cantica I, Hell* (1949; New York: Penguin, 1984), p. 56.
70. Maurice Hewlitt, quoted in ibid., p. 55.
71. Brabazon, p. 234.
72. Introduction to *Hell*, p. 63.
73. Walter L. Arnstein, *Britain Yesterday and Today: 1830 to the Present*, 5th ed. (Lexington, Mass.: D.C. Heath and Co., 1988), p. 338.
74. Asa Briggs, *A Social History of England* (New York: Viking, 1983), p. 273.
75. Barry Supple, "The Economy: Adjustment, Affluence, Decline," in *The Cambridge Historical Encyclopedia of Great Britain and Ireland*, ed. Christopher Haigh (Cambridge: Cambridge University Press, 1985), p. 325.
76. Briggs, p. 282.
77. Dorothy L. Sayers, "The Meaning of Heaven and Hell," in *Introductory Papers on Dante*, p. 66.

78. Hone, p. 150. This play has never been published.
79. Brabazon, p. 240.
80. Father Patrick McLaughlin, Director of St. Anne's House from 1943 to 1958, died 16 July 1988 in London. See Sayers Society *Bulletin* #78, p. 1.
81. Brabazon, p. 241.
82. Dorothy L. Sayers, "Living to Work," in *Unpopular Opinions*, p. 155.
83. Dorothy L. Sayers, "The Meaning of Purgatory," in *Introductory Papers on Dante*, pp. 74, 84.
84. Ibid., p. 93.
85. Dorothy L. Sayers, "Dante's Virgil," in *Further Papers on Dante*, pp. 53–77.
86. Briggs, pp. 292–302.
87. Dorothy L. Sayers, "The Comedy of the *Comedy*," in *Introductory Papers on Dante*, p. 168.
88. Ibid., p. 151.
89. Letter from Edgar Fleming to Ann Fleming 13 June 1950, quoted in Brabazon, p. 253.
90. Hone, p. 171.
91. Brabazon, p. 255.
92. Ibid., p. 256.
93. Dorothy L. Sayers, *The Emperor Constantine: A Chronicle* (Grand Rapids, Michigan: William B. Eerdmans Publishing Co., 1976).
94. Robert B. Harmon and Margaret A. Burger, *An Annotated Guide to the Works of Dorothy L. Sayers* (New York: Garland, 1977), p. 128.
95. Sayers, *The Emperor Constantine*, pp. 182, 181.
96. Dorothy L. Sayers, "The Cornice of Sloth," in *Further Papers on Dante*, p. 119.
97. Reynolds, p. 182.
98. Ibid., p. 186.
99. Ibid., p. 206.
100. Hone, p. 178.
101. Dorothy L. Sayers, "The Pantheon Papers," *Punch* 225 (2 November 1953), pp. 16–19; 226 (6 January 1954), p. 60 and 13 January 1954, p. 84; and 226 (2 January 1954), p. 124.
102. Brabazon, p. 258.
103. Kathleen Nott, *The Emperor's Clothes* (London: Heinemann, 1954).
104. E. L. Mascall, "What Happened to Dorothy L. Sayers that Good Friday?," *Seven* 3, p. 9.
105. Brabazon, p. 264; for the entire discussion, see pp. 262–65.
106. Mascall, p. 18.
107. See *Seven* 3, pp. 35–44 for Dorothy L. Sayers's part of "A Debate Deferred," "Part I: The Dogma in the Manger: A Reply to Kathleen Nott." Nott's remarks follow as "Notes Towards a Reply."
108. Dorothy L. Sayers, "The Fourfold Interpretation of the *Comedy*," in *Introductory Papers on Dante*, pp. 116–17.
109. Dorothy L. Sayers, Letter to E. V. Rieu 24 August 1956, quoted in

Brabazon, p. 267.

110. Brabazon, p. 265.
111. Barbara Reynolds, Preface to *Introductory Papers on Dante*, p. ix.
112. Reynolds, p. 149.
113. Hone, p. 186.
114. Brabazon, p. 269.
115. Hone, p. 186.
116. Brabazon, p. 271. Item 10.33 of the Sayers Society Archives lists her estate at £34, 539, all left to her son Anthony Fleming (p. 32).
117. Inscription of memorial plaque presented by the Dorothy L. Sayers Society, quoted in Brabazon, p. 273.
118. Alzina Stone Dale, *Maker and Craftsman: The Story of Dorothy L. Sayers* (Grand Rapids, Mich.: William B. Eerdmans Publishing Co., 1978), p. 153.
119. Hone, p. 188; Brabazon, p. 267.
120. Reynolds, p. 178.
121. Ibid., p. 153.
122. Sayers, "The Comedy of the *Comedy*," p. 174.

9 The Sayers Solution

Dorothy L. Sayers's life and her achievements, like the great *Comedy* whose translation crowned them, fall into three stages – her youth, when she wrote her detective novels; her maturity, when she produced her overtly religious works; and her later years, when she translated Dante. In her major projects and the essays, speeches, and reviews that cluster about them, she responded to her biographical and historical milieu as an exceptionally gifted individual who happened to be a traditionally Christian Englishwoman living in the first half of the twentieth century. The sheer perversity that brings about so much human misery is generally dignified, though vaguely, as "the human condition," and most people simply endure its effects with gritted teeth or hangdog resignation. Dorothy Sayers, on the other hand, called it by a specific name – the mystery of wickedness – and resolutely set about solving each of its manifestations she encountered. As her perceptions of it widened, the successive spheres of her creative efforts to seek out its solution broadened throughout her life.

One of hell's worst torments, Dorothy Sayers believed, must be work that has no purpose. From her own experience, she understood how working to no end felt. In her youth she discovered that achieving the literary career that her talent and her training suited her for would have been far easier if she had been a young man. In the 1920s, few opportunities allowed a woman who wanted to be a serious author to show what she could do, and the first jobs she did get, like her brief attempts at teaching and her work in publishing at Blackwell's, failed to satisfy her thirst for intellectual challenge and the desire to express herself that just then was propelling her into poetry. Unschooled about men and sexuality as she and most young women of her class and time were, her emotions got in her way, too, betraying her first with Eric Whelpton, then with John Cournos, near-disastrously with "Bill," the father of her child, and finally into her marriage to Mac. Idealistically, she made the classic mistake of many women in love: she tried to change every one of them, and, shatteringly, she learned she couldn't.

Dorothy Sayers overcame heartbreak and made a living for herself and her family with a gallant, gritty determination to succeed. Today's successful crime-mystery-suspense novels differ from mainstream writing because they demand highly skilled plotting around convincingly motivated and disparate characters, expert knowledge of settings and unusual professions, and scrupulous familiarity with locale. In large measure Dorothy Sayers set those standards for the form, and she did so brilliantly. The theory of detective fiction with which she anchored her mystery stories arose from her disillusion with work that had no meaning and with its other face, love that had no worthwhile object. Rather than accepting the professional restrictions her society imposed on women and allowing herself to wallow in the slough of her despond over the wrong men, she met the riddles of her situation head on by creating solvable puzzles of her own. In creating Wimsey and his world, she could vicariously enjoy not just the physical comforts her poverty denied her – the elegant clothing, Bunter's sumptuous cooking, the ravishing Daimler – but the intellectual satisfactions that her society found virtually inconceivable for a woman to want – the rare edition of Dante, the time to perfect the performance of a Scarlatti sonata, and most of all, the inner delight at matching wits with an evil opponent worthy of one's best and overcoming him with nothing less rigourous than uncompromising truth, the core of her religious faith.

In her mystery novels of the 1920s, Dorothy Sayers had had to confront some of her most intimate enemies, like the bitter disillusionment with Whelpton that she worked off in *Clouds of Witness* and Mac's resentment of her growing popularity, which darkens *The Unpleasantness at the Bellona Club*. In the aftermath of Black Friday, however, Dorothy Sayers needed more than the early Lord Peter Wimsey could give. She could and did offer her public, starved for escape from their humdrum worries, one kind of security in a dismayingly changing world, a stunning variety of detective stories where intellect could win out and right could triumph, but she was learning that the wickedness Wimsey was battling was a good deal more complex than it might first have seemed.

Brian Garfield has argued that "the literature of crime and suspense can provoke images and questions of the most complex intellectual and emotional force; it can explore the most critical of ethical and behavioral dilemmas."[1] Since for Dorothy L. Sayers the chief such problem was man's sinful nature, the only solution she could find acceptable would have to be based on the Christian dogma she wholeheartedly upheld. The villains of her first novels are swollen with the intellectual pride that successfully tempts them to put themselves above the laws that order human behavior – both society's and God's. But for the grace of God Sayers herself, with her formidable mind, might have fallen victim to that failing, but in the mid-1930s she began to scrutinize herself deeply, first in her attempts at autobiography and then by bringing Harriet Vane to life, the creative artist to Peter's performing one. She achieved artistic equilibrium by creating a new form of detective fiction, more concerned with the riddles of human values than with the thrill of the chase. *The Nine Tailors* throws the pride he took in his brilliant detection back in Wimsey's own face, making him pay for it in body and in spirit. *Gaudy Night* purges the pride that kept Peter and Harriet apart, at the same time laying the issue of intellectual pride to rest; so far as Sayers is concerned in this novel, the climax of her career as a detective novelist, work can only have value so long as it is anchored in truth. For dramatic purposes she let Wimsey trap one last killer in *Busman's Honeymoon*, and during the harrowing eve of the murderer's execution, she made Peter face the real sinner every believing Christian must confront at the end – himself.[2]

In *The Nine Tailors* Lord Peter Wimsey and his creator put the bedeviling problem directly. Doing evil to bring about a good end may be one thing, but doing good so as to result in evil is quite different – Sayers's succinct and prophetic comment on the glowering international tension of the mid-1930s. Faced with the appalling devastation of World War I and righteously determined never to let it happen again, Britain and the United States allowed the French thirst for revenge on an old enemy to prevail in the Treaty of Versailles, imposing terms that Germany could not meet, and igniting the ruinous, worldwide financial crisis that eventually helped bring Adolf Hitler to power. In her wartime essays Dorothy Sayers laid the responsibility for the Second World War directly at the feet of persons like Neville Chamberlain, who tried so hard to be good that they unleashed unspeakable evils – at last resulting in the paradox of the atomic bomb, in Sayers's view an evil force which had to be wielded to end the war.

England's triumph in tragedy at Dunkirk and the "English war" of 1940–41, one tiny island ringed by Hitler's hosts, like the immortal doomed defenses at Thermopylae and Roncevaux, fired Dorothy Sayers's heart and her imagination. Even before Hitler marched into Poland, she had already begun her artistic answer to her nation's dilemma[3] by personalizing the widened scope of human pride which led to errors of judgment like the British position at Versailles in her 1937 Canterbury Cathedral play, *The Zeal of Thy House*, where God casts down the architect who presumes to put his own human talent above his Lord's. She subsequently spent most of World War II restating that theme in her sequence of religious dramas. In *The Devil to Pay*, her Faust is a modern-day reformer, hell-bent on saving mankind even if he has to surrender his soul, foreshadowing one of the most original characters in all her work, Judas in *The Man Born to Be King*, whose injured pride and jealous anger destroy his finest gift from God, the soaring potential of his intellect, which, abused and perverted, brought him to fall into Satan's very maw by betraying his Friend.

Dorothy Sayers's religious plays, especially *The Man Born to Be King*, are the artistic corollaries to the theories she pronounced over and over in her wartime essays, like *Begin Here*, which call on Britain to seize the chance to build a better world out of the ashes of the old. The most important theoretical work of her maturity, however, is unquestionably *The Mind of the Maker*, which insists that all individuals must take responsibility for learning the meaning of life and then turning the evil that surrounds them into good, through work that has a positive reason for being. No book reveals more of Dorothy Sayers's personality than *The Mind of the Maker* does; few books have more effectively brought the mystery of the Triune God into the grasp of human intellect; no book has more brilliantly linked the enigma of the artist's creativity to his Creator's. Born out of her country's battles and her own, *The*

Mind of the Maker confirms Dorothy Sayers as a consummate Christian artist of our times.

Sayers's detective stories arose as much from her response to the wickedness she encountered as a young woman as from her need to support herself, and her wartime plays and essays confirm her Christian stance, rather than revealing any change in her thinking about the steps she believed Britain and the West should take in the face of godless totalitarianism. When she turned so gladly to Dante in the last year of World War II, she was directly facing one of the world's noblest answers to the ultimate horror of the pit – mindless evil for evil's sake. Throughout her life, in spite of a largely unearned reputation for being difficult to get along with, Dorothy Sayers had been able and willing to collaborate on novels and plays, the very kind of artistic projects in which literary prima donnas are least able to endure sharing the spotlight. She never tolerated fools gladly, and indeed with the multitude of tasks that bombarded her – many more of them undertaken for others than some of her critics care to admit – she hardly had time to do so. Readiness to see another's point of view is paramount in translation, a field where she had already excelled, and she approached the *Divine Comedy* as though she were a performing artist, like Wimsey, interpreting the work of a creative genius to audiences who need help to appreciate its glories. Her reasons for maintaining Dante's demanding *terza rima* remain valid, but scholars have remarked that the limitations of the English language make for occasional discomfiting stretches in her rendition, especially in *Hell*, which perhaps because of its very nature reads less smoothly than her version of *Purgatory*. Anyone acquainted with her definitive introductions and notes, however, must acknowledge the generous presence of a master teacher in them, and nearly all of her readers find an irresistible energy in the translation itself, a compulsion to read on; Dorothy L. Sayers succeeded in bringing the *Divine Comedy* to more general readers than ever before.[4] At the close of her life, she devoted herself to putting her own talents in the service of an author she readily acknowledged as her superior and as a man she could at last love as a woman of her capabilities should. As vivid and as accurate as her translation of the *Divine Comedy* is, its chief accomplishment is to make its heroic message accessible to readers of good will: that the individual must confront the worst – his own sins – in hell, work them out of his soul in purgatory, and once cleansed, rise rejoicing to his God in Paradise.

Dorothy Sayers knew she had not received the gift that the religious mystic shares with a creative artist like Dante: that sudden flash of near-divine insight when life, kept separate by pieces of man's mystery of wickedness, fall together into marvelous shining wholeness. But she knew she did have the powerful gift of synthesis to fit them painstakingly together bit by bit, and when, with a dash of intuition, it worked – as at her best she could make it work – she fairly earned the right to feel "like God on the seventh day." She also could declare, near the end of her life, that the only way she could love her Lord and be saved was through her intellect: "This alone, Lord, in Thee and in me, have I never betrayed."[5]

Dorothy L. Sayers's translation of the *Divine Comedy*; *The Mind of the Maker*; *The Man Born to Be King* – these and fine moments in her other works speak for themselves of the quality of Dorothy Sayers's honorable craftsmanship. Beyond these, however, and in a class by themselves, the intense humanity of Peter Wimsey and Harriet Vane and all the good and wicked people around them remain most alive in the reader's imagination in the same manner as Dante's affirming images are summed up, according to Charles Williams, in the real Beatrice whom Dante loved. Perhaps readers love Dorothy Sayers's detective fiction best of all because in these works her solutions to the mystery of wickedness seem more approachable, less demanding of ourselves, than in her later works. Perhaps in the Wimsey novels we share what she loved first and best herself, even if not always wisely. Perhaps we have not yet grown into the solution as she always knew it, that the old creeds are right and that men and women must work desperately hard all their days to earn a glimpse of truth, sometimes even enduring and overcoming evil so that the good they want may come to pass: a better world, a happy life, a soul at peace.

On the fiftieth anniversary of her first religious drama and the thirtieth anniversary of her death, Canterbury Cathedral performed *The Zeal of Thy House* again, and the morning afterward the Cathedral's Dean, the Very Reverend John Simpson, offered a Service of Thanksgiving for her life and work:

> Not many in this century have made truth and excellence their pursuit. We are only too familiar with the pursuit of self-fulfillment, of power, of compassion, kindness, even of a form of justice. But all these are at best only pale reflections, and at worst perversions, of what in God's plan they are meant to be, unless underpinned by truth and excellence. A person who makes truth and excellence his or her pursuit is indeed a person of deep insight, worthy of honour, worthy of emulation.
> . . . we give thanks to God for Dorothy L. Sayers, a woman of great scholarship, talent, Christian faith, and, above all, commitment to truth.

Notes

1. Brian Garfield, *I, Witness*, quoted in "Books," *Time* 17 April 1978, p. 98.
2. Nancy-Lou Patterson has commented that as the "wounded healer" of shamanistic language, Lord Peter attained his power to help and heal by his death and rebirth in World War I. This reading, while containing interesting psychological insights, neglects the integral Christian orientation of both Lord Peter and his maker, Dorothy L. Sayers. See Patterson, "'All Nerves and Nose': Lord Peter Wimsey as Wounded Healer in the Novels of Dorothy L. Sayers," *Mythlore* 54 (Summer 1988), pp. 13–16.
3. Carolyn Heilbrun, in *Writing a Woman's Life* (New York: Norton, 1988), p. 59, has argued that Dorothy L. Sayers underwent a change of direction in middle age, marking what Heilbrun calls "that often radical shift, either in work or emphasis, that some women, up to then unconsciously courageous, consciously make in their later years." While in many other cases this process may be discernible, Dorothy L. Sayers seems to have been remarkably consistent in her beliefs as well as in her work. Her moving into drama and theology seems an intensification of her early position, not a new direction; and it would seem that she was consciously courageous about all of her undertakings throughout her life.
4. Barbara Reynolds, *The Passionate Intellect* (Kent, Ohio: Kent State University Press, 1989), p. 117.
5. Letter from Dorothy L. Sayers to John Wren-Lewis, Good Friday of 1954; quoted in Reynolds, p. 210.

Chronology

Dorothy L. Sayers's Life[1]		*Literary and World Events*
	1841–44	Poe's seminal detective stories
	1863	J. S. LeFanu became widely known
	1867	Earliest detective novel, *The Dead Letter*, by Seeley Regester (Mrs. Metta M. F. Victor)
	1868	First full-length English detective-mystery novel, *The Moonstone*, by Wilkie Collins
	1874	Reading of detective fiction condemned at Temple Bar
	1875	First examination of women at Oxford
	1878	*The Leavenworth Case*, by Anna Katherine Green, "mother of detective fiction"
	1879	Opening of Somerville Hall
	1881	Changed to Somerville College
	1887	*A Study in Scarlet*, by Arthur Conan Doyle; first Sherlock Holmes story
Dorothy Leigh Sayers born at #1 Brewer Street, Oxford; baptized 26 July 1893 by her father	13 June 1893	
	1894	All Oxford qualifying B.A. examinations opened to women
	1897	Queen Victoria's

		Diamond Jubilee
Sayers family moved to Bluntisham-cum-Earith	1898	
Dorothy began to study Latin with her father and to write poems; studied later with governesses	1900	
	1901	Death of Queen Victoria
	1905–9	Baroness Orczy's popular armchair detective stories
Dorothy's French had out-stripped her Latin; she met her cousin Ivy Shrimpton and exchanged letters and poems	1906	
Dorothy demonstrated technical poetic prowess with "The Gargoyle"	1908	G. K. Chesterton's *The Man Who Was Thursday*; Mary Roberts Rinehart's *The Circular Staircase*
Dorothy entered Godolphin School, Salisbury	17 Jan. 1909	
won three Distinctions	17 Sept. 1909	
DLS confirmed at Salisbury Cathedral	1910	
Illness forced Dorothy to leave school	1911	
Dorothy won Gilchrist Scholarship to Oxford; Eric Whelpton began at Hertford College, Oxford; John Cournos arrived in England from U.S.	1912	E. C. Bentley's *Trent's Last Case*
Dorothy acted, debated, wrote satires	1913	Suffragette demonstrations in London; Thomas Mann's *Death in Venice*; D. H. Lawrence's *Sons and Lovers*
Dorothy took summer trip to Continent; Ivy returned to Oxford	1914	Outbreak of World War I in August

211

Dorothy took Class I Honours in French and Degree Course Certificate; began reading detective fiction	1915	Margaret Sanger jailed for writing *Family Limitation*
Dorothy began teaching at Hull in autumn; Whelpton was invalided in Sept.; by Dec. Dorothy's *Op. I* was published	1916	First zeppelin raids on Paris; Battle of Verdun; British draft began
Teaching at Hull ended in April; Dorothy took editing job at Blackwell's, Oxford; she wrote poems and translated Thomas's *Tristan*	1917	Bobbed hair a fashion craze
Whelpton arrived in Oxford in the spring; "Mac" Fleming left Army as a Captain and did not return to his wife	1918	22 million dead of influenza; women over 30 receive the vote in Britain; Armistice signed 11 Nov.
Dorothy left Blackwell's in spring; Dorothy left for France in autumn to take job with Whelpton at L'Ecole des Roches	1919	Fleming's *How to See the Battlefields*; Treaty of Versailles
Dorothy returned to London in Sept. and experimented with detective stories, including the first brief glimpse of Lord Peter Wimsey; in Oct. she was one of first women to receive Oxford B.A. and M.A.	1920	*The Mysterious Affair at Styles*, Agatha Christie's first published novel
DLS completed *Whose Body?* by mid-October, but found no publisher; Cournos at Oxford	1921	Founding of the BBC
In April Dorothy acquired first agent	1922	Joyce's *Ulysses* published; 500 copies burned on

and in May took job at
Benson's; she began
*Clouds of Witness; Whose
Body?* was sold after
five rejections; Oct.
relationship with
Cournos ended; Dec.
DLS brought home "a
man ('Bill') and a
motor-cycle."

Dorothy became
pregnant in April; 11
May *Whose Body?*
published in New York
and in London in
Oct.; DLS worked on
Clouds of Witness and
stayed at Benson's till
Nov.   1923

arrival in U.S.;
Mercedes-Daimler
dominated auto racing

John Anthony born 3   1924   Labour Party came to
January; 28 Jan.   power for first time
Dorothy returned to
Benson's and Ivy took
over child's care; in
April DLS broke off
with "Bill"; Cournos
married Sybil Norton

Fleming's divorce was   1925
finalized

Clouds of Witness   1926   21 April Princess
published 8 Feb.;   Elizabeth of York born
Dorothy married
Fleming 13 April in
London

Unnatural Death published 1927   German economy
(as *The Dawson Pedigree*   collapsed
in U.S.)

DLS helped form   1928   Women's suffrage in
Detection Club; her   Britain reduced from
father died in Sept.;   30 to 21 ("flapper
Mac's health declined;   vote")
DLS edited First Series
of *Great Short Stories of
Detection, Mystery, and
Horror* for Gollancz (in
U.S. called *The Omnibus
of Crime*); *Lord Peter*

213

Views the Body published		
DLS brought Witham house; her mother died in July; *Tristan in Brittany* published; Dorothy acquired new agent, David Higham	1929	29 Oct. U.S. Stock Market collapse
The Documents in the Case published 4 July; Dorothy and Mac had summer vacation in Galloway; *Strong Poison* published in autumn; DLS initiated BBC series "The Scoop"	1930	French Maginot Line begun
Five Red Herrings published (in U.S. *Suspicious Characters*) DLS left Benson's; she began research into campanology; *The Floating Admiral* and Second Series of *Great Short Stories* . . . published	1931	Britain abandoned gold standard; closure of all German banks
DLS worked on "My Edwardian Childhood" (unpubl.); *Have His Carcase* published in April	1932	Depression in major British industries; widespread unemployment
Murder Must Advertise published in Feb.; *Hangman's Holiday* in May; *Nine Tailors* completed by Nov.; DLS took trip with Muriel St. Clare Byrne to decide about her marriage and her son	1933	Hitler named German Chancellor; first concentration camps created
Nine Tailors published; June, DLS attended Somerville Gaudy while working on "Cat o' Mary" (unpub.); Dec., DLS informally "adopted" Anthony;	1934	Churchill warned Britain of German air menace; Nazi blood bath in Germany

214

Third Series *Great Short Stories . . .* published 10 Feb. through summer DLS worked on *Busman's Honeymoon* (play) with Muriel St. Clare Byrne; *Gaudy Night* published in Nov.	1935	Show trials in USSR; Italy invades Ethiopia
DLS worked on "Thrones, Dominations" (unpub.); Nov. completed novel adaptation of *Busman's Honeymoon*; Dec. *Busman's Honeymoon* opened in London; *Papers Relating to the Family of Wimsey* privately printed; DLS hired first secretary	1936	George V died; German troops occupied Rhineland; Spanish Civil War began; 11 Dec. Edward VIII abdicated
Feb. DLS completed *The Zeal of Thy House*; wrote "Gaudy Night" (essay); June, *The Zeal of Thy House* presented at Canterbury and novel *Busman's Honeymoon* published; August DLS visited Venice with Marjorie Barber	1937	Neville Chamberlain became Prime Minister
DLS collected material for Collins project; BBC began to adapt her detective novels for radio; DLS managed tour of *The Zeal of Thy House*; Val Gielgud produced *He That Should Come* for BBC	1938	Sept. Chamberlain signed Munich Pact with Hitler: "peace in our time"; Oct. Hitler invaded Czechoslovakia
In the Teeth of the Evidence published; June *The Devil to Pay* presented at Canterbury and published; DLS wrote *Love All* and *Begin Here*;	1939	Aug. Nazis signed pact with USSR; 1 Sept. Hitler invaded Poland; 3 Sept. Britain declared war; women and children evacuated

Anthony entered
Malvern College; DLS
had brief contact with
the Ministry of
Information

Dr. James Welch
proposed BBC series
on the life of Christ to
DLS; DLS began
connection with St.
Anne's; April DLS
started *Bridgeheads*
series; *Love All*
presented in London;
DLS began scripts for
*The Man Born to Be
King*

Val Gielgud agreed to
produce *The Man Born
to Be King*; DLS began
correspondence with
Patrick McLaughlin;
July *The Mind of the
Maker* published; Oct.
"The Other Six Deadly
Sins" published; by
Dec. the first five plays
of *The Man* . . .
completed; 21 Dec. to

10 Oct. *The Man Born to
Be King* (series)
presented by the BBC;
DLS probably wrote
"Talboys" this year
(last Wimsey story);
DLS gave address
"The Creative Mind";
Anthony won Domus
History Scholarship to
Balliol College, Oxford;
St. Anne's used to
convert "thinking

1940

1941

1942

from London; USSR
invaded Finland

British Home Guard
called up; rationing
started; 9 April Nazis
invaded Norway; May,
Churchill became
Prime Minister; 25
May Dunkirk
evacuation began; June
France fell;
August–Sept. the
Battle of Britain; Oct.
London Blitz began;
Nov. Coventry
destroyed

U.S. Congress passed
Lend-Lease legislation;
10 May peak of Blitz;
22 June Nazis invaded
USSR; August
Roosevelt and
Churchill formulated
Atlantic Charter; Oct.
Japan invaded
Philippines and sank
Prince of Wales and
Repulse; 7 Dec. Japan
attacked Pearl Harbor
and U.S. declared war
8 Dec.

British Thousand-Bomber
Raid on Cologne; Nazi
attacks on historic
British cities; turning
point of war with U.S.
victories at Midway,
the Coral Sea, and
Guadalcanal and
British defeat of
Rommel at El Alamein

pagans"

DLS offered Doctorate of Divinity by Archbishop of Canterbury, but she refused	1943	Feb. Nazis surrendered at Stalingrad; 8 Sept. Italy surrendered; Allied 24-hour bombing raids began; Solomons Campaign completed
16 Aug. DLS commented on *Divine Comedy*; Nov. DLS joined St. Anne's Advisory Council; Dec. she began translating the *Inferno*	1944	4 June Rome fell to Allies; No. Atlantic U-Boat threat ended; 6 June Allied invasion in Normandy; Nazi rockets used on Britain; Dec. Nazi counteroffensive Battle of the Bulge
Apr. Penguin offered DLS contract for *Divine Comedy* translation; *The Just Vengeance* commissioned for Lichfield Cathedral	1945	Labour Party won majority; 7 May Nazi Germany surrendered; 6 August first atomic bomb dropped at Hiroshima; 14 Aug. Japanese surrendered
Anthony entered Balliol College; DLS lectured at Summer School of Italian Studies; Anthony accidentally discovered parentage; Detection Club resurrected; *The Just Vengeance* presented at Lichfield	1946	Churchill gave "Iron Curtain" speech at Fulton, Missouri; severe winter fuel crisis in Britain
Mac's health deteriorated; DLS initiated *Essays Presented to Charles Williams*	1947	British India partitioned; severe economic policies and nationalization of key industries in Britain
Four Sacred Plays published; May, *Hell* (translation) completed; July, Anthony obtained First Class Honours in politics, philosophy and economics; Sept., DLS	1948	U.S. began Marshall Plan aid to Europe; British gradually lifted rationing and controls of raw materials; British National Health Service begun

217

worked on German translation of *The Man Born to Be King*		
DLS revived *The Zeal of Thy House*; she began *The Emperor Constantine* for 1951 Colchester Cathedral Festival and started translation of *Purgatory*; 10 Nov. *Inferno* published	1949	Devaluation of British pound; NATO Treaty signed; Berlin airlift
DLS sat for portrait by Sir William Hurchison; Apr. Mac hospitalized; May, DLS received Hon. Doctorate from U. of Durham; 9 June Mac died of stroke; 24 Aug. DLS took first holiday since start of World War II	1950	25 June No. Korea invaded So. Korea; United Nations forces sent under U.S. initiative
July *The Emperor Constantine* staged at Colchester and published in Aug.	1951	Churchill became British Prime Minister again with Conservative victory; denationalization of certain basic British industries
DLS experimented with small play on Dante	1952	George VII died; anti-British riots in Egypt; 6 Nov. U.S. explodes first hydrogen bomb
DLS appealed for restoration of St. Thomas's Church, London; wrote juvenile holiday calendars	1953	Coronation of Elizabeth II; death of Stalin; inauguration of U.S. President Eisenhower
Spring, attack on DLS and other writers by Kathleen Nott in *The Emperor's Clothes*; Sept. DLS completed *Purgatory* (trans.); Oct. *Introductory Papers on Dante*	1954	Food rationing in Britain discontinued
May, *Purgatory* published	1955	Commercial television

		broadcasting began in Britain; Universal Copyright Convention took effect
DLS postponed *Paradise* translation to translate *The Song of Roland*	1956	Suez Crisis; Soviet invasion of Hungary
DLS became Churchwarden of St. Anne's and St. Thomas's; May, *Further Papers on Dante* published; 17 Dec. DLS died at her home in Witham	1957	USSR launches first Sputniks
Jan. Memorial Service for Dorothy L. Sayers at St. Margaret's Church, Westminster	1958	
"Talboys" discovered	1961	
Paradise translation published, as completed by Barbara Reynolds	1962	
The Poetry of Search and the Poetry of Statement published	1963	
Barbara Reynolds published two additional authorized Sayers articles on Dante	1965	
"Striding Folly" published in book form with "Talboys" and "The Haunted Policeman"	1972	
Janet Hitchman discovered Anthony's parentage and published it in her *Such a Strange Lady*, the first biography of DLS	1973	
DLS's home in Witham threatened by demolition; citizens form "Witham &	1974–75	

219

Countryside Society"
to resist

DLS's home restored and   1975
reopened in Nov. by
Ian Carmichael

Jan. citizens call meeting   1976
to form Dorothy L.
Sayers Society; Ralph
Clarke elected
chairman; Nov. First
Annual Convention of
the Society (continuing
to present)

Wilkie Collins: A Critical   1977
and Biographical Study by
DLS, ed. by E. R.
Gregory, published

DLS Society arranged   1978
Thanksgiving Service
for DLS at St. Paul's,
Covent Garden;
Colleen Gilbert's
Bibliography of the Works
of DLS published

Ralph Hone's *Dorothy L.*   1979
Sayers published

James Brabazon's *Dorothy*   1981
L. Sayers published

Nov. death of Anthony   1986
Fleming

Aug. Performance of *The*   1987
Zeal of Thy House at
Canterbury;
Archbishop of
Canterbury becomes
patron of the Society;
Ralph Clarke elected
president, Dr. Reynolds
chairman.

220

Note

1. This chronology of major events in the life of Dorothy L. Sayers is drawn largely from her two most authoritative biographies, by Ralph E. Hone and James Brabazon.

Select Bibliography

Two primary sources of research material on the life and works of Dorothy L. Sayers exist. In Britain, the Dorothy L. Sayers Society, Rose Cottage, Malthouse Lane, Hurstpierpoint, West Sussex, BN6 9JY, England, was founded in 1976 "to promote the study of [her] life, works and thoughts, . . . to encourage the performance of her plays and the publication of books by and about her, to preserve original material for posterity and to provide assistance for researchers." The Society holds annual seminars, offers a list of approximately 700 items for research purposes, and publishes six bulletins per year to its membership. In the United States, the Marion E. Wade Center at Wheaton College, Wheaton, Illinois 60187, opened its collection of the Dorothy L. Sayers Papers acquired from the Anthony Fleming Estate to responsible researchers on 1 February 1989. This collection is immense, with correspondence to and from Miss Sayers alone including over 30,000 pages.

The Major Works of Dorothy L. Sayers

Detective Fiction (in chronological order; first British publication and most recent paperback publication are given):

Whose Body?, London: T. Fisher Unwin, 1923; New York: Avon, 1961. Novel.

Clouds of Witness, London: T. Fisher Unwin, 1926; New York: Avon, 1966. Novel.

Unnatural Death, London: Ernest Benn, 1927; New York: Avon, 1964. Novel (initially published in the United States as *The Dawson Pedigree*).

The Unpleasantness at the Bellona Club, London: Ernest Benn, 1928; New York: Avon, 1963. Novel.

Lord Peter Views the Body, London: Gollancz, 1928; New York: Avon, 1969. Collection of short fiction.

The Documents in the Case, London: Ernest Benn, 1930; New York: Avon, 1968. Novel (in collaboration with Robert Eustace).

Strong Poison, London: Gollancz, 1930; New York: Avon, 1971. Novel.

The Five Red Herrings, London: Gollancz, 1931; New York: Avon, 1968. Novel.

The Floating Admiral, London: Hodder and Staunton, 1931; New York: Charter, 1980. Collaborative novel, with members of The Detection Club; DLS contributed the Introduction, Chapter VII, and the Solution.

Have His Carcase, London: Gollancz, 1932; New York: Avon, 1968. Novel.

Murder Must Advertise, London: Gollancz, 1933; New York: Avon, 1967. Novel.

Ask a Policeman, London: A. Barker, 1933; New York: Berkeley, 1984. Collaborative novel, with members of The Detection Club; DLS contributed "The Conclusions of Mr. Roger Sheringham."

Hangman's Holiday, London: Gollancz, 1933; New York: Avon, 1969. Collection of short fiction.

The Nine Tailors, London: Gollancz, 1934; New York: Harcourt Brace Jovanovich, 1962. Novel.

Gaudy Night, London: Gollancz, 1936; New York: Avon, 1968. Novel.

Busman's Honeymoon, London: Gollancz, 1937; New York: Avon, 1968. Novel adaptation of play.

Double Death, London: Gollancz, 1939. Collaborative novel, with members of The Detection Club.

No Flowers by Request, Published as a serial in *The Daily Sketch*, 1953; New York: Berkeley, 1984. Collaborative novel, with members of The Detection Club; DLS contributed Chapter I.

Striding Folly, Including Three Final Lord Peter Wimsey Stories, London: New English Library, 1972. Collection of short fiction, including "Talboys," written in 1942.

Lord Peter, New York: Avon, 1972. Collection of all twenty-one short stories involving Lord Peter Wimsey, plus Carolyn Heinbrun's article "Sayers, Lord Peter and God" and E. C. Bentley's parody "Greedy Night."

Drama (in chronological order; first publication and currently accessible published versions are given):

Busman's Honeymoon, London: Gollancz, 1937; Kent, Ohio: Kent State University Press, 1984 (includes *Love All*). Detective comedy, written in collaboration with Muriel St. Clare Byrne.

The Zeal of Thy House, London: Gollancz, 1937; in *Four Sacred Plays* (London: Gollancz, 1948). Religious drama for Canterbury Cathedral Festival.

The Devil to Pay, London: Gollancz, 1939; in *Four Sacred Plays*. Religious drama for Canterbury Cathedral Festival.

He That Should Come, London: Gollancz, 1939; in *Four Sacred Plays*. Nativity play for radio.

Love All, published posthumously with *Busman's Honeymoon*, 1984 (see above); romantic comedy produced in London, April 1940.

The Man Born to Be King, London: Gollancz, 1943. Twelve-part play cycle on the life of Christ, written for radio and first presented by the BBC December 1941–October 1942.

The Just Vengeance, London: Gollancz, 1946; in *Four Sacred Plays*. Religious play for Lichfield Cathedral Festival.

The Emperor Constantine, London: Gollancz, 1951. Religious-historical play for Colchester Cathedral Festival.

Translations (in chronological order):

Tristan in Brittany, London: Ernest Benn, 1929. Extant fragments of the twelfth-century *Tristan* by Thomas of Britain; DLS fitted these together with brief prose condensations of Joseph Bedier's 1902–5 summary.

The Heart of Stone, Witham, Essex: J. H. Clarke, 1946. Four Canzoni of Dante's "Pietra" Group.

The Comedy of Dante Alighieri, the Florentine, Harmondsworth: Penguin Books, 1949–63. *Terza rima* translation; DLS completed Cantica I, *Hell*, with Introduction and Notes, in 1949 and Cantica II, *Purgatory*, with Introduction and Notes, in 1955. Before her death in 1957, she had finished twenty cantos of *Paradise*, which was completed by Dr. Barbara Reynolds with Introduction and Notes in 1962.

The Song of Roland, Harmondsworth: Penguin Books, 1957. Translation from the Old French DLS began at Oxford and completed forty years later.

Essays and Addresses:

Introduction to *Great Short Stories of Detection, Mystery, and Horror*, London: Gollancz, 1928 (retitled *The Omnibus of Crime* in the U.S.).

"The Present Status of the Mystery Story," *London Mercury*, November 1930. Critical article.

Introduction to *Great Short Stories of Detection, Mystery, and Horror, Second Series*, London: Gollancz, 1931 (retitled *The Second Omnibus of Crime* in the U.S.).

Introduction to *Great Short Stories of Detection, Mystery, and Horror, Third Series*, London: Gollancz, 1934 (retitled *The Third Omnibus of Crime* in the U.S.).

"Wimsey Papers," *The Spectator*, November 1939–January 1940. Articles.

Begin Here, London: Gollancz, 1940. Book-length wartime essay.

The Mind of the Maker, London: Methuen, 1941. Book-length religious-aesthetic essay.

Unpopular Opinions, London: Gollancz, 1946. Articles and addresses on theological, political, and critical topics.

Creed or Chaos?, London: Methuen, 1947. Essays on theology.

Introductory Papers on Dante, London: Methuen, 1954. Eight papers first delivered to student audiences.

Further Papers on Dante, London: Methuen, 1957. Eight essays intended for nonscholarly readers.

The Poetry of Search and the Poetry of Statement, London: Gollancz, 1963. Twelve posthumously published essays for a general audience, five dealing with Dante and the others on related topics.

A Matter of Eternity, Grand Rapids, Mich.: Eerdmans, 1973. Selections from DLS's devotional and theological writings.

The Whimsical Christian, New York: Macmillan, 1978. Reprinted religious essays.

Principal Unpublished Works:

"My Edwardian Childhood," Autobiographical fragment, thirty-three pages; written around 1932.
"Cat o'Mary," Fragmentary autobiographical novel, 209 pages; written around 1934.
"Thrones, Dominations," Fragmentary detective novel featuring Lord Peter Wimsey and Harriet Vane after their marriage, six chapters; written around 1938–39.

Works on Dorothy L. Sayers and Her Writings

Bibliographies:

Gilbert, Colleen B., *A Bibliography of the Works of Dorothy L. Sayers*, London: Macmillan, 1978.
Harmon, Robert B. and Margaret A. Burger, *An Annotated Guide to the Works of Dorothy L. Sayers*, New York: Garland, 1977.

Biographies:

Brabazon, James, *Dorothy L. Sayers: A Biography*, New York: Charles Scribner's Sons, 1981. Authorized by Anthony Fleming.
Dale, Alzina Stone, *Maker and Craftsman: The Story of Dorothy L. Sayers*, Grand Rapids, Mich.: Eerdmans, 1978. Accurate, sprightly, and intended for a youthful audience.
Hitchman, Janet, *Such a Strange Lady–An Introduction to Dorothy L. Sayers*, London: New English Library, 1975. The first biography of DLS to appear.
Hone, Ralph E., *Dorothy L. Sayers: A Literary Biography*, Kent, Ohio: Kent State University Press, 1979. Erudite, reliable, and immensely readable.

Works by Persons Connected to Dorothy L. Sayers:

Byrne, Muriel St. Clare and Catherine Hope Mansfield, *Somerville College, 1879–1921*, Oxford: Oxford University Press, 1927.

Cournos, John, *Autobiography*, New York: Liveright, 1935.

Fleming, Atherton, *The Craft of the Short Story* (under pseudonym Donald Maconochie), London: Pitman, 1936.

——, *The Gourmet's Book of Food and Drink*, London: John Lane, The Bodley Head, 1933.

——, *How to See the Battlefields*, London: Cassell, 1919.

Frankenberg, Charis U., *Not Old, Madam–Vintage*, Lavenham, England: Galaxy Books, 1975.

Higham, David, *Literary Gent*, New York: Coward, McCann and Geoghegan, 1978.

Reynolds, Barbara, *The Passionate Intellect: Dorothy L. Sayers' Encounter with Dante*, Kent, Ohio: Kent State University Press, 1989.

Schreurs, Ann, *Memoir* of her father, Atherton (Mac) Fleming, the Dorothy L. Sayers Historical and Literary Society, July 1976.

Whelpton, Eric, *The Making of a European*, London: Johnson, 1974.

Williams, Charles, *The Figure of Beatrice: A Study in Dante*, London: Faber and Faber, 1941.

Critical Studies of the Works of Dorothy L. Sayers:

Gaillard, Dawson, *Dorothy L. Sayers*, New York: Ungar, 1981. A discussion of DLS's mystery fiction.

Hannay, Margaret (ed.), *As Her Whimsey Took Her: Critical Essays on the Work of Dorothy L. Sayers*, Kent, Ohio: Kent State University Press, 1979. Essays covering all aspects of DLS's work.

Heilbrun, Carolyn, "Sayers, Lord Peter, and God." See above. Originally published in *The American Scholar* 37 (Spring 1968).

——, *Writing Women's Lives*, New York: Norton, 1988.

Leavis, Q. D., "The Case of Miss Dorothy Sayers," *Scrutiny* 6 (December 1937).

Nott, Kathleen, "Lord Peter Views the Soul," in *The Emperor's Clothes*, London: Heinemann, 1954.

Reynolds, Barbara, "The Origin of Lord Peter Wimsey," address to the Dorothy L. Sayers Historical and Literary Society, June 1976; *Times Literary Supplement* 22 April 1977.

Studies of Mystery Fiction:

Dale, Alzina Stone and Barbara Sloan Hendershott, *Mystery Reader's Walking Guide: England*, Lincolnwood, Illinois: Passport Books, 1988.

Mann, Jessica, *Deadlier Than the Male: Why Are Respectable English Women So Good at Murder?*, New York: Macmillan, 1981.

Symons, Julian, *Bloody Murder: From the Detective Story to the Crime Novel: A History*, London: Faber and Faber, 1972.

Watson, Colin, *Snobbery with Violence–Crime Stories and Their Audience*, London: Eyre and Spottiswoode, 1971.

Studies of English Culture, 1850–present:

Aslet, Clive, *The Last Country Houses*, New Haven, Conn.: Yale University Press, 1982.

Briggs, Asa, *A Social History of England*, New York: Viking, 1983.

Girouard, Mark, *The Return to Camelot: Chivalry and the English Gentleman*, New Haven, Conn.: Yale University Press, 1981.

Morris, Jan (ed.), *The Oxford Book of Oxford*, Oxford: Oxford University Press, 1978.

Quiney, Anthony, *The English Country Town*, London: Thames and Hudson, 1987.

Index

Works by Dorothy L. Sayers

General

231